Swinburne

The Works of
Algernon Charles Swinburne

❊

with an Introduction by Laurence Binyon,
and Bibliography

Wordsworth Poetry Library

This edition published 1995 by Wordsworth Editions Ltd,
Cumberland House, Crib Street, Ware, Hertfordshire SG12 9ET.

ISBN 1-85326-443-1

Printed and bound in Denmark by Nørhaven.

The paper in this book is produced from pure wood
pulp, without the use of chlorine or any other substance
harmful to the environment. The energy used in its
production consists almost entirely of hydroelectricity
and heat generated from waste materials, thereby
conserving fossil fuels and contributing little to the
greenhouse effect.

INTRODUCTION

By LAURENCE BINYON

BORN in London on April 5, 1837, two months before the Queen's accession, Swinburne survived Victoria by eight years. Dates claim him as a complete Victorian; and, much as he delighted to flout Victorian respectabilities, as a poet he is of his period, in the sense that in the long sequence of English poets he finds there his due time and fitting place, being neither a survival nor an anticipation.

The first and the obvious thing to say about Swinburne is that he was a man of genius. However one may qualify his work, however imperfect be the sympathy with his aim and achievement, the genius in it is something incontestable and unassailable. And his genius, like his personality, was strange and singular. He is like no other English poet, either in his work or in himself. We have a vivid record of the impression he made on many observers. With his small figure, rigidly held, his hands beside him automatically fluttering, the long solid neck above sloping shoulders supporting a massive head and a fiery cloud of hair, he seemed in his youth 'not quite human', a kind of apparition in the world of mortals. Henry Adams, meeting him at a country house in 1862, when his name was still unknown, found himself reminded of 'a tropical bird, high-crested, long-beaked, quick-moving, with rapid utterance and screams of humour, quite unlike any English lark or nightingale. One could hardly call him a crimson macaw among owls, and yet no ordinary contrast availed.' Wonder at his exotic appearance was soon lost in excited astonishment at 'the Walpurgis-night of his talk' and his 'incredible memory' as he chanted his own poems or Greek verse for hours on end.

In portraits made at the time Swinburne is seen in repose. And what strikes one above all in these portraits is the fixed look of the eyes; not the wide eyes of a visionary, yet eyes unresponsive to immediate surroundings, eyes of a calm and fearless arrogance, with a look of enclosed remoteness. In ordinary unconvivial society, and when not under the stimulus of excitement, he was distinguished by his dignity and ceremonial manners. For there was a dualism in Swinburne's nature. An extreme excitability, bursting out with fantastic violence when he felt or imagined an affront and equally exuberant in enthusiasm for his chosen idols, alternated with a remarkable sweetness and gentleness. Again, as Sir Edmund Gosse pointed out, 'his imagination was always swinging, like a pendulum, between north and south', between the bare moors of Northumberland and the sunny slopes of the Isle of Wight, which were both equally impressed upon his memories of boyhood: and as a poet he would be possessed now by the spirit of the grim Border Ballads, now by the *Fleurs du Mal* and *Mademoiselle de Maupin*. At a deeper level of his nature was an impulse to absolute self-surrender, to ecstatic worship, alternating or combined with an impulse to virile revolt against all restrictions from without. A friend noted his 'self-esteem, solid as a rock' amid the storm of scandal raised by *Poems and Ballads*. And yet, once caged at Putney, how extraordinary is his docile submission to the prohibitions of Watts-Dunton!

The impact of Swinburne's personality on all he met in his early manhood was matched by the overwhelming effect on a whole generation of *Atalanta in Calydon* and *Poems and Ballads*. His first volume, the two plays *The Queen Mother* and *Rosamund*, had made no stir, had hardly been noticed. But *Atalanta* took its readers by storm; and, though *Poems and Ballads* so outraged the decorous, the fascination of this new voice, of this daring rebel with his torrents of eloquence and marvellous melodies, which it was a physical pleasure to declaim, caused in the youth of that time an unparalleled excitement and enthusiasm. The question we ask to-day is: Can that excitement and enthusiasm ever be recaptured? Will they be replaced by a more sober and durable appreciation?

Swinburne's centenary found him not so much depreciated as ignored, at least by those who are writing, and those who are interested in, the poetry of to-day. Whereas to his contemporaries he seemed to be opening up new vistas, to be inaugurating a new kind of poetry, to us he seems to come at the close of a tradition. He conquered a new kingdom, but he left no heirs. The writers of light verse have profited by his metrical inventions, but in serious poetry his example has been singularly unfruitful. Swinburne has been indeed the chief enemy of his own reputation. No poet of his stature has repeated and diluted himself so recklessly. If we are to enjoy him and give him his due, we must definitely limit our reading of him. But selection is difficult. It is not only that Swinburne wrote far too much, but that even his best poems are apt to be in the nature of a surfeit. Poe was right; there is a time-limit to our capacity for being thrilled. With Swinburne too often a high exhilaration subsides in a sense of fatigue.

There is a story that Swinburne, Rossetti, and

Meredith once went down to Hampton Court from Waterloo and each composed a poem in the train. Swinburne's was *Faustine*. He wanted to see how many stanzas he could make on that one rhyme. The rhymes exhausted, the poem was complete. This no doubt is far from being the whole explanation of the poem; but it hints at a peculiarity in Swinburne's gift, what one might almost call his interminability. Of *Mater Triumphalis* he said himself that it seemed to be going on for ever, so he had to cut it short—as if there were no inner necessity in the conception to control the form: and it is this lack of interior form that is Swinburne's chief defect as an artist. One would think that he was incapable of self-criticism, or how could he bear to reiterate those easy rhymes, those hackneyed images, that recur for ever in his later verse? He was aware of his weakness, he noted the danger of 'a dulcet and luscious form of verbosity', and he could parody without mercy his own obsessions:

> It's plain as a newspaper leader
>   That a rhymester who scribbles like me
> May feel perfectly sure that his reader
>   Is sick of the sea.

But this awareness had no effect. A spark kindled, the poet flamed, and almost as if by a sort of automatism the familiar ringing cadences rushed out.

Yet this sort of automatism was once something very different: it was the divine madness seizing on, possessing the poet, driving him on, unconscious of himself. If Swinburne never makes us think of the sculptor seeking to liberate his thought from the marble, if we have to renounce the pleasure of watching the poem shape itself as a living thing, we have the experience of another pleasure. We seem to watch a trained runner leaping into his stride and glorying in his speed, never flagging for a moment, till at last he breasts the tape. It was the 'splendour and speed' of the *Atalanta* choruses that swept the youth of England off their feet. And not only this; for in *Atalanta* lyrics and blank verse alike announced a formed style, quite new and perfectly mastered.

How had this style, already so mature, been formed? The effect of it in 1866 was all the greater because the early poems had never been published, and Swinburne appeared suddenly as a master. Yet if his own wish had been carried out—it was vetoed by Watts-Dunton—a volume of Early Poems would have been published in 1876 containing pieces that had not been printed before. Much of this early work has been printed since Swinburne's death, but a good deal of material still exists in manuscript. One cannot help thinking that the poet's reputation would have suffered less if these Juvenilia had been accessible to readers than it suffered from the publication of the last dozen of his volumes of verse. For, at least in the early poems, whatever their immaturity, we watch a poet growing, a style being formed; whereas in the later work there is no growth, only repetition.

This stage of growth has been acutely analysed by M. Georges Lafourçade, whose *Jeunesse de Swinburne* is the most full, penetrating, amply documented study of the poet that has yet appeared. Swinburne, rather surprisingly, was not precocious. At Eton he wrote a poem, *The Triumph of Gloriana*, the manuscript of which is in the British Museum, on a visit of Queen Victoria to the school in 1851. It is in the style of Pope, and the couplets are handled with fluent ease, though with no individual note. In couplets, again, is *The Temple of Janus* (also in the British Museum), a poem sent in for the Newdigate Prize at Oxford in 1857. It was supposed by Gosse to be lost. Most of it is printed by M. Lafourçade. In the main the influence is that of Shelley, still more apparent in the *Ode to Mazzini* of the same date (printed in *Posthumous Poems*, 1917); but the very first couplet,

> Earth and the changeless powers that keep her fair,
> The glories of the planet-lighted air,

has a cadence which will be exactly repeated in the brilliant Prologue to *Tristram of Lyonesse*, written in 1871.

> Love that is first and last of all things made
> The light that has the living world for shade,

and we are hardly surprised to find that the last line ends with the word that was to end so many poems to come,

> A blind grey dawn moved on the shadowy sea.

But far more interesting is *The Death of Sir John Franklin* (*Posthumous Poems*), long supposed to have been sent in for the Newdigate in 1858, and, like its predecessor, rejected. M. Lafourçade discovered that this poem really dates from 1860, Swinburne's last year at Oxford, and competed not for the Newdigate but for a special prize. This is a noble poem, unusually massive and deliberate in movement, unusually shapely, and though with some slight echo of Shakespeare is already almost in the mature Swinburnian manner. It represents an escape from the pre-Raphaelite phase of the three preceding years. Stimulated by the close companionship of Rossetti, Morris, and Burne-Jones, Swinburne had been seduced from his

own instinctive preferences and chosen models—the
Bible, the Elizabethan dramatists, Aeschylus, Shelley
—and produced a mass of verse of medieval atmosphere
and inspiration, imitating Morris or early Morality
Plays with marvellous skill and success. Some of
these pieces were included in *Poems and Ballads*; but
this pre-Raphaelite phase was transitory; the adopted
style was pictorial, Swinburne's natural style was rhe-
torical (I use the word in no depreciatory sense); and
though it brought a sense of colour and an unusual
distinctness into poems like *The Sundew*, which are no
mere pastiche, this faded out too in time. The Bible,
the Greeks, the Elizabethans remained.

And Shelley? Assuredly Shelley counted for a good
deal in his development, not only through shared
political enthusiasms but through the great expansion
of lyric measures that Shelley effected. I have heard
the relation between the two expressed as being that
of an amateur, a divine amateur, to a professional.
And certainly Shelley as a craftsman is prone to
lapses of haste and carelessness which are never found
in Swinburne. But let us take an example:

We have seen thee, O Love, thou art fair; thou art goodly,
    O Love;
Thy wings make light in the air as the wings of a dove.
Thy feet are as winds that divide the stream of the sea;
Earth is thy covering to hide thee, the garment of thee.
Thou art swift and subtle and blind as a flame of fire;
Before thee the laughter, behind thee the tears of desire;
And twain go forth beside thee, a man with a maid;
Her eyes are the eyes of a bride whom delight makes afraid;
As the breath in the buds that stir is her bridal breath;
But Fate is the name of her; and his name is Death.

And now for Shelley:

    Ah, sister, Desolation is a delicate thing:
    It walks not on the earth, it floats not on the air,

But treads with killing footstep, and fans with silent wing
The tender hopes which in their hearts the best and gentlest
  bear;
Who, soothed to false repose by the fanning plumes above
And the music-stirring motion of its soft and busy feet
Dream visions of aërial joy, and call the monster, Love
And wake and find the shadow Pain, as he whom now we greet.

The underlying thought is very similar in both passages. But there is a difference. We are exhilarated
by the Swinburne as by the lovely motions of a dancer,
but hardly moved. The language is, so to speak, a
non-conductor, it is there for its own sake. But with
the Shelley (for all that the atmosphere of *Prometheus*
is so rarefied) there are vibrations that come from a
world of felt experience and intimately modulate the
rhythm. The language is communicative. Swinburne
hardly ever catches the rhythmical secret of such a
lyric as *When the lamp is shattered*, and chiefly because
the rhythm so spontaneously obeys the emotion, as
pliant boughs obey the wind. In *The Triumph of Time*,
Swinburne's masterpiece in lyric, inspired by bitter
experience, there are exquisite modulations; but the
main impression is made by the powerful, flexible
'tune', if one may so call it; and our admiration is for
the superb and confident abundance which sustains
the poet through such a long succession of stanzas
without a falter, and this when the poem, so far from
being empty rhetoric, traces so closely the turns and
changes of profound feeling. If not so magical an
artist in rhythm as is sometimes assumed, as a master
of lyric *metre* Swinburne is incomparable. He has no
rival. Take for instance the *Christmas Antiphones* in
Songs before Sunrise. Here is no dancing measure with
elaborate reverberations; the small, cramping stanza
with a triple rhyme in it, seems simple but is actually

most difficult, and the poet has chosen to increase the difficulty very greatly by an internal rhyme:

> Thou whose birth on earth
> Angels sang to men,
> While thy stars made mirth,
> Saviour, at thy birth,
> This day born again.

The ingenuity which could compose sixty stanzas on this pattern and make it all smooth and simple is almost incredible; and yet the impression is not of ingenuity but of perfect ease. In the more elaborate metres which Swinburne invented in such astounding variety this extraordinary ease of mastery is, of course, more obvious. We may sometimes wish that the voice would falter and the skill fail; but no, the stanzas are threaded together like pearls on a string, each perfect; there are rarely, as with other poets, the one or two surpassing stanzas which outshine and dim the rest.

The Elizabethans, as we all know, were a passion with Swinburne from his boyhood till his death. (As early as 1849, when he was thirteen, he composed a tragedy, *The Unhappy Revenge*, on the Elizabethan model, which exists in manuscript.) Swinburne thought that 'the fusion of lyric with dramatic form gives the highest type of poetry'. If by this he meant the kind of fiery and exalted speech characteristic of the dialogue of the Elizabethans, it was for him an unfortunate belief. Swinburne was better advised when he composed *Atalanta* on a Greek model; for his essentially lyric genius the scheme which provided a chorus for lyric outlets and dialogue for the drama was much more propitious. And the proof is that *Atalanta* has won, and will probably always win, enthusiastic admirers, while the plays on the Elizabethan model interest rather than carry away. *Atalanta* is surely Swinburne's master-work. The movement of the blank verse is rather artificial, it does not allow for the natural pauses to take breath, yet it is highly individual and has both volume and vehemence. No one since Milton had employed elision so deliberately and resourcefully. Passages of the choruses may be analysed into almost nonsense, yet enchant the ear. Perhaps the chief fault of the poem is the central anti-theistic chorus, or rather its place in the tragedy, before anything has happened, and also its disproportionate violence and weight; for, as M. de Reul remarks, such invectives would be more fitted to follow the superhuman calamities of the House of Atreus. It seems incongruous also in the mouth of a group of girls. But if this is somewhat of an excrescence, it does not seriously mar the total effect of the drama. Althea, though her motive for letting her son die may not appeal to us, is a truly tragic figure; and the play moves magnificently to its close with the plangent lyric laments and antiphons that precede Meleager's death and Atalanta's brief farewell.

Perhaps even more intoxicating in their effect than *Atalanta* were the *Poems and Ballads* of the following year, all the more because they provoked at the same time such violent denunciation. There are those who, like Mr. Harold Nicolson, find the Second Series of *Poems and Ballads* (1878) superior to the first. Yet we fancy that those who on the occasion of his centenary took up Swinburne again will have felt his genius more strongly and vividly in the volume of 1866 than in any subsequent volume, even the *Songs before Sunrise*. Mr. Nicolson dismisses the majority of the poems

on the ground that sensuality provides essentially
ephemeral motives and that the experiences they
embody are eccentric. Yet they represent a very real
side of the poet's abnormal temperament, with its
abnormal stimulations; Chastelard in Swinburne's
play gives us, as M. Lafourçade shows, the clue.
True, it is not the joyous paganism of Marlowe, of
whom Swinburne had written that he had 'done
justice once for all to that much misused and belied
thing, the purely sensuous and outward side of love';
these poems breathe the hothouse air of Romanticism
in its last stage, with its thirst for sensation at all cost,

Exceeding pleasure out of extreme pain.

Many things contributed to this phase of ferment
in the young poet, conscious of extraordinary powers,
arrogant and defiant: adoration of beauty for its own
sake: an impish desire to shock: enthusiasm for the
theories of the Marquis de Sade (addressed in *Dolores*
as 'thy prophet, thy preacher, thy poet') and for the
antinomianism of Blake: the rejection of the one love
of his life. Revolting from the over-sentimental conception of love imposed on the time, he tore through
the surface of make-believe to reveal the fury of Lust
as a terrible and tremendous force, incarnate through
the ages in one 'fatal' woman after another, insatiate
and unappeased against a background of sombre
grandeur, charged with doom, 'the thunder of the
trumpets of the Night'. But already in *Hesperia* sounds
the note of reaction from the mood of *Dolores*.

For desire is a respite from love, and the flesh not the heart
    is her fuel;
She was sweet to me once, who am fled and escaped from the
    rage of her reign.

In *Songs before Sunrise* the renunciation is complete.

As Swinburne said himself, 'The impulse failed.' The theme was exhausted. The new inspiration was something worthier and more durable. The events of the Italian Risorgimento provided the ostensible motive; but beyond them was discerned and adored the symbolic figure of Liberty, conceived as the fullest expression of the human soul in all its potentialities. At the same time the furious invectives against the God of this world (Blake's conception) begin to give place to a positive worship of the Spirit of Man, a divine humanity. *Hertha*, the most complete and compact expression of this 'religion', was Swinburne's favourite among all his poems. Exalted and impassioned as it is, masterly in the handling of the metre, it is remote from most readers' sympathies, even though it embodies Swinburne's central convictions. In *Songs before Sunrise* the poetry has become more abstract, the reiteration of the same images has set in, and these extravagant ecstasies of lyrism poured out before a radiant phantom do not print themselves upon the mind with the edge and sting of the earlier *Poems and Ballads*. Yet this volume and the second *Poems and Ballads* (which contains *Ave atque Vale*) yield a harvest of lyrics, notable not only for metrical splendour, but sometimes also for hard thought, which are indispensable for a true appreciation of Swinburne.

Persistent in all this poetry, whether celebrating passion or freedom, is the symbol of the sea. The mere sight of the sea sufficed to set Swinburne in a quiver of excitement. A wild bright morning, blown spray, and bursting waves, intoxicated him. He swam in the salt water with a physical ecstasy. Now and then we get a line that is vivid to the eye—

or where the wind's feet shine along the sea—

but there is no concrete picture, rather a sense of dazzle and movement and light. It is an idea more than an image. The symbolism shifts and changes; the sea is now the mother of Aphrodite, the 'bitter blossom' born of the foam, and now mingles with the remote and dazzling idea of Liberty, and now is the splendid lover, and now the lustral waters of healing and forgetfulness. Swinburne's imagery is not pictorial and deals little in colour; it is the elements, Water, Fire, Wind, that are his constant inspiration and give a restless brightness to his verse.

'The first duty of a singer is to sing.' So Swinburne confidently pronounced. How many poets to-day would approach their art from this angle? Since Swinburne's death, and before, the movement in poetry has been in quite another direction. One could not go on from Swinburne on his own lines; his poetry represents something completed, and therefore incapable of growth. What is characteristic of the last half-century is the increasing desire not to invent new 'tunes', but to incorporate into metre the inexhaustibly varied rhythms of speech. It started with Gerard Hopkins, who said of Swinburne: 'his poetry seems a powerful effort at establishing a new standard of poetical diction . . . but to waive every other objection it is essentially archaic . . . a perfect style must be of its age.' Whether this be a cogent criticism or not, there is no doubt about the modern effort to be contemporary not only in diction but in theme, to admit as material everything that comes within the writer's experience. And Swinburne therefore, with his poetical diction and limited themes, is out of touch with more modern production.

It may be that with reaction against harsh matter

and deflated rhythms there will come a revived enjoyment of Swinburne's clear and confident singing voice. But, because his sensibilities were so different from those of other men and so extreme in themselves, he is likely to remain to a certain degree isolated and remote. We must take him for what he is; we expect from him no broad and deep humanity, no tender intimacies of perception; but he has done things that no other English poet has done, and in his own special sphere he is supreme.

FURTHER READING

T.S. Elliot, 'Swinburne as Poet', in *The Sacred Wood*, 1920.
D. Bush, *Mythology and the Romantic Tradition in English Poetry*, 1937.
C.K. Hyder (ed.), *Swinburne: The Critical Heritage*, 1970.
J. McGann, *Swinburne: An Experiment in Criticism*, 1972.

Biographies
G. Lafourcade (2 vols), London, 1932.
J.O. Fuller, 1971.
P. Henderson, 1974.
D. Thomas, 1979.

A BALLAD OF LIFE

I FOUND in dreams a place of wind and flowers,
  Full of sweet trees and colour of glad grass,
  In midst whereof there was
A lady clothed like summer with sweet hours.
Her beauty, fervent as a fiery moon,
  Made my blood burn and swoon
    Like a flame rained upon.
Sorrow had filled her shaken eyelids' blue,
And her mouth's sad red heavy rose all through
    Seemed sad with glad things gone.

She held a little cithern by the strings,
  Shaped heartwise, strung with subtle-coloured hair
  Of some dead lute-player
That in dead years had done delicious things.
The seven strings were named accordingly;
  The first string charity,
    The second tenderness,
The rest were pleasure, sorrow, sleep, and sin,
And loving-kindness, that is pity's kin
    And is most pitiless.

There were three men with her, each garmented
  With gold and shod with gold upon the feet;
  And with plucked ears of wheat
The first man's hair was wound upon his head:
His face was red, and his mouth curled and sad;
  All his gold garment had
    Pale stains of dust and rust.
A riven hood was pulled across his eyes;
The token of him being upon this wise
    Made for a sign of Lust.

The next was Shame, with hollow heavy face
  Coloured like green wood when flame kindles it.
  He hath such feeble feet
They may not well endure in any place.
His face was full of grey old miseries,
  And all his blood's increase
    Was even increase of pain.
The last was Fear, that is akin to Death;
He is Shame's friend, and always as Shame saith
    Fear answers him again.

My soul said in me; This is marvellous,
  Seeing the air's face is not so delicate
  Nor the sun's grace so great,
If sin and she be kin or amorous.
And seeing where maidens served her on their
    knees,
  I bade one crave of these
    To know the cause thereof.
Then Fear said: I am Pity that was dead.
And Shame said: I am Sorrow comforted.
    And Lust said: I am Love.

Thereat her hands began a lute-playing
  And her sweet mouth a song in a strange tongue;
  And all the while she sung
There was no sound but long tears following
Long tears upon men's faces, waxen white
  With extreme sad delight.
    But those three following men
Became as men raised up among the dead;
Great glad mouths open and fair cheeks made red
    With child's blood come again.

Then I said: Now assuredly I see
  My lady is perfect, and transfigureth
  All sin and sorrow and death,
Making them fair as her own eyelids be,
Or lips wherein my whole soul's life abides;
  Or as her sweet white sides
    And bosom carved to kiss.
Now therefore, if her pity further me,
Doubtless for her sake all my days shall be
    As righteous as she is.

Forth, ballad, and take roses in both arms,
  Even till the top rose touch thee in the throat
Where the least thornprick harms;
  And girdled in thy golden singing-coat,
Come thou before my lady and say this;
  Borgia, thy gold hair's colour burns in me,
    Thy mouth makes beat my blood in feverish
      rhymes;
  Therefore so many as these roses be,
    Kiss me so many times.
Then it may be, seeing how sweet she is,
  That she will stoop herself none otherwise
    Than a blown vine-branch doth,
  And kiss thee with a soft laughter on thine eyes,
    Ballad, and on thy mouth.

A BALLAD OF DEATH

Kneel down, fair Love, and fill thyself with tears,
Girdle thyself with sighing for a girth
Upon the sides of mirth,
Cover thy lips and eyelids, let thine ears

Be filled with rumour of people sorrowing;
Make thee soft raiment out of woven sighs
Upon the flesh to cleave,
Set pains therein and many a grievous thing,
And many sorrows after each his wise
For armlet and for gorget and for sleeve.

O Love's lute heard about the lands of death,
Left hanged upon the trees that were therein;
O Love and Time and Sin,
Three singing mouths that mourn now underbreath,
Three lovers, each one evil spoken of;
O smitten lips wherethrough this voice of mine
Came softer with her praise;
Abide a little for our lady's love.
The kisses of her mouth were more than wine,
And more than peace the passage of her days.

O Love, thou knowest if she were good to see.
O Time, thou shalt not find in any land
Till, cast out of thine hand,
The sunlight and the moonlight fail from thee,
Another woman fashioned like as this.
O Sin, thou knowest that all thy shame in her
Was made a goodly thing;
Yea, she caught Shame and shamed him with her kiss,
With her fair kiss, and lips much lovelier
Than lips of amorous roses in late spring.

By night there stood over against my bed
Queen Venus with a hood striped gold and black,
Both sides drawn fully back
From brows wherein the sad blood failed of red,

And temples drained of purple and full of death.
Her curled hair had the wave of sea-water
And the sea's gold in it.
Her eyes were as a dove's that sickeneth.
Strewn dust of gold she had shed over her,
And pearl and purple and amber on her feet.

Upon her raiment of dyed sendaline
Were painted all the secret ways of love
And covered things thereof,
That hold delight as grape-flowers hold their wine;
Red mouths of maidens and red feet of doves,
And brides that kept within the bride-chamber
Their garment of soft shame,
And weeping faces of the wearied loves
That swoon in sleep and awake wearier,
With heat of lips and hair shed out like flame.

The tears that through her eyelids fell on me
Made mine own bitter where they ran between
As blood had fallen therein,
She saying; Arise, lift up thine eyes and see
If any glad thing be or any good
Now the best thing is taken forth of us;
Even she to whom all praise
Was as one flower in a great multitude,
One glorious flower of many and glorious,
One day found gracious among many days:

Even she whose handmaiden was Love—to whom
At kissing times across her stateliest bed
Kings bowed themselves and shed
Pale wine, and honey with the honeycomb,

And spikenard bruisèd for a burnt-offering;
Even she between whose lips the kiss became
As fire and frankincense;
Whose hair was as gold raiment on a king,
Whose eyes were as the morning purged with flame,
Whose eyelids as sweet savour issuing thence.

Then I beheld, and lo on the other side
My lady's likeness crowned and robed and dead.
Sweet still, but now not red,
Was the shut mouth whereby men lived and died.
And sweet, but emptied of the blood's blue shade,
The great curled eyelids that withheld her eyes.
And sweet, but like spoilt gold,
The weight of colour in her tresses weighed.
And sweet, but as a vesture with new dyes,
The body that was clothed with love of old.

Ah! that my tears filled all her woven hair
And all the hollow bosom of her gown—
Ah! that my tears ran down
Even to the place where many kisses were,
Even where her parted breast-flowers have place,
Even where they are cloven apart—who knows not
    this?
Ah! the flowers cleave apart
And their sweet fills the tender interspace;
Ah! the leaves grown thereof were things to kiss
Ere their fine gold was tarnished at the heart.

Ah! in the days when God did good to me,
Each part about her was a righteous thing;
Her mouth an almsgiving,
The glory of her garments charity,

The beauty of her bosom a good deed,
In the good days when God kept sight of us;
Love lay upon her eyes,
And on that hair whereof the world takes heed;
And all her body was more virtuous
Than souls of women fashioned otherwise.

Now, ballad, gather poppies in thine hands
And sheaves of brier and many rusted sheaves
Rain-rotten in rank lands,
Waste marigold and late unhappy leaves
And grass that fades ere any of it be mown;
And when thy bosom is filled full thereof
Seek out Death's face ere the light altereth,
And say 'My master that was thrall to Love
Is become thrall to Death.'
Bow down before him, ballad, sigh and groan,
But make no sojourn in thy outgoing;
For haply it may be
That when thy feet return at evening
Death shall come in with thee.

THE TRIUMPH OF TIME

BEFORE our lives divide for ever,
　While time is with us and hands are free,
(Time, swift to fasten and swift to sever
　Hand from hand, as we stand by the sea)
I will say no word that a man might say
Whose whole life's love goes down in a day;
For this could never have been; and never,
　Though the gods and the years relent, shall be.

Is it worth a tear, is it worth an hour,
　To think of things that are well outworn?
Of fruitless husk and fugitive flower,
　The dream foregone and the deed forborne?
Though joy be done with and grief be vain,
Time shall not sever us wholly in twain;
Earth is not spoilt for a single shower;
　But the rain has ruined the ungrown corn.

It will grow not again, this fruit of my heart,
　Smitten with sunbeams, ruined with rain.
The singing seasons divide and depart,
　Winter and summer depart in twain.
It will grow not again, it is ruined at root,
The bloodlike blossom, the dull red fruit;
Though the heart yet sickens, the lips yet smart,
　With sullen savour of poisonous pain.

I have given no man of my fruit to eat;
　I trod the grapes, I have drunken the wine.
Had you eaten and drunken and found it sweet,
　This wild new growth of the corn and vine,
This wine and bread without lees or leaven,
We had grown as gods, as the gods in heaven,
Souls fair to look upon, goodly to greet,
　One splendid spirit, your soul and mine.

In the change of years, in the coil of things,
　In the clamour and rumour of life to be,
We, drinking love at the furthest springs,
　Covered with love as a covering tree,
We had grown as gods, as the gods above,
Filled from the heart to the lips with love,
Held fast in his hands, clothed warm with his wings,
　O love, my love, had you loved but me!

We had stood as the sure stars stand, and moved
  As the moon moves, loving the world; and seen
Grief collapse as a thing disproved,
  Death consume as a thing unclean.
Twain halves of a perfect heart, made fast
Soul to soul while the years fell past;
Had you loved me once, as you have not loved;
  Had the chance been with us that has not been.

I have put my days and dreams out of mind,
  Days that are over, dreams that are done.
Though we seek life through, we shall surely find
  There is none of them clear to us now, not one.
But clear are these things; the grass and the sand,
Where, sure as the eyes reach, ever at hand,
With lips wide open and face burnt blind,
  The strong sea-daisies feast on the sun.

The low downs lean to the sea; the stream,
  One loose thin pulseless tremulous vein,
Rapid and vivid and dumb as a dream,
  Works downward, sick of the sun and the rain;
No wind is rough with the rank rare flowers;
The sweet sea, mother of loves and hours,
Shudders and shines as the grey winds gleam,
  Turning her smile to a fugitive pain.

Mother of loves that are swift to fade,
  Mother of mutable winds and hours.
A barren mother, a mother-maid,
  Cold and clean as her faint salt flowers.
I would we twain were even as she,
Lost in the night and the light of the sea,
Where faint sounds falter and wan beams wade,
  Break, and are broken, and shed into showers.

The loves and hours of the life of a man,
  They are swift and sad, being born of the sea.
Hours that rejoice and regret for a span,
  Born with a man's breath, mortal as he;
Loves that are lost ere they come to birth,
Weeds of the wave, without fruit upon earth.
I lose what I long for, save what I can,
  My love, my love, and no love for me!

It is not much that a man can save
  On the sands of life, in the straits of time,
Who swims in sight of the great third wave
  That never a swimmer shall cross or climb.
Some waif washed up with the strays and spars
That ebb-tide shows to the shore and the stars;
Weed from the water, grass from a grave,
  A broken blossom, a ruined rhyme.

There will no man do for your sake, I think,
  What I would have done for the least word said.
I had wrung life dry for your lips to drink,
  Broken it up for your daily bread:
Body for body and blood for blood,
As the flow of the full sea risen to flood
That yearns and trembles before it sink,
  I had given, and lain down for you, glad and dead.

Yea, hope at highest and all her fruit,
  And time at fullest and all his dower,
I had given you surely, and life to boot,
  Were we once made one for a single hour.
But now, you are twain, you are cloven apart,
Flesh of his flesh, but heart of my heart;
And deep in one is the bitter root,
  And sweet for one is the lifelong flower.

To have died if you cared I should die for you, clung
   To my life if you bade me, played my part
As it pleased you—these were the thoughts that stung,
   The dreams that smote with a keener dart
Than shafts of love or arrows of death;
These were but as fire is, dust, or breath,
Or poisonous foam on the tender tongue
   Of the little snakes that eat my heart.

I wish we were dead together to-day,
   Lost sight of, hidden away out of sight,
Clasped and clothed in the cloven clay,
   Out of the world's way, out of the light,
Out of the ages of worldly weather,
Forgotten of all men altogether,
As the world's first dead, taken wholly away,
   Made one with death, filled full of the night.

How we should slumber, how we should sleep,
   Far in the dark with the dreams and the dews!
And dreaming, grow to each other, and weep,
   Laugh low, live softly, murmur and muse;
Yea, and it may be, struck through by the dream,
Feel the dust quicken and quiver, and seem
Alive as of old to the lips, and leap
   Spirit to spirit as lovers use.

Sick dreams and sad of a dull delight;
   For what shall it profit when men are dead
To have dreamed, to have loved with the whole soul's
     might,
   To have looked for day when the day was fled?
Let come what will, there is one thing worth,
To have had fair love in the life upon earth:
To have held love safe till the day grew night,
   While skies had colour and lips were red.

Would I lose you now? would I take you then,
　　If I lose you now that my heart has need?
And come what may after death to men,
　　What thing worth this will the dead years breed?
Lose life, lose all; but at least I know,
O sweet life's love, having loved you so,
Had I reached you on earth, I should lose not again,
　　In death nor life, nor in dream or deed.

Yea, I know this well: were you once sealed mine,
　　Mine in the blood's beat, mine in the breath,
Mixed into me as honey in wine,
　　Not time, that sayeth and gainsayeth,
Nor all strong winds had severed us then;
Not wrath of gods, nor wisdom of men,
Nor all things earthly, nor all divine,
　　Nor joy nor sorrow, nor life nor death.

I had grown pure as the dawn and the dew,
　　You had grown strong as the sun or the sea.
But none shall triumph a whole life through:
　　For death is one, and the fates are three.
At the door of life, by the gate of breath,
There are worse things waiting for men than death;
Death could not sever my soul and you,
　　As these have severed your soul from me.

You have chosen and clung to the chance they sent
　　　　you,
　　Life sweet as perfume and pure as prayer.
But will it not one day in heaven repent you?
　　Will they solace you wholly, the days that were?
Will you lift up your eyes between sadness and bliss,
Meet mine, and see where the great love is,
And tremble and turn and be changed? Content you;
　　The gate is strait; I shall not be there.

But you, had you chosen, had you stretched hand,
   Had you seen good such a thing were done,
I too might have stood with the souls that stand
   In the sun's sight, clothed with the light of the sun;
But who now on earth need care how I live?
Have the high gods anything left to give,
Save dust and laurels and gold and sand?
   Which gifts are goodly; but I will none.

O all fair lovers about the world,
   There is none of you, none, that shall comfort me.
My thoughts are as dead things, wrecked and whirled
   Round and round in a gulf of the sea;
And still, through the sound and the straining stream,
Through the coil and chafe, they gleam in a dream,
The bright fine lips so cruelly curled,
   And strange swift eyes where the soul sits free.

Free, without pity, withheld from woe,
   Ignorant; fair as the eyes are fair.
Would I have you change now, change at a blow
   Startled and stricken, awake and aware?
Yea, if I could, would I have you see
My very love of you filling me,
And know my soul to the quick, as I know
   The likeness and look of your throat and hair?

I shall not change you. Nay, though I might,
   Would I change my sweet one love with a word?
I had rather your hair should change in a night,
   Clear now as the plume of a black bright bird;
Your face fail suddenly, cease, turn grey,
Die as a leaf that dies in a day.
I will keep my soul in a place out of sight,
   Far off, where the pulse of it is not heard.

Far off it walks, in a bleak blown space,
　　Full of the sound of the sorrow of years.
I have woven a veil for the weeping face,
　　Whose lips have drunken the wine of tears;
I have found a way for the failing feet,
A place for slumber and sorrow to meet;
There is no rumour about the place,
　　Nor light, nor any that sees or hears.

I have hidden my soul out of sight, and said
　　'Let none take pity upon thee, none
Comfort thy crying: for lo, thou art dead,
　　Lie still now, safe out of sight of the sun.
Have I not built thee a grave, and wrought
Thy grave-clothes on thee of grievous thought,
With soft spun verses and tears unshed,
　　And sweet light visions of things undone?

'I have given thee garments and balm and myrrh,
　　And gold, and beautiful burial things.
But thou, be at peace now, make no stir;
　　Is not thy grave as a royal king's?
Fret not thyself though the end were sore;
Sleep, be patient, vex me no more.
Sleep; what hast thou to do with her?
　　The eyes that weep, with the mouth that sings?'

Where the dead red leaves of the years lie rotten,
　　The cold old crimes and the deeds thrown by,
The misconceived and the misbegotten,
　　I would find a sin to do ere I die,
Sure to dissolve and destroy me all through,
That would set you higher in heaven, serve you
And leave you happy, when clean forgotten,
　　As a dead man out of mind, am I.

Your lithe hands draw me, your face burns through
   me,
  I am swift to follow you, keen to see;
But love lacks might to redeem or undo me;
  As I have been, I know I shall surely be;
'What should such fellows as I do?' Nay,
My part were worse if I chose to play;
For the worst is this after all; if they knew me,
  Not a soul upon earth would pity me.

And I play not for pity of these; but you,
  If you saw with your soul what man am I,
You would praise me at least that my soul all through
  Clove to you, loathing the lives that lie;
The souls and lips that are bought and sold,
The smiles of silver and kisses of gold,
The lapdog loves that whine as they chew,
  The little lovers that curse and cry.

There are fairer women, I hear; that may be;
  But I, that I love you and find you fair,
Who are more than fair in my eyes if they be,
  Do the high gods know or the great gods care?
Though the swords in my heart for one were seven,
Should the iron hollow of doubtful heaven,
That knows not itself whether night-time or day be,
  Reverberate words and a foolish prayer?

I will go back to the great sweet mother,
  Mother and lover of men, the sea.
I will go down to her, I and none other,
  Close with her, kiss her and mix her with me;
Cling to her, strive with her, hold her fast:
O fair white mother, in days long past
Born without sister, born without brother,
  Set free my soul as thy soul is free.

O fair green-girdled mother of mine,
    Sea, that art clothed with the sun and the rain,
Thy sweet hard kisses are strong like wine,
    Thy large embraces are keen like pain.
Save me and hide me with all thy waves,
Find me one grave of thy thousand graves,
Those pure cold populous graves of thine
    Wrought without hand in a world without stain.

I shall sleep, and move with the moving ships,
    Change as the winds change, veer in the tide;
My lips will feast on the foam of thy lips,
    I shall rise with thy rising, with thee subside;
Sleep, and not know if she be, if she were,
Filled full with life to the eyes and hair,
As a rose is fulfilled to the roseleaf tips
    With splendid summer and perfume and pride.

This woven raiment of nights and days,
    Were it once cast off and unwound from me,
Naked and glad would I walk in thy ways,
    Alive and aware of thy ways and thee;
Clear of the whole world, hidden at home,
Clothed with the green and crowned with the foam,
A pulse of the life of thy straits and bays,
    A vein in the heart of the streams of the sea.

Fair mother, fed with the lives of men,
    Thou art subtle and cruel of heart, men say.
Thou hast taken, and shalt not render again;
    Thou art full of thy dead, and cold as they.
But death is the worst that comes of thee;
Thou art fed with our dead, O mother, O sea,
But when hast thou fed on our hearts? or when,
    Having given us love, hast thou taken away?

O tender-hearted, O perfect lover, .
  Thy lips are bitter, and sweet thine heart.
The hopes that hurt and the dreams that hover,
  Shall they not vanish away and apart?
But thou, thou art sure, thou art older than earth;
Thou art strong for death and fruitful of birth;
Thy depths conceal and thy gulfs discover;
  From the first thou wert; in the end thou art.

And grief shall endure not for ever, I know.
  As things that are not shall these things be;
We shall live through seasons of sun and of snow,
  And none be grievous as this to me.
We shall hear, as one in a trance that hears,
The sound of time, the rhyme of the years;
Wrecked hope and passionate pain will grow
  As tender things of a spring-tide sea.

Sea-fruit that swings in the waves that hiss,
  Drowned gold and purple and royal rings.
And all time past, was it all for this?
  Times unforgotten, and treasures of things?
Swift years of liking and sweet long laughter,
That wist not well of the years thereafter
Till love woke, smitten at heart by a kiss,
  With lips that trembled and trailing wings?

There lived a singer in France of old
  By the tideless dolorous midland sea.
In a land of sand and ruin and gold
  There shone one woman, and none but she.
And finding life for her love's sake fail,
Being fain to see her, he bade set sail,
Touched land, and saw her as life grew cold,
  And praised God, seeing; and so died he.

Died, praising God for his gift and grace:
  For she bowed down to him weeping, and said
'Live;' and her tears were shed on his face
  Or ever the life in his face was shed.
The sharp tears fell through her hair, and stung
Once, and her close lips touched him and clung
Once, and grew one with his lips for a space;
  And so drew back, and the man was dead.

O brother, the gods were good to you.
  Sleep, and be glad while the world endures.
Be well content as the years wear through;
  Give thanks for life, and the loves and lures;
Give thanks for life, O brother, and death,
For the sweet last sound of her feet, her breath,
For gifts she gave you, gracious and few,
  Tears and kisses, that lady of yours.

Rest, and be glad of the gods; but I,
  How shall I praise them, or how take rest?
There is not room under all the sky
  For me that know not of worst or best,
Dream or desire of the days before,
Sweet things or bitterness, any more.
Love will not come to me now though I die,
  As love came close to you, breast to breast.

I shall never be friends again with roses;
  I shall loathe sweet tunes, where a note grown
    strong
Relents and recoils, and climbs and closes,
  As a wave of the sea turned back by song.
There are sounds where the soul's delight takes fire,
Face to face with its own desire;
A delight that rebels, a desire that reposes;
  I shall hate sweet music my whole life long.

The pulse of war and the passion of wonder,
  The heavens that murmur, the sounds that shine,
The stars that sing and the loves that thunder,
  The music burning at heart like wine,
An armed archangel whose hands raise up
All senses mixed in the spirit's cup
Till flesh and spirit are molten in sunder—
  These things are over, and no more mine.

These were a part of the playing I heard
  Once, ere my love and my heart were at strife;
Love that sings and hath wings as a bird,
  Balm of the wound and heft of the knife.
Fairer than earth is the sea, and sleep
Than overwatching of eyes that weep,
Now time has done with his one sweet word,
  The wine and leaven of lovely life.

I shall go my ways, tread out my measure,
  Fill the days of my daily breath
With fugitive things not good to treasure,
  Do as the world doth, say as it saith;
But if we had loved each other—O sweet,
Had you felt, lying under the palms of your feet,
The heart of my heart, beating harder with pleasure
  To feel you tread it to dust and death—

Ah, had I not taken my life up and given
  All that life gives and the years let go,
The wine and honey, the balm and leaven,
  The dreams reared high and the hopes brought low?
Come life, come death, not a word be said;
Should I lose you living, and vex you dead?
I never shall tell you on earth; and in heaven,
  If I cry to you then, will you hear or know?

ITYLUS

SWALLOW, my sister, O sister swallow,
　How can thine heart be full of the spring?
　　A thousand summers are over and dead.
What hast thou found in the spring to follow?
　What hast thou found in thine heart to sing?
　　What wilt thou do when the summer is shed?

O swallow, sister, O fair swift swallow,
　Why wilt thou fly after spring to the south,
　　The soft south whither thine heart is set?
Shall not the grief of the old time follow?
　Shall not the song thereof cleave to thy mouth?
　　Hast thou forgotten ere I forget?

Sister, my sister, O fleet sweet swallow,
　Thy way is long to the sun and the south;
　　But I, fulfilled of my heart's desire,
Shedding my song upon height, upon hollow,
　From tawny body and sweet small mouth
　　Feed the heart of the night with fire.

I the nightingale all spring through,
　O swallow, sister, O changing swallow,
　　All spring through till the spring be done,
Clothed with the light of the night on the dew,
　Sing, while the hours and the wild birds follow,
　　Take flight and follow and find the sun.

Sister, my sister, O soft light swallow,
　Though all things feast in the spring's guest-
　　　chamber,
　　How hast thou heart to be glad thereof yet?
For where thou fliest I shall not follow,
　Till life forget and death remember,
　　Till thou remember and I forget.

Swallow, my sister, O singing swallow,
  I know not how thou hast heart to sing.
    Hast thou the heart? is it all past over?
Thy lord the summer is good to follow,
  And fair the feet of thy lover the spring:
    But what wilt thou say to the spring thy lover?

O swallow, sister, O fleeting swallow,
  My heart in me is a molten ember
    And over my head the waves have met.
But thou wouldst tarry or I would follow,
  Could I forget or thou remember,
    Couldst thou remember and I forget.

O sweet stray sister, O shifting swallow,
  The heart's division divideth us.
    Thy heart is light as a leaf of a tree;
But mine goes forth among sea-gulfs hollow
  To the place of the slaying of Itylus,
    The feast of Daulis, the Thracian sea.

O swallow, sister, O rapid swallow,
  I pray thee sing not a little space.
    Are not the roofs and the lintels wet?
The woven web that was plain to follow,
  The small slain body, the flowerlike face,
    Can I remember if thou forget?

O sister, sister, thy first-begotten!
  The hands that cling and the feet that follow,
    The voice of the child's blood crying yet
Who hath remembered me? who hath forgotten?
  Thou hast forgotten, O summer swallow,
    But the world shall end when I forget.

HYMN TO PROSERPINE

After the Proclamation in Rome of the Christian Faith

Vicisti, Galilæe.

I HAVE lived long enough, having seen one thing,
    that love hath an end;
Goddess and maiden and queen, be near me now and
    befriend.
Thou art more than the day or the morrow, the
    seasons that laugh or that weep;
For these give joy and sorrow; but thou, Proserpina,
    sleep.
Sweet is the treading of wine, and sweet the feet of the
    dove;
But a goodlier gift is thine than foam of the grapes or
    love.
Yea, is not even Apollo, with hair and harpstring of
    gold,
A bitter God to follow, a beautiful God to behold?
I am sick of singing: the bays burn deep and chafe:
    I am fain
To rest a little from praise and the grievous pleasure
    and pain.
For the Gods we know not of, who give us our daily
    breath,
We know they are cruel as love or life, and lovely as
    death.
O Gods dethroned and deceased, cast forth, wiped
    out in a day!
From your wrath is the world released, redeemed
    from your chains, men say.
New Gods are crowned in the city; their flowers have
    broken your rods;

They are merciful, clothed with pity, the young compassionate Gods.

But for me their new device is barren, the days are
bare;

Things long past over suffice, and men forgotten that
were.

Time and the Gods are at strife; ye dwell in the midst
thereof,

Draining a little life from the barren breasts of
love.

I say to you, cease, take rest; yea, I say to you all, be
at peace,

Till the bitter milk of her breast and the barren bosom
shall cease,

Wilt thou yet take all, Galilean? but these thou shalt
not take,

The laurel, the palms and the pæan, the breasts of the
nymphs in the brake;

Breasts more soft than a dove's, that tremble with
tenderer breath;

And all the wings of the Loves, and all the joy before
death;

All the feet of the hours that sound as a single
lyre,

Dropped and deep in the flowers, with strings that
flicker like fire.

More than these wilt thou give, things fairer than all
these things?

Nay, for a little we live, and life hath mutable
wings.

A little while and we die; shall life not thrive as it
may?

For no man under the sky lives twice, outliving his
day.

And grief is a grievous thing, and a man hath enough
    of his tears:
Why should he labour, and bring fresh grief to blacken
    his years?
Thou hast conquered, O pale Galilean; the world has
    grown grey from thy breath;
We have drunken of things Lethean, and fed on the
    fullness of death.
Laurel is green for a season, and love is sweet for
    a day;
But love grows bitter with treason, and laurel outlives
    not May.
Sleep, shall we sleep after all? for the world is not
    sweet in the end;
For the old faiths loosen and fall, the new years ruin
    and rend.
Fate is a sea without shore, and the soul is a rock that
    abides;
But her ears are vexed with the roar and her face with
    the foam of the tides.
O lips that the live blood faints in, the leavings of
    racks and rods!
O ghastly glories of saints, dead limbs of gibbeted
    Gods!
Though all men abase them before you in spirit, and
    all knees bend,
I kneel not neither adore you, but standing, look to
    the end.
All delicate days and pleasant, all spirits and sorrows
    are cast
Far out with the foam of the present that sweeps to
    the surf of the past:
Where beyond the extreme sea-wall, and between the
    remote sea-gates,

Waste water washes, and tall ships founder, and deep
    death waits:
Where, mighty with deepening sides, clad about with
    the seas as with wings,
And impelled of invisible tides, and fulfilled of un-
    speakable things,
White-eyed and poisonous-finned, shark-toothed and
    serpentine-curled,
Rolls, under the whitening wind of the future, the
    wave of the world.
The depths stand naked in sunder behind it, the
    storms flee away;
In the hollow before it the thunder is taken and snared
    as a prey;
In its sides is the north-wind bound; and its salt is
    of all men's tears;
With light of ruin, and sound of changes, and pulse
    of years:
With travail of day after day, and with trouble of
    hour upon hour;
And bitter as blood is the spray; and the crests are
    as fangs that devour:
And its vapour and storm of its steam as the sighing
    of spirits to be;
And its noise as the noise in a dream; and its depth as
    the roots of the sea:
And the height of its heads as the height of the utmost
    stars of the air;
And the ends of the earth at the might thereof tremble,
    and time is made bare.
Will ye bridle the deep sea with reins, will ye chasten
    the high sea with rods?
Will ye take her to chain her with chains, who is older
    than all ye Gods?

And ye as a wind shall go by, as a fire shall ye pass and
    be past;

Ye are Gods, and behold, ye shall die, and the waves
    be upon you at last.

In the darkness of time, in the deeps of the years, in
    the changes of things,

Ye shall sleep as a slain man sleeps, and the world
    shall forget you for kings.

Though the feet of thine high priests tread where thy
    lords and our forefathers trod,

Though these that were Gods are dead, and thou
    being dead art a God,

Though before thee the throned Cytherean be fallen,
    and hidden her head,

Yet thy kingdom shall pass, Galilean, thy dead shall
    go down to thee dead.

Of the maiden thy mother men sing as a goddess with
    grace clad around;

Thou art throned where another was king; where
    another was queen she is crowned.

Yea, once we had sight of another: but now she is
    queen, say these.

Not as thine, not as thine was our mother, a blossom
    of flowering seas,

Clothed round with the world's desire as with raiment,
    and fair as the foam,

And fleeter than kindled fire, and a goddess, and
    mother of Rome.

For thine came pale and a maiden, and sister to
    sorrow; but ours,

Her deep hair heavily laden with odour and colour
    of flowers,

White rose of the rose-white water, a silver splendour,
    a flame,

Bent down unto us that besought her, and earth grew
    sweet with her name.
For thine came weeping, a slave among slaves, and
    rejected; but she
Came flushed from the full-flushed wave, and imperial,
    her foot on the sea.
And the wonderful waters knew her, the winds and
    the viewless ways,
And the roses grew rosier, and bluer the sea-blue
    stream of the bays.
Ye are fallen, our lords, by what token? we wist that
    ye should not fall.
Ye were all so fair that are broken; and one more fair
    than ye all.
But I turn to her still, having seen she shall surely
    abide in the end;
Goddess and maiden and queen, be near me now and
    befriend.
O daughter of earth, of my mother, her crown and
    blossom of birth,
I am also, I also, thy brother; I go as I came unto
    earth.
In the night where thine eyes are as moons are in
    heaven, the night where thou art,
Where the silence is more than all tunes, where sleep
    overflows from the heart,
Where the poppies are sweet as the rose in our world,
    and the red rose is white,
And the wind falls faint as it blows with the fume of
    the flowers of the night,
And the murmur of spirits that sleep in the shadow
    of Gods from afar
Grows dim in thine ears and deep as the deep dim
    soul of a star,

In the sweet low light of thy face, under heavens
    untrod by the sun,
Let my soul with their souls find place, and forget
    what is done and undone.
Thou art more than the Gods who number the days
    of our temporal breath;
For these give labour and slumber; but thou, Proser-
    pina, death.
Therefore now at thy feet I abide for a season in
    silence. I know
I shall die as my fathers died, and sleep as they sleep;
    even so.
For the glass of the years is brittle wherein we gaze
    for a span;
A little soul for a little bears up this corpse which is
    man.[1]
So long I endure, no longer; and laugh not again,
    neither weep.
For there is no God found stronger than death; and
    death is a sleep.

BEFORE THE MIRROR

Verses written under a picture.

Inscribed to J. A. Whistler

I

WHITE rose in red rose-garden
    Is not so white;
Snowdrops that plead for pardon
    And pine for fright

---

[1] ψυχάριον εἶ βαστάζον νεκρόν.
                         EPICTETUS.

Because the hard East blows
Over their maiden rows
  Grow not as this face grows from pale to bright.

Behind the veil, forbidden,
  Shut up from sight,
Love, is there sorrow hidden,
  Is there delight?
Is joy thy dower or grief,
White rose of weary leaf,
  Late rose whose life is brief, whose loves are light?

Soft snows that hard winds harden
  Till each flake bite
Fill all the flowerless garden
  Whose flowers took flight
Long since when summer ceased,
And men rose up from feast,
  And warm west wind grew east, and warm day
    night.

II

'Come snow, come wind or thunder
  High up in air,
I watch my face, and wonder
  At my bright hair;
Nought else exalts or grieves
The rose at heart, that heaves
  With love of her own leaves and lips that pair.

'She knows not loves that kissed her
  She knows not where.
Art thou the ghost, my sister,
  White sister there,

Am I the ghost, who knows?
My hand, a fallen rose,
   Lies snow-white on white snows, and takes no care.

'I cannot see what pleasures
   Or what pains were;
What pale new loves and treasures
   New years will bear;
What beam will fall, what shower,
What grief or joy for dower;
   But one thing knows the flower; the flower is fair.'

III

Glad, but not flushed with gladness,
   Since joys go by;
Sad, but not bent with sadness,
   Since sorrows die;
Deep in the gleaming glass
She sees all past things pass,
   And all sweet life that was lie down and lie.

There glowing ghosts of flowers
   Draw down, draw nigh;
And wings of swift spent hours
   Take flight and fly;
She sees by formless gleams,
She hears across cold streams,
   Dead mouths of many dreams that sing and sigh.

Face fallen and white throat lifted,
   With sleepless eye
She sees old loves that drifted,
   She knew not why,
Old loves and faded fears
Float down a stream that hears
   The flowing of all men's tears beneath the sky.

IN MEMORY OF WALTER SAVAGE LANDOR

BACK to the flower-town, side by side,
    The bright months bring,
New-born, the bridegroom and the bride,
    Freedom and spring.

The sweet land laughs from sea to sea,
    Filled full of sun;
All things come back to her, being free;
    All things but one.

In many a tender wheaten plot
    Flowers that were dead
Live, and old suns revive; but not
    That holier head.

By this white wandering waste of sea,
    Far north, I hear
One face shall never turn to me
    As once this year:

Shall never smile and turn and rest
    On mine as there,
Nor one most sacred hand be prest
    Upon my hair.

I came as one whose thoughts half linger,
    Half run before;
The youngest to the oldest singer
    That England bore.

I found him whom I shall not find
    Till all grief end,
In holiest age our mightiest mind,
    Father and friend.

But thou, if anything endure,
    If hope there be,
O spirit that man's life left pure,
    Man's death set free,

Not with disdain of days that were
    Look earthward now;
Let dreams revive the reverend hair,
    The imperial brow;

Come back in sleep, for in the life
    Where thou art not
We find none like thee. Time and strife
    And the world's lot

Move thee no more; but love at least
    And reverent heart
May move thee, royal and released,
    Soul, as thou art.

And thou, his Florence, to thy trust
    Receive and keep,
Keep safe his dedicated dust,
    His sacred sleep.

So shall thy lovers come from far,
    Mix with thy name
As morning-star with evening-star
    His faultless fame.

A SONG IN TIME OF ORDER. 1852

Push hard across the sand,
    For the salt wind gathers breath;
Shoulder and wrist and hand,
    Push hard as the push of death.

The wind is as iron that rings,
    The foam-heads loosen and flee;
It swells and welters and swings,
    The pulse of the tide of the sea.

And up on the yellow cliff
    The long corn flickers and shakes;
Push, for the wind holds stiff,
    And the gunwale dips and rakes.

Good hap to the fresh fierce weather,
    The quiver and beat of the sea!
While three men hold together,
    The kingdoms are less by three.

Out to the sea with her there,
    Out with her over the sand;
Let the kings keep the earth for their share!
    We have done with the sharers of land.

They have tied the world in a tether,
    They have bought over God with a fee;
While three men hold together,
    The kingdoms are less by three.

We have done with the kisses that sting,
    The thief's mouth red from the feast,
The blood on the hands of the king
    And the lie at the lips of the priest.

Will they tie the winds in a tether,
    Put a bit in the jaws of the sea?
While three men hold together,
    The kingdoms are less by three.

Let our flag run out straight in the wind!
    The old red shall be floated again
When the ranks that are thin shall be thinned,
    When the names that were twenty are ten;

When the devil's riddle is mastered
    And the galley-bench creaks with a Pope,
We shall see Buonaparte the bastard
    Kick heels with his throat in a rope.

While the shepherd sets wolves on his sheep
    And the emperor halters his kine,
While Shame is a watchman asleep
    And Faith is a keeper of swine,

Let the wind shake our flag like a feather,
    Like the plumes of the foam of the sea!
While three men hold together,
    The kingdoms are less by three.

All the world has its burdens to bear,
    From Cayenne to the Austrian whips;
Forth, with the rain in our hair
    And the salt sweet foam in our lips;

In the teeth of the hard glad weather,
    In the blown wet face of the sea;
While three men hold together,
    The kingdoms are less by three.

A SONG IN TIME OF REVOLUTION. 1860

THE heart of the rulers is sick, and the high-priest
    covers his head:
For this is the song of the quick that is heard in the
    ears of the dead.

The poor and the halt and the blind are keen and
    mighty and fleet:
Like the noise of the blowing of wind is the sound of
    the noise of their feet.

The wind has the sound of a laugh in the clamour of
    days and of deeds:
The priests are scattered like chaff, and the rulers
    broken like reeds.

The high-priest sick from qualms, with his raiment
    bloodily dashed;
The thief with branded palms, and the liar with
    cheeks abashed;

They are smitten, they tremble greatly, they are
    pained for their pleasant things:
For the house of the priests made stately, and the
    might in the mouth of the kings.

They are grieved and greatly afraid; they are taken,
    they shall not flee:
For the heart of the nations is made as the strength of
    the springs of the sea.

They were fair in the grace of gold, they walked with
    delicate feet:
They were clothed with the cunning of old, and the
    smell of their garments was sweet.

For the breaking of gold in their hair they halt as a
man made lame:
They are utterly naked and bare; their mouths are
bitter with shame.

Wilt thou judge thy people now, O king that wast
found most wise?
Wilt thou lie any more, O thou whose mouth is
emptied of lies?

Shall God make a pact with thee, till his hook be
found in thy sides?
Wilt thou put back the time of the sea, or the place of
the season of tides?

Set a word in thy lips, to stand before God with a
word in thy mouth:
That 'the rain shall return in the land, and the tender
dew after drouth'.

But the arm of the elders is broken, their strength is
unbound and undone:
They wait for a sign of a token; they cry, and there
cometh none.

Their moan is in every place, the cry of them filleth
the land:
There is shame in the sight of their face, there is fear
in the thews of their hand.

They are girdled about the reins with a curse for the
girdle thereon:
For the noise of the rending of chains the face of their
colour is gone.

For the sound of the shouting of men they are
    grievously stricken at heart:
They are smitten asunder with pain, their bones are
    smitten apart.

There is none of them all that is whole; their lips gape
    open for breath;
They are clothed with sickness of soul, and the shape
    of the shadow of death.

The wind is thwart in their feet; it is full of the shout-
    ing of mirth;
As one shaketh the sides of a sheet, so it shaketh the
    ends of the earth.

The sword, the sword is made keen; the iron has
    opened its mouth;
The corn is red that was green; it is bound for the
    sheaves of the south.

The sound of a word was shed, the sound of the wind
    as a breath,
In the ears of the souls that were dead, in the dust of
    the deepness of death;

Where the face of the moon is taken, the ways of the
    stars undone,
The light of the whole sky shaken, the light of the
    face of the sun:

Where the waters are emptied and broken, the waves
    of the waters are stayed;
Where God has bound for a token the darkness that
    maketh afraid;

Where the sword was covered and hidden, and dust
    had grown in its side,
A word came forth which was bidden, the crying of
    one that cried:

The sides of the two-edged sword shall be bare, and
    its mouth shall be red,
For the breath of the face of the Lord that is felt in
    the bones of the dead.

TO VICTOR HUGO

In the fair days when God
  By man as godlike trod,
And each alike was Greek, alike was free,
  God's lightning spared, they said,
  Alone the happier head
Whose laurels screened it; fruitless grace for thee,
  To whom the high gods gave of right
Their thunders and their laurels and their light.

  Sunbeams and bays before
  Our master's servants wore,
For these Apollo left in all men's lands;
  But far from these ere now
  And watched with jealous brow
Lay the blind lightnings shut between God's hands,
  And only loosed on slaves and kings
The terror of the tempest of their wings.

  Born in those younger years
  That shone with storms of spears

And shook in the wind blown from a dead world's pyre,
    When by her back-blown hair
    Napoleon caught the fair
And fierce Republic with her feet of fire,
    And stayed with iron words and hands
Her flight, and freedom in a thousand lands:

    Thou sawest the tides of things
    Close over the heads of kings,
And thine hand felt the thunder, and to thee
    Laurels and lightnings were
    As sunbeams and soft air
Mixed each in other, or as mist with sea
    Mixed, or as memory with desire,
Or the lute's pulses with the louder lyre.

    For thee man's spirit stood
    Disrobed of flesh and blood,
And bare the heart of the most secret hours;
    And to thine hand more tame
    Than birds in winter came
High hopes and unknown flying forms of powers,
    And from thy table fed, and sang
Till with the tune men's ears took fire and rang.

    Even all men's eyes and ears
    With fiery sound and tears
Waxed hot, and cheeks caught flame and eyelids light
    At those high songs of thine
    That stung the sense like wine,
Or fell more soft than dew or snow by night,
    Or wailed as in some flooded cave
Sobs the strong broken spirit in a wave.

But we, our master, we
Whose hearts, uplift to thee,
Ache with the pulse of thy remembered song,
We ask not nor await
From the clenched hands of fate,
As thou, remission of the world's old wrong;
Respite we ask not, nor release;
Freedom a man may have, he shall not peace.

Though thy most fiery hope
Storm heaven, to set wide ope
The all-sought-for gate whence God or Chance debars
All feet of men, all eyes—
The old night resumes her skies,
Her hollow hiding-place of clouds and stars,
Where nought save these is sure in sight;
And, paven with death, our days are roofed with
night.

One thing we can; to be
Awhile, as men may, free;
But not by hope or pleasure the most stern
Goddess, most awful-eyed,
Sits, but on either side
Sit sorrow and the wrath of hearts that burn,
Sad faith that cannot hope or fear,
And memory grey with many a flowerless year.

Not that in stranger's wise
I lift not loving eyes
To the fair foster-mother France, that gave
Beyond the pale fleet foam
Help to my sires and home,
Whose great sweet breast could shelter those and save
Whom from her nursing breasts and hands
Their land cast forth of old on gentler lands.

Not without thoughts that ache
For theirs and for thy sake,
I, born of exiles, hail thy banished head;
I whose young song took flight
Toward the great heat and light
On me a child from thy far splendour shed,
From thine high place of soul and song,
Which, fallen on eyes yet feeble, made them strong.

Ah, not with lessening love
For memories born hereof,
I look to that sweet mother-land and see
The old fields and fair full streams,
And skies, but fled like dreams
The feet of freedom and the thought of thee;
And all between the skies and graves
The mirth of mockers and the shame of slaves.

She, killed with noisome air,
Even she! and still so fair,
Who said 'Let there be freedom,' and there was
Freedom; and as a lance
The fiery eyes of France
Touched the world's sleep and as a sleep made pass
Forth of men's heavier ears and eyes
Smitten with fire and thunder from new skies.

Are they men's friends indeed
Who watch them weep and bleed?
Because thou hast loved us, shall the gods love thee?
Thou, first of men and friend,
Seest thou, even thou, the end?
Thou knowest what hath been, knowest thou what
    shall be?
Evils may pass and hopes endure;
But fate is dim, and all the gods obscure.

O nursed in airs apart,
O poet highest of heart,
Hast thou seen time, who hast seen so many things?
　　Are not the years more wise,
　　More sad than keenest eyes,
The years with soundless feet and sounding wings?
　　Passing we hear them not, but past
The clamour of them thrills us, and their blast.

　　Thou art chief of us, and lord;
　　Thy song is as a sword
Keen-edged and scented in the blade from flowers;
　　Thou art lord and king; but we
　　Lift younger eyes, and see
Less of high hope, less light on wandering hours;
　　Hours that have borne men down so long,
Seen the right fail, and watched uplift the wrong.

　　But thine imperial soul,
　　As years and ruins roll
To the same end, and all things and all dreams
　　With the same wreck and roar
　　Drift on the dim same shore,
Still in the bitter foam and brackish streams
　　Tracks the fresh water-spring to be
And sudden sweeter fountains in the sea.

　　As once the high God bound
　　With many a rivet round
Man's saviour, and with iron nailed him through,
　　At the wild end of things,
　　Where even his own bird's wings
Flagged, whence the sea shone like a drop of dew,
　　From Caucasus beheld below
Past fathoms of unfathomable snow;

So the strong God, the chance
    Central of circumstance,
Still shows him exile who will not be slave;
    All thy great fame and thee
    Girt by the dim strait sea
With multitudinous walls of wandering wave;
    Shows us our greatest from his throne
Fate-stricken, and rejected of his own.

    Yea, he is strong, thou say'st,
    A mystery many-faced,
The wild beasts know him and the wild birds flee;
    The blind night sees him, death
    Shrinks beaten at his breath,
And his right hand is heavy on the sea:
    We know he hath made us, and is king;
We know not if he care for anything.

    Thus much, no more, we know;
    He bade what is be so,
Bade light be and bade night be, one by one;
    Bade hope and fear, bade ill
    And good redeem and kill,
Till all men be aweary of the sun
    And his world burn in its own flame
And bear no witness longer of his name.

    Yet though all this be thus,
    Be those men praised of us
Who have loved and wrought and sorrowed and not
        sinned
    For fame or fear or gold,
    Nor waxed for winter cold,
Nor changed for changes of the worldly wind;

Praised above men of men be these,
Till this one world and work we know shall cease.

Yea, one thing more than this,
We know that one thing is,
The splendour of a spirit without blame,
That not the labouring years
Blind-born, nor any fears,
Nor men nor any goods can tire or tame;
But purer power with fiery breath
Fills, and exalts above the gulfs of death.

Praised above men be thou,
Whose laurel-laden brow,
Made for the morning, droops not in the night;
Praised and beloved, that none
Of all thy great things done
Flies higher than thy most equal spirit's flight;
Praised, that nor doubt nor hope could bend
Earth's loftiest head, found upright to the end.

DOLORES

Notre-Dame des Sept Douleurs

COLD eyelids that hide like a jewel
   Hard eyes that grow soft for an hour;
The heavy white limbs, and the cruel
   Red mouth like a venomous flower;
When these are gone by with their glories,
   What shall rest of thee then, what remain,
O mystic and sombre Dolores,
   Our Lady of Pain?

Seven sorrows the priests give their Virgin;
   But thy sins, which are seventy times seven,
Seven ages would fail thee to purge in,
   And then they would haunt thee in heaven:
Fierce midnights and famishing morrows,
   And the loves that complete and control
All the joys of the flesh, all the sorrows
   That wear out the soul.

O garment not golden but gilded,
   O garden where all men may dwell,
O tower not of ivory, but builded
   By hands that reach heaven from hell;
O mystical rose of the mire,
   O house not of gold but of gain,
O house of unquenchable fire,
   Our Lady of Pain!

O lips full of lust and of laughter,
   Curled snakes that are fed from my breast,
Bite hard, lest remembrance come after
   And press with new lips where you pressed.
For my heart too springs up at the pressure,
   Mine eyelids too moisten and burn;
Ah, feed me and fill me with pleasure,
   Ere pain come in turn.

In yesterday's reach and to-morrow's,
   Out of sight though they lie of to-day,
There have been and there yet shall be sorrows
   That smite not and bite not in play.
The life and the love thou despisest,
   These hurt us indeed, and in vain,
O wise among women, and wisest,
   Our Lady of Pain.

Who gave thee thy wisdom? what stories
  That stung thee, what visions that smote?
Wert thou pure and a maiden, Dolores,
  When desire took thee first by the throat?
What bud was the shell of a blossom
  That all men may smell to and pluck?
What milk fed thee first at what bosom?
  What sins gave thee suck?

We shift and bedeck and bedrape us,
  Thou art noble and nude and antique;
Libitina thy mother, Priapus
  Thy father, a Tuscan and Greek.
We play with light loves in the portal,
  And wince and relent and refrain;
Loves die, and we know thee immortal,
  Our Lady of Pain.

Fruits fail and love dies and time ranges;
  Thou art fed with perpetual breath,
And alive after infinite changes,
  And fresh from the kisses of death;
Of languors rekindled and rallied,
  Of barren delights and unclean,
Things monstrous and fruitless, a pallid
  And poisonous queen.

Could you hurt me, sweet lips, though I hurt you?
  Men touch them, and change in a trice
The lilies and languors of virtue
  For the raptures and roses of vice;
Those lie where thy foot on the floor is,
  These crown and caress thee and chain,
O splendid and sterile Dolores,
  Our Lady of Pain.

There are sins it may be to discover,
    There are deeds it may be to delight.
What new work wilt thou find for thy lover,
    What new passions for daytime or night?
What spells that they know not a word of
    Whose lives are as leaves overblown?
What tortures undreamt of, unheard of,
    Unwritten, unknown?

Ah beautiful passionate body
    That never has ached with a heart!
On thy mouth though the kisses are bloody,
    Though they sting till it shudder and smart,
More kind than the love we adore is,
    They hurt not the heart or the brain,
O bitter and tender Dolores,
    Our Lady of Pain.

As our kisses relax and redouble,
    From the lips and the foam and the fangs
Shall no new sin be born for men's trouble,
    No dream of impossible pangs?
With the sweet of the sins of old ages
    Wilt thou satiate thy soul as of yore?
Too sweet is the rind, say the sages,
    Too bitter the core.

Hast thou told all thy secrets the last time,
    And bared all thy beauties to one?
Ah, where shall we go then for pastime,
    If the worst that can be has been done?
But sweet as the rind was the core is;
    We are fain of thee still, we are fain,
O sanguine and subtle Dolores,
    Our Lady of Pain.

By the hunger of change and emotion,
　　By the thirst of unbearable things,
By despair, the twin-born of devotion,
　　By the pleasure that winces and stings,
The delight that consumes the desire,
　　The desire that outruns the delight,
By the cruelty deaf as a fire
　　And blind as the night,

By the ravenous teeth that have smitten
　　Through the kisses that blossom and bud,
By the lips intertwisted and bitten
　　Till the foam has a savour of blood,
By the pulse as it rises and falters,
　　By the hands as they slacken and strain,
I adjure thee, respond from thine altars,
　　Our Lady of Pain.

Wilt thou smile as a woman disdaining
　　The light fire in the veins of a boy?
But he comes to thee sad, without feigning,
　　Who has wearied of sorrow and joy;
Less careful of labour and glory
　　Than the elders whose hair has uncurled;
And young, but with fancies as hoary
　　And grey as the world.

I have passed from the outermost portal
　　To the shrine where the sin is a prayer;
What care though the service be mortal?
　　O our Lady of Torture, what care?
All thine the last wine that I pour is,
　　The last in the chalice we drain,
O fierce and luxurious Dolores,
　　Our Lady of Pain.

All thine the new wine of desire,
   The fruit of four lips as they clung
Till the hair and the eyelids took fire,
   The foam of a serpentine tongue,
The froth of the serpents of pleasure,
   More salt than the foam of the sea,
Now felt as a flame, now at leisure
   As wine shed for me.

Ah thy people, thy children, thy chosen,
   Marked cross from the womb and perverse!
They have found out the secret to cozen
   The gods that constrain us and curse;
They alone, they are wise, and none other;
   Give me place, even me, in their train,
O my sister, my spouse, and my mother,
   Our Lady of Pain.

For the crown of our life as it closes
   Is darkness, the fruit thereof dust;
No thorns go as deep as a rose's,
   And love is more cruel than lust.
Time turns the old days to derision,
   Our loves into corpses or wives;
And marriage and death and division
   Make barren our lives.

And pale from the past we draw nigh thee,
   And satiate with comfortless hours;
And we know thee, how all men belie thee,
   And we gather the fruit of thy flowers;
The passion that slays and recovers,
   The pangs and the kisses that rain
On the lips and the limbs of thy lovers,
   Our Lady of Pain.

The desire of thy furious embraces
   Is more than the wisdom of years,
On the blossom though the blood lie in traces,
   Though the foliage be sodden with tears.
For the lords in whose keeping the door is
   That opens on all who draw breath
Gave the cypress to love, my Dolores,
   The myrtle to death.

And they laughed, changing hands in the measure.
   And they mixed and made peace after strife;
Pain melted in tears, and was pleasure;
   Death tingled with blood, and was life.
Like lovers they melted and tingled,
   In the dusk of thine innermost fane;
In the darkness they murmured and mingled,
   Our Lady of Pain.

In a twilight where virtues are vices,
   In thy chapels, unknown of the sun,
To a tune that enthralls and entices,
   They are wed, and the twain were as one.
For the tune from thine altar hath sounded
   Since God bade the world's work begin,
And the fume of thine incense abounded,
   To sweeten the sin.

Love listens, and paler than ashes,
   Through his curls as the crown on them slips,
Lifts languid wet eyelids and lashes,
   And laughs with insatiable lips.
Thou shalt hush him with heavy caresses,
   With music that scares the profane;
Thou shalt darken his eyes with they tresses,
   Our Lady of Pain.

Thou shalt blind his bright eyes though he wrestle,
   Thou shalt chain his light limbs though he strive;
In his lips all thy serpents shall nestle,
   In his hands all thy cruelties thrive.
In the daytime thy voice shall go through him,
   In his dreams he shall feel thee and ache;
Thou shalt kindle by night and subdue him
   Asleep and awake.

Thou shalt touch and make redder his roses
   With juice not of fruit nor of bud;
When the sense in the spirit reposes,
   Thou shalt quicken the soul through the blood.
Thine, thine the one grace we implore is,
   Who would live and not languish or feign,.
O sleepless and deadly Dolores,
   Our Lady of Pain.

Dost thou dream, in a respite of slumber,
   In a lull of the fires of thy life,
Of the days without name, without number,
   When thy will stung the world into strife;
When, a goddess, the pulse of thy passion
   Smote kings as they revelled in Rome;
And they hailed thee re-risen, O Thalassian,
   Foam-white, from the foam?

When thy lips had such lovers to flatter;
   When the city lay red from thy rods,
And thine hands were as arrows to scatter
   The children of change and their gods;
When the blood of thy foemen made fervent
   A sand never moist from the main,
As one smote them, their lord and thy servant,
   Our Lady of Pain.

On sands by the storm never shaken,
   Nor wet from the washing of tides;
Nor by foam of the waves overtaken,
   Nor winds that the thunder bestrides;
But red from the print of thy paces,
   Made smooth for the world and its lords,
Ringed round with a ring of fair faces,
   And splendid with swords.

There the gladiator, pale for thy pleasure,
   Drew bitter and perilous breath;
There torments lay hold on the treasure
   Of limbs too delicious for death;
When thy gardens were lit with live torches;
   When the world was a steed for thy rein;
When the nations lay prone in thy porches,
   Our Lady of Pain.

When, with flame all around him aspirant,
   Stood flushed, as a harp-player stands,
The implacable beautiful tyrant,
   Rose-crowned, having death in his hands;
And a sound as the sound of loud water
   Smote far through the flight of the fires,
And mixed with the lightning of slaughter
   A thunder of lyres.

Dost thou dream of what was and no more is,
   The old kingdoms of earth and the kings?
Dost thou hunger for these things, Dolores,
   For these, in a world of new things?
But thy bosom no fasts could emaciate,
   No hunger compel to complain
Those lips that no bloodshed could satiate,
   Our Lady of Pain.

As of old when the world's heart was lighter,
   Through thy garments the grace of thee glows,
The white wealth of thy body made whiter
   By the blushes of amorous blows,
And seamed with sharp lips and fierce fingers,
   And branded by kisses that bruise;
When all shall be gone that now lingers,
   Ah, what shall we lose?

Thou wert fair in the fearless old fashion,
   And thy limbs are as melodies yet,
And move to the music of passion
   With lithe and lascivious regret.
What ailed us, O gods, to desert you
   For creeds that refuse and restrain?
Come down and redeem us from virtue,
   Our Lady of Pain.

All shrines that were Vestal are flameless,
   But the flame has not fallen from this;
Though obscure be the god, and though nameless
   The eyes and the hair that we kiss;
Low fires that love sits by and forges
   Fresh heads for his arrows and thine;
Hair loosened and soiled in mid orgies
   With kisses and wine.

Thy skin changes country and colour,
   And shrivels or swells to a snakes'.
Let it brighten and bloat and grow duller,
   We know it, the flames and the flakes,
Red brands on it smitten and bitten,
   Round skies where a star is a stain,
And the leaves with thy litanies written,
   Our Lady of Pain.

On thy bosom though many a kiss be,
    There are none such as knew it of old.
Was it Alciphron once or Arisbe,
    Male ringlets or feminine gold,
That thy lips met with under the statue,
    Whence a look shot out sharp after thieves
From the eyes of the garden-god at you
    Across the fig-leaves?

Then still, through dry seasons and moister,
    One god had a wreath to his shrine;
Then love was the pearl of his oyster,[1]
    And Venus rose red out of wine.
We have all done amiss, choosing rather
    Such loves as the wise gods disdain;
Intercede for us thou with thy father,
    Our Lady of Pain.

In spring he had crowns of his garden,
    Red corn in the heat of the year,
Then hoary green olives that harden
    When the grape-blossom freezes with fear;
And milk-budded myrtles with Venus
    And vine-leaves with Bacchus he trod;
And ye said, 'We have seen, he hath seen us,
    A visible God.'

What broke off the garlands that girt you?
    What sundered you spirit and clay?
Weak sins yet alive are as virtue
    To the strength of the sins of that day.

[1] Nam te præcipuè in suis urbibus colit ora
    Hellespontia, cæteris ostreosior oris.
                        CATULL. *Carm.* xviii

For dried is the blood of thy lover,
  Ipsithilla, contracted the vein;
Cry aloud, 'Will he rise and recover,
  Our Lady of Pain?'

Cry aloud; for the old world is broken:
  Cry out; for the Phrygian is priest,
And rears not the bountiful token
  And spreads not the fatherly feast.
From the midmost of Ida, from shady
  Recesses that murmur at morn,
They have brought and baptized her, Our Lady,
  A goddess new-born.

And the chaplets of old are above us,
  And the oyster-bed teems out of reach;
Old poets outsing and outlove us,
  And Catullus makes mouths at our speech.
Who shall kiss, in thy father's own city,
  With such lips as he sang with, again?
Intercede for us all of thy pity,
  Our Lady of Pain.

Out of Dindymus heavily laden
  Her lions draw bound and unfed
A mother, a mortal, a maiden,
  A queen over death and the dead.
She is cold, and her habit is lowly,
  Her temple of branches and sods;
Most fruitful and virginal, holy,
  A mother of gods.

She hath wasted with fire thine high places,
  She hath hidden and marred and made sad
The fair limbs of the Loves, the fair faces
  Of gods that were goodly and glad.

She slays, and her hands are not bloody;
    She moves as a moon in the wane,
White-robed, and thy raiment is ruddy,
    Our Lady of Pain.

They shall pass and their places be taken,
    The gods and the priests that are pure.
They shall pass, and shalt thou not be shaken?
    They shall perish, and shalt thou endure?
Death laughs, breathing close and relentless
    In the nostrils and eyelids of lust,
With a pinch in his fingers of scentless
    And delicate dust.

But the worm shall revive thee with kisses;
    Thou shalt change and transmute as a god,
As the rod to a serpent that hisses,
    As the serpent again to a rod.
Thy life shall not cease though thou doff it;
    Thou shalt live until evil be slain,
And good shall die first, said thy prophet,
    Our Lady of Pain.

Did he lie? did he laugh? does he know it,
    Now he lies out of reach, out of breath,
Thy prophet, thy preacher, thy poet,
    Sin's child by incestuous Death?
Did he find out in fire at his waking,
    Or discern as his eyelids lost light,
When the bands of the body were breaking
    And all came in sight?

Who has known all the evil before us,
    Or the tyrannous secrets of time?
Though we match not the dead men that bore us
    At a song, at a kiss, at a crime—

Though the heathen outface and outlive us,
  And our lives and our longings are twain—
Ah, forgive us our virtues, forgive us,
  Our Lady of Pain.

Who are we that embalm and embrace thee
  With spices and savours of song?
What is time, that his children should face thee?
  What am I, that my lips do thee wrong?
I could hurt thee—but pain would delight thee;
  Or caress thee—but love would repel;
And the lovers whose lips would excite thee
  Are serpents in hell.

Who now shall content thee as they did,
  Thy lovers, when temples were built
And the hair of the sacrifice braided
  And the blood of the sacrifice spilt,
In Lampsacus fervent with faces,
  In Aphaca red from thy reign,
Who embraced thee with awful embraces,
  Our Lady of Pain?

Where are they, Cotytto or Venus,
  Astarte or Ashtaroth, where?
Do their hands as we touch come between us?
  Is the breath of them hot in thy hair?
From their lips have thy lips taken fever,
  With the blood of their bodies grown red?
Hast thou left upon earth a believer
  If these men are dead?

They were purple of raiment and golden,
  Filled full of thee, fiery with wine,
Thy lovers, in haunts unbeholden,
  In marvellous chambers of thine.

They are fled, and their footprints escape us,
   Who appraise thee, adore, and abstain,
O daughter of death and Priapus,
   Our Lady of Pain.

What ails us to fear overmeasure,
   To praise thee with timorous breath,
O mistress and mother of pleasure,
   The one thing as certain as death?
We shall change as the things that we cherish,
   Shall fade as they faded before,
As foam upon water shall perish,
   As sand upon shore.

We shall know what the darkness discovers,
   If the grave-pit be shallow or deep;
And our fathers of old, and our lovers,
   We shall know if they sleep not or sleep.
We shall see whether hell be not heaven,
   Find out whether tares be not grain,
And the joys of thee seventy times seven,
   Our Lady of Pain.

THE GARDEN OF PROSERPINE

HERE, where the world is quiet;
   Here, where all trouble seems
Dead winds' and spent waves' riot
   In doubtful dreams of dreams;
I watch the green field growing
For reaping folk and sowing,
For harvest-time and mowing,
   A sleepy world of streams.

I am tired of tears and laughter,
   And men that laugh and weep;
Of what may come hereafter
   For men that sow to reap:
I am weary of days and hours,
Blown buds of barren flowers,
Desires and dreams and powers
   And everything but sleep.

Here life has death for neighbour,
   And far from eye or ear
Wan waves and wet winds labour,
   Weak ships and spirits steer;
They drive adrift, and whither
They wot not who make thither;
But no such winds blow hither,
   And no such things grow here.

No growth of moor or coppice,
   No heather-flower or vine,
But bloomless buds of poppies,
   Green grapes of Proserpine,
Pale beds of blowing rushes
Where no leaf blooms or blushes
Save this whereout she crushes
   For dead men deadly wine.

Pale, without name or number,
   In fruitless fields of corn,
They bow themselves and slumber
   All night till light is born;
And like a soul belated,
In hell and heaven unmated,
By cloud and mist abated
   Comes out of darkness morn.

Though one were strong as seven,
   He too with death shall dwell,
Nor wake with wings in heaven,
   Nor weep for pains in hell;
Though one were fair as roses,
His beauty clouds and closes;
And well though love reposes,
   In the end it is not well.

Pale, beyond porch and portal,
   Crowned with calm leaves, she stands
Who gathers all things mortal
   With cold immortal hands;
Her languid lips are sweeter
Than love's who fears to greet her
To men that mix and meet her
   From many times and lands.

She waits for each and other,
   She waits for all men born;
Forgets the earth her mother,
   The life of fruits and corn;
And spring and seed and swallow
Take wing for her and follow
Where summer song rings hollow
   And flowers are put to scorn.

There go the loves that wither,
   The old loves with wearier wings;
And all dead years draw thither,
   And all disastrous things;
Dead dreams of days forsaken,
Blind buds that snows have shaken,
Wild leaves that winds have taken,
   Red strays of ruined springs.

We are not sure of sorrow,
　　And joy was never sure;
To-day will die to-morrow;
　　Time stoops to no man's lure;
And love, grown faint and fretful,
With lips but half regretful
Sighs, and with eyes forgetful
　　Weeps that no loves endure.

From too much love of living,
　　From hope and fear set free,
We thank with brief thanksgiving
　　Whatever gods may be
That no life lives for ever;
That dead men rise up never;
That even the weariest river
　　Winds somewhere safe to sea.

Then star nor sun shall waken,
　　Nor any change of light:
Nor sound of waters shaken,
　　Nor any sound or sight:
Nor wintry leaves nor vernal,
Nor days nor things diurnal;
Only the sleep eternal
　　In an eternal night.

HESPERIA

Out of the golden remote wild west where the sea
　　without shore is,
　Full of the sunset, and sad, if at all, with the fulness
　　　of joy,

As a wind sets in with the autumn that blows from the
　　region of stories,
　Blows with a perfume of songs and of memories
　　　beloved from a boy,
Blows from the capes of the past oversea to the bays
　　of the present,
　Filled as with shadow of sound with the pulse of
　　　invisible feet,
Far out to the shallows and straits of the future, by
　　rough ways or pleasant,
　Is it thither the wind's wings beat? is it hither to me,
　　　O my sweet?
For thee, in the stream of the deep tide-wind blowing
　　in with the water,
　Thee I behold as a bird borne in with the wind
　　　from the west,
Straight from the sunset, across white waves whence
　　rose as a daughter
　Venus thy mother, in years when the world was a
　　　water at rest.
Out of the distance of dreams, as a dream that abides
　　after slumber,
　Strayed from the fugitive flock of the night, when
　　　the moon overhead
Wanes in the wan waste heights of the heaven, and
　　stars without number
　Die without sound, and are spent like lamps that
　　　are burnt by the dead,
Comes back to me, stays by me, lulls me with touch
　　of forgotten caresses,
　One warm dream clad about with a fire as of life
　　　that endures;
The delight of thy face, and the sound of thy feet, and
　　the wind of thy tresses,

And all of a man that regrets, and all of a maid that
allures.
But thy bosom is warm for my face and profound as
a manifold flower,
Thy silence as music, thy voice as an odour that
fades in a flame;
Not a dream, not a dream is the kiss of thy mouth,
and the bountiful hour
That makes me forget what was sin, and would
make me forget were it shame.
Thine eyes that are quiet, thine hands that are tender,
thy lips that are loving,
Comfort and cool me as dew in the dawn of a moon
like a dream;
And my heart yearns baffled and blind, moved vainly
toward thee, and moving
As the refluent seaweed moves in the languid exube-
rant stream,
Fair as a rose is on earth, as a rose under water in
prison,
That stretches and swings to the slow passionate
pulse of the sea,
Closed up from the air and the sun, but alive, as a
ghost rearisen,
Pale as the love that revives as a ghost rearisen in
me.
Fom the bountiful infinite west, from the happy
memorial places
Full of the stately repose and the lordly delight of
the dead,
Where the fortunate islands are lit with the light of
ineffable faces,
And the sound of a sea without wind is about them,
and sunset is red,

Come back to redeem and release me from love that
      recalls and represses,
  That cleaves to my flesh as a flame, till the serpent
      has eaten his fill;
From the bitter delights of the dark, and the feverish,
      the furtive caresses
  That murder the youth in a man or ever his heart
      have its will.
Thy lips cannot laugh and thine eyes cannot weep;
      thou art pale as a rose is,
  Paler and sweeter than leaves that cover the blush
      of the bud;
And the heart of the flower is compassion, and pity
      the core it encloses,
  Pity, not love, that is born of the breath and decays
      with the blood.
As the cross that a wild nun clasps till the edge of it
      bruises her bosom,
  So love wounds as we grasp it, and blackens and
      burns as a flame;
I have loved overmuch in my life; when the live bud
      bursts with the blossom,
  Bitter as ashes or tears is the fruit, and the wine
      thereof shame.
As a heart that its anguish divides is the green bud
      cloven asunder;
  As the blood of a man self-slain is the flush of the
      leaves that allure;
And the perfume as poison and wine to the brain, a
      delight and a wonder;
  And the thorns are too sharp for a boy, too slight
      for a man, to endure.
Too soon did I love it, and lost love's rose; and I
      cared not for glory's:

Only the blossoms of sleep and of pleasure were
    mixed in my hair.
Was it myrtle or poppy thy garland was woven with,
    O my Dolores?
Was it pallor of slumber, or blush as of blood, that
    I found in thee fair?
For desire is a respite from love, and the flesh not the
    heart is her fuel;
She was sweet to me once, who am fled and escaped
    from the rage of her reign;
Who behold as of old time at hand as I turn, with her
    mouth growing cruel,
And flushed as with wine with the blood of her
    lovers, Our Lady of Pain.
Low down where the thicket is thicker with thorns
    than with leaves in the summer,
In the brake is a gleaming of eyes and a hissing of
    tongues that I knew;
And the lithe long throats of her snakes reach round
    her, their mouths overcome her,
And her lips grow cool with their foam, made
    moist as a desert with dew.
With the thirst and the hunger of lust though her
    beautiful lips be so bitter,
With the cold foul foam of the snakes they soften
    and redden and smile;
And her fierce mouth sweetens, her eyes wax wide
    and her eyelashes glitter,
And she laughs with a savour of blood in her face,
    and a savour of guile.
She laughs, and her hands reach hither, her hair
    blows hither and hisses,
As a low-lit flame in a wind, back-blown till it
    shudder and leap;

Let her lips not again lay hold on my soul, nor her
    poisonous kisses,
  To consume it alive and divide from thy bosom,
    Our Lady of Sleep.
Ah daughter of sunset and slumber, if now it return
    into prison,
  Who shall redeem it anew? but we, if thou wilt,
    let us fly;
Let us take to us, now that the white skies thrill with
    a moon unarisen,
  Swift horses of fear or of love, take flight and depart
    and not die.
They are swifter than dreams, they are stronger than
    death; there is none that hath ridden,
  None that shall ride in the dim strange ways of his
    life as we ride;
By the meadows of memory, the highlands of hope,
    and the shore that is hidden,
  Where life breaks loud and unseen, a sonorous
    invisible tide;
By the sands where sorrow has trodden, the salt pools
    bitter and sterile,
  By the thundering reef and the low sea-wall and
    the channel of years,
Our wild steeds press on the night, strain hard
    through pleasure and peril,
  Labour and listen and pant not or pause for the
    peril that nears;
And the sound of them trampling the way cleaves
    night as an arrow asunder,
  And slow by the sand-hill and swift by the down
    with its glimpses of grass,
Sudden and steady the music, as eight hoofs trample
    and thunder,

Rings in the ear of the low blind wind of the night
    as we pass;
Shrill shrieks in our faces the blind bland air that was
    mute as a maiden,
  Stung into storm by the speed of our passage, and
    deaf where we past;
And our spirits too burn as we bound, thine holy but
    mine heavy-laden,
  As we burn with the fire of our flight; ah love, shall
    we win at the last?

DEDICATION OF *POEMS AND BALLADS*
1865

THE sea gives her shells to the shingle,
  The earth gives her streams to the sea:
They are many, but my gift is single,
  My verses, the firstfruits of me.
Let the wind take the green and the grey leaf,
  Cast forth without fruit upon air;
Take rose-leaf and vine-leaf and bay-leaf
  Blown loose from the hair.

The night shakes them round me in legions,
  Dawn drives them before her like dreams;
Time sheds them like snows on strange regions,
  Swept shoreward on infinite streams;
Leaves pallid and sombre and ruddy,
  Dead fruits of the fugitive years;
Some stained as with wine and made bloody,
  And some as with tears.

Some scattered in seven years' traces,
   As they fell from the boy that was then;
Long left among idle green places,
   Or gathered but now among men;
On seas full of wonder and peril,
   Blown white round the capes of the north;
Or in islands where myrtles are sterile
   And loves bring not forth.

O daughters of dreams and of stories
   That life is not wearied of yet,
Faustine, Fragoletta, Dolores,
   Félise and Yolande and Juliette,
Shall I find you not still, shall I miss you,
   When sleep, that is true or that seems,
Comes back to me hopeless to kiss you,
   O daughters of dreams?

They are past as a slumber that passes,
   As the dew of a dawn of old time;
More frail than the shadows on glasses,
   More fleet than a wave or a rhyme.
As the waves after ebb drawing seaward,
   When their hollows are full of the night,
So the birds that flew singing to me-ward
   Recede out of sight.

The songs of dead seasons, that wander
   On wings of articulate words;
Lost leaves that the shore-wind may squander,
   Light flocks of untameable birds;
Some sang to me dreaming in class-time
   And truant in hand as in tongue;
For the youngest were born of boy's pastime,
   The eldest are young.

Is there shelter while life in them lingers,
　　Is there hearing for songs that recede,
Tunes touched from a harp with man's fingers
　　Or blown with boy's mouth in a reed?
Is there place in the land of your labour,
　　Is there room in your world of delight,
Where change has not sorrow for neighbour
　　And day has not night?

In their wings though the sea-wind yet quivers,
　　Will you spare not a space for them there
Made green with the running of rivers
　　And gracious with temperate air;
In the fields and the turreted cities,
　　That cover from sunshine and rain
Fair passions and bountiful pities
　　And loves without stain?

In a land of clear colours and stories,
　　In a region of shadowless hours,
Where earth has a garment of glories
　　And a murmur of musical flowers;
In woods where the spring half uncovers
　　The flush of her amorous face,
By the waters that listen for lovers,
　　For these is there place?

For the song-birds of sorrow, that muffle
　　Their music as clouds do their fire:
For the storm-birds of passion, that ruffle
　　Wild wings in a wind of desire;

In the stream of the storm as it settles
   Blown seaward, borne far from the sun,
Shaken loose on the darkness like petals
   Dropt one after one?

Though the world of your hands be more gracious
   And lovelier in lordship of things
Clothed round by sweet art with the spacious
   Warm heaven of her imminent wings,
Let them enter, unfledged and nigh fainting,
   For the love of old loves and lost times;
And receive in your palace of painting
   This revel of rhymes.

Though the seasons of man full of losses
   Make empty the years full of youth,
If but one thing be constant in crosses,
   Change lays not her hand upon truth;
Hopes die, and their tombs are for token
   That the grief as the joy of them ends
Ere time that breaks all men has broken
   The faith between friends.

Though the many lights dwindle to one light,
   There is help if the heaven has one;
Though the skies be discrowned of the sunlight
   And the earth dispossessed of the sun,
They have moonlight and sleep for repayment,
   When, refreshed as a bride and set free,
With stars and sea-winds in her raiment,
   Night sinks on the sea.

THE LAST ORACLE

(A.D. 361)

εἴπατε τῷ βασιλῆϊ, χαμαὶ πέσε δαίδαλος αὐλά·
οὐκέτι Φοῖβος ἔχει καλύβαν, οὐ μάντιδα δάφνην,
οὐ παγὰν λαλέουσαν · ἀπέσβετο καὶ λάλον ὕδωρ.

YEARS have risen and fallen in darkness or in twilight,
  Ages waxed and waned that knew not thee nor
    thine,
While the world sought light by night and sought not
    thy light,
  Since the sad last pilgrim left thy dark mid shrine.
Dark the shrine and dumb the fount of song thence
    welling,
  Save for words more sad than tears of blood, that
    said:
Tell the king, on earth has fallen the glorious dwelling,
  And the watersprings that spake are quenched and dead.
Not a cell is left the God, no roof, no cover;
  In his hand the prophet laurel flowers no more.
And the great king's high sad heart, thy true last lover,
  Felt thine answer pierce and cleave it to the core.
    And he bowed down his hopeless head
      In the drift of the wild world's tide,
    And dying, *Thou hast conquered*, he said,
      Galilean; he said it, and died.
    And the world that was thine and was ours
    When the Graces took hands with the Hours
    Grew cold as a winter wave
    In the wind from a wide-mouthed grave,
    As a gulf wide open to swallow
      The light that the world held dear.
  O father of all of us, Paian, Apollo,
    Destroyer and healer, hear!

Age on age thy mouth was mute, thy face was hidden,
  And the lips and eyes that loved thee blind and
      dumb;
Song forsook their tongues that held thy name for-
      bidden,
  Light their eyes that saw the strange God's kingdom
      come.
Fire for light and hell for heaven and psalms for pæans
  Filled the clearest eyes and lips most sweet of song,
When for chant of Greeks the wail of Galileans
  Made the whole world moan with hymns of wrath
      and wrong.
Yea, not yet we see thee, father, as they saw thee,
  They that worshipped when the world was theirs
      and thine,
They whose words had power by thine own power to
      draw thee
  Down from heaven till earth seemed more than
      heaven divine.
        For the shades are about us that hover
            When darkness is half withdrawn
        And the skirts of the dead night cover
            The face of the live new dawn.
        For the past is not utterly past
        Though the word on its lips be the last,
        And the time be gone by with its creed
        When men were as beasts that bleed,
        As sheep or as swine that wallow,
            In the shambles of faith and of fear.
      O father of all of us, Paian, Apollo,
            Destroyer and healer, hear!

Yet it may be, lord and father, could we know it,
  We that love thee for our darkness shall have light

More than ever prophet hailed of old or poet
  Standing crowned and robed and sovereign in thy
    sight.
To the likeness of one God their dreams enthralled
    thee,
  Who wast greater than all Gods that waned and
    grew;
Son of God the shining son of Time they called thee,
  Who wast older, O our father, than they knew.
For no thought of man made Gods to love or honour
  Ere the song within the silent soul began,
Nor might earth in dream or deed take heaven upon
    her
  Till the word was clothed with speech by lips of
    man.
      And the word and the life wast thou,
        The spirit of man and the breath;
      And before thee the Gods that bow
        Take life at thine hands and death.
      For these are as ghosts that wane,
      That are gone in an age or twain;
      Harsh, merciful, passionate, pure,
      They perish, but thou shalt endure;
      Be their flight with the swan or the swallow,
        They pass as the flight of a year.
    O father of all of us, Paian, Apollo,
        Destroyer and healer, hear!

Thou the word, the light, the life, the breath, the
    glory,
  Strong to help and heal, to lighten and to slay,
Thine is all the song of man, the world's whole story;
  Not of morning and of evening is thy day.
Old and younger Gods are buried or begotten

From uprising to downsetting of thy sun,
Risen from eastward, fallen to westward and for-
    gotten,
    And their springs are many, but their end is one.
Divers births of godheads find one death appointed,
    As the soul whence each was born makes room for
        each;
God by God goes out, discrowned and disanointed,
    But the soul stands fast that gave them shape and
        speech.
            Is the sun yet cast out of heaven?
                Is the song yet cast out of man?
            Life that had song for its leaven
                To quicken the blood that ran
            Through the veins of the songless years
            More bitter and cold than tears,
            Heaven that had thee for its one
            Light, life, word, witness, O sun,
            Are they soundless and sightless and hollow,
                Without eye, without speech, without ear?
        O father of all of us, Paian, Apollo,
                Destroyer and healer, hear!

Time arose and smote thee silent at his warning,
    Change and darkness fell on men that fell from
        thee;
Dark thou satest, veiled with light, behind the morn-
    ing,
    Till the soul of man should lift up eyes and see.
Till the blind mute soul get speech again and eye-
    sight,
    Man may worship not the light of life within;
In his sight the stars whose fires grow dark in thy sight
    Shine as sunbeams on the night of death and sin.

Time again is risen with mightier word of warning,
  Change hath blown again a blast of louder breath;
Clothed with clouds and stars and dreams that melt
    in morning,
    Lo, the Gods that ruled by grace of sin and death!
      They are conquered, they break, they are
        stricken,
        Whose might made the whole world pale;
      They are dust that shall rise not or quicken
        Though the world for their death's sake wail.
      As a hound on a wild beast's trace,
      So time has their godhead in chase;
      As wolves when the hunt makes head,
      They are scattered, they fly, they are fled;
      They are fled beyond hail, beyond hollo,
        And the cry of the chase, and the cheer.
    O father of all of us, Paian, Apollo,
      Destroyer and healer, hear!

Day by day thy shadow shines in heaven beholden,
  Even the sun, the shining shadow of thy face:
King, the ways of heaven before thy feet grow golden;
  God, the soul of earth is kindled with thy grace.
In thy lips the speech of man whence Gods were
    fashioned,
  In thy soul the thought that makes them and un-
    makes;
By the light and heat incarnate and impassioned,
  Soul to soul of man gives light for light and takes.
As they knew thy name of old time could we know it,
  Healer called of sickness, slayer invoked of wrong,
Light of eyes that saw thy light, God, king, priest, poet,
  Song should bring thee back to heal us with thy
    song.

For thy kingdom is past not away,
   Nor thy power from the place thereof hurled;
Out of heaven they shall cast not the day,
   They shall cast not out song from the world.
By the song and the light they give
We know thy works that they live;
With the gift thou hast given us of speech
We praise, we adore, we beseech,
We arise at thy bidding and follow,
   We cry to thee, answer, appear,
O father of all of us, Paian, Apollo,
   Destroyer and healer, hear!

A FORSAKEN GARDEN

In a coign of the cliff between lowland and highland,
   At the sea-down's edge between windward and lee,
Walled round with rocks as an inland island,
   The ghost of a garden fronts the sea.
A girdle of brushwood and thorn encloses
   The steep square slope of the blossomless bed
Where the weeds that grew green from the graves of
    its roses
       Now lie dead.

The fields fall southward, abrupt and broken,
   To the low last edge of the long lone land.
If a step should sound or a word be spoken,
   Would a ghost not rise at the strange guest's hand?
So long have the grey bare walks lain guestless,
   Through branches and briars if a man make way,
He shall find no life but the sea-wind's, restless
       Night and day.

The dense hard passage is blind and stifled
   That crawls by a track none turn to climb
To the strait waste place that the years have rifled
   Of all but the thorns that are touched not of time.
The thorns he spares when the rose is taken;
   The rocks are left when he wastes the plain.
The wind that wanders, the weeds wind-shaken,
       These remain.

Not a flower to be pressed of the foot that falls not;
   As the heart of a dead man the seed-plots are dry;
From the thicket of thorns whence the nightingale
   calls not,
   Could she call, there were never a rose to reply.
Over the meadows that blossom and wither
   Rings but the note of a sea-bird's song;
Only the sun and the rain come hither
       All year long.

The sun burns sere and the rain dishevels
   One gaunt bleak blossom of scentless breath.
Only the wind here hovers and revels
   In a round where life seems barren as death.
Here there was laughing of old, there was weeping,
   Haply, of lovers none ever will know,
Whose eyes went seaward a hundred sleeping
       Years ago.

Heart handfast in heart as they stood, 'Look thither.'
   Did he whisper? 'look forth from the flowers to the
   . sea;
For the foam-flowers endure when the rose-blossoms
   wither,
   And men that love lightly may die—but we?'

And the same wind sang and the same waves whitened,
  And or ever the garden's last petals were shed,
In the lips that had whispered, the eyes that had
    lightened,
        Love was dead.

Or they loved their life through, and then went
    whither?
  And were one to the end—but what end who knows?
Love deep as the sea as a rose must wither,
  As the rose-red seaweed that mocks the rose.
Shall the dead take thought for the dead to love them?
  What love was ever as deep as a grave?
They are loveless now as the grass above them
      Or the wave.

All are at one now, roses and lovers,
  Not known of the cliffs and the fields and the sea.
Not a breath of the time that has been hovers
  In the air now soft with a summer to be.
Not a breath shall there sweeten the seasons hereafter
  Of the flowers or the lovers that laugh now or weep,
When as they that are free now of weeping and
    laughter
      We shall sleep.

Here death may deal not again for ever;
  Here change may come not till all change end.
From the graves they have made they shall rise up
    never,
  Who have left nought living to ravage and rend.
Earth, stones, and thorns of the wild ground growing,
  While the sun and the rain live, these shall be;
Till a last wind's breath upon all these blowing
      Roll the sea.

Till the slow sea rise and the sheer cliff crumble,
   Till terrace and meadow the deep gulfs drink,
Till the strength of the waves of the high tides humble
   The fields that lessen, the rocks that shrink,
Here now in his triumph where all things falter,
    Stretched out on the spoils that his own hand
      spread,
As a god self-slain on his own strange altar,
      Death lies dead.

AVE ATQUE VALE

In memory of Charles Baudelaire

Nous devrions pourtant lui porter quelques fleurs;
Les morts, les pauvres morts, ont de grandes douleurs,
Et quand Octobre souffle, émondeur des vieux arbres,
Son vent mélancolique à l'entour de leurs marbres,
Certe, ils doivent trouver les vivants bien ingrats.
                  Les Fleurs du Mal.

I

SHALL I strew on thee rose or rue or laurel,
    Brother, on this that was the veil of thee?
      Or quiet sea-flower moulded by the sea,
Or simplest growth of meadow-sweet or sorrel,
    Such as the summer-sleepy Dryads weave,
   Waked up by snow-soft sudden rains at eve?
Or wilt thou rather, as on earth before,
    Half-faded fiery blossoms, pale with heat
    And full of bitter summer, but more sweet
To thee than gleamings of a northern shore
    Trod by no tropic feet?

II

For always thee the fervid languid glories
    Allured of heavier suns in mightier skies;
    Thine ears knew all the wandering watery sighs
Where the sea sobs round Lesbian promontories,
    The barren kiss of piteous wave to wave
    That knows not where is that Leucadian grave
Which hides too deep the supreme head of song.
    Ah, salt and sterile as her kisses were,
    The wild sea winds her and the green gulfs bear
Hither and thither, and vex and work her wrong,
    Blind gods that cannot spare.

III

Thou sawest, in thine old singing season, brother,
    Secrets and sorrows unbeheld of us:
    Fierce loves, and lovely leaf-buds poisonous,
Bare to thy subtler eye, but for none other
    Blowing by night in some unbreathed-in clime;
    The hidden harvest of luxurious time,
Sin without shape, and pleasure without speech;
    And where strange dreams in a tumultuous sleep
    Make the shut eyes of stricken spirits weep;
And with each face thou sawest the shadow on each,
    Seeing as men sow men reap.

IV

O sleepless heart and sombre soul unsleeping,
    That were athirst for sleep and no more life
    And no more love, for peace and no more strife!
Now the dim gods of death have in their keeping
    Spirit and body and all the springs of song,
    Is it well now where love can do no wrong,

Where stingless pleasure has no foam or fang
    Behind the unopening closure of her lips?
    Is it not well where soul from body slips
And flesh from bone divides without a pang
    As dew from flower-bell drips?

V

It is enough; the end and the beginning
    Are one thing to thee, who art past the end.
    O hand unclasped of unbeholden friend,
For thee no fruits to pluck, no palms for winning,
    No triumph and no labour and no lust,
    Only dead yew-leaves and a little dust.
O quiet eyes wherein the light saith nought,
    Whereto the day is dumb, nor any night
    With obscure finger silences your sight,
Nor in your speech the sudden soul speaks thought,
    Sleep, and have sleep for light.

VI

Now all strange hours and all strange loves are over,
    Dreams and desires and sombre songs and sweet,
    Hast thou found place at the great knees and feet
Of some pale Titan-woman like a lover,
    Such as thy vision here solicited,
    Under the shadow of her fair vast head,
The deep division of prodigious breasts,
    The solemn slope of mighty limbs asleep,
    The weight of awful tresses that still keep
The savour and shade of old-world pine-forests
    Where the wet hill-winds weep?

VII

Hast thou found any likeness for thy vision?
    O gardener of strange flowers, what bud, what
        bloom,
    Hast thou found sown, what gathered in the
        gloom?
What of despair, of rapture, of derision,
    What of life is there, what of ill or good?
    Are the fruits grey like dust or bright like blood?
Does the dim ground grow any seed of ours,
    The faint fields quicken any terrene root,
    In low lands where the sun and moon are mute
And all the stars keep silence? Are there flowers
    At all, or any fruit?

VIII

Alas, but though my flying song flies after,
    O sweet strange elder singer, thy more fleet
    Singing, and footprints of thy fleeter feet,
Some dim derision of mysterious laughter
    From the blind tongueless warders of the dead,
    Some gainless glimpse of Proserpine's veiled head,
Some little sound of unregarded tears
    Wept by effaced unprofitable eyes,
    And from pale mouths some cadence of dead
        sighs—
These only, these the hearkening spirit hears,
    Sees only such things rise.

IX

Thou art far too far for wings of words to follow,
    Far too far off for thought or any prayer.
    What ails us with thee, who art wind and air?
What ails us gazing where all seen is hollow?

Yet with some fancy, yet with some desire,
Dreams pursue death as winds a flying fire,
Our dreams pursue òur dead and do not find.
Still, and more swift than they, the thin flame
flies,
The low light fails us in elusive skies,
Still the foiled earnest ear is deaf, and blind
Are still the eluded eyes.

X

Not thee, O never thee, in all time's changes,
Not thee, but this the sound of thy sad soul,
The shadow of thy swift spirit, this shut scroll
I lay my hand on, and not death estranges
My spirit from communion of thy song—
These memories and these melodies that throng
Veiled porches of a Muse funereal—
These I salute, these touch, these clasp and fold
As though a hand were in my hand to hold,
Or through mine ears a mourning musical
Of many mourners rolled.

XI

I among these, I also, in such station
As when the pyre was charred, and piled the sods,
And offering to the dead made, and their gods,
The old mourners had, standing to make libation,
I stand, and to the gods and to the dead
Do reverence without prayer or praise, and shed
Offering to these unknown, the gods of gloom,
And what of honey and spice my seedlands bear,
And what I may of fruits in this chilled air,
And lay, Orestes-like, across the tomb
A curl of severed hair.

XII

But by no hand nor any treason stricken,
    Not like the low-lying head of Him, the King,
    The flame that made of Troy a ruinous thing,
Thou liest, and on this dust no tears could quicken
    There fall no tears like theirs that all men hear
    Fall tear by sweet imperishable tear
Down the opening leaves of holy poets' pages.
    Thee not Orestes, not Electra mourns;
    But bending us-ward with memorial urns
The most high Muses that fulfil all ages
    Weep, and our God's heart yearns.

XIII

For, sparing of his sacred strength, not often
    Among us darkling here the lord of light
    Makes manifest his music and his might
In hearts that open and in lips that soften
    With the soft flame and heat of songs that shine.
    Thy lips indeed he touched with bitter wine,
And nourished them indeed with bitter bread;
    Yet surely from his hand thy soul's food came,
    The fire that scarred thy spirit at his flame
Was lighted, and thine hungering heart he fed
    Who feeds our hearts with fame.

XIV

Therefore he too now at thy soul's sunsetting,
    God of all suns and songs, he too bends down
    To mix his laurel with thy cypress crown,
And save thy dust from blame and from forgetting.

Therefore he too, seeing all thou wert and art,
Compassionate, with sad and sacred heart,
Mourns thee of many his children the last dead,
And hallows with strange tears and alien sighs
Thine unmelodious mouth and sunless eyes,
And over thine irrevocable head
Sheds light from the under skies.

XV

And one weeps with him in the ways Lethean,
And stains with tears her changing bosom chill:
That obscure Venus of the hollow hill,
That thing transformed which was the Cytherean,
With lips that lost their Grecian laugh divine
Long since, and face no more called Erycine;
A ghost, a bitter and luxurious god.
Thee also with fair flesh and singing spell
Did she, a sad and second prey, compel
Into the footless places once more trod.
And shadows hot from hell.

XVI

And now no sacred staff shall break in blossom,
No choral salutation lure to light
A spirit sick with perfume and sweet night
And love's tired eyes and hands and barren bosom.
There is no help for these things; none to mend
And none to mar; not all our songs, O friend,
Will make death clear or make life durable.
Howbeit with rose and ivy and wild vine
And with wild notes about this dust of thine

At least I fill the place where white dreams dwell
    And wreathe an unseen shrine.

XVII

Sleep, and if life was bitter to thee, pardon,
    If sweet, give thanks; thou hast no more to live;
    And to give thanks is good, and to forgive.
Out of the mystic and the mournful garden
    Where all day through thine hands in barren
        braid
    Wove the sick flowers of secrecy and shade,
Green buds of sorrow and sin, and remnants grey,
    Sweet-smelling, pale with poison, sanguine-
        hearted,
    Passions that sprang from sleep and thoughts that
        started,
Shall death not bring us all as thee one day
    Among the days departed?

XVIII

For thee, O now a silent soul, my brother,
    Take at my hands this garland, and farewell.
    Thin is the leaf, and chill the wintry smell,
And chill the solemn earth, a fatal mother,
    With sadder than the Niobean womb,
    And in the hollow of her breasts a tomb.
Content thee, howsoe'er, whose days are done;
    There lies not any troublous thing before,
    Nor sight nor sound to war against thee more,
For whom all winds are quiet as the sun,
    All waters as the shore.

A BALLAD OF FRANÇOIS VILLON

Prince of all Ballad-makers

BIRD of the bitter bright grey golden morn
  Scarce risen upon the dusk of dolorous years,
First of us all and sweetest singer born
    Whose far shrill note the world of new men hears
    Cleave the cold shuddering shade as twilight
      clears;
When song new-born put off the old world's attire
And felt its tune on her changed lips expire,
  Writ foremost on the roll of them that came
Fresh girt for service of the latter lyre,
  Villon, our sad bad glad mad brother's name!

Alas the joy, the sorrow, and the scorn,
  That clothed thy life with hopes and sins and fears,
And gave thee stones for bread and tares for corn
    And plume-plucked gaol-birds for thy starveling
      peers
    Till death clipt close their flight with shameful
      shears;
Till shifts came short and loves were hard to hire,
When lilt of song nor twitch of twangling wire
  Could buy thee bread or kisses; when light fame
Spurned like a ball and haled through brake and
      briar,
  Villon, our sad bad glad mad brother's name!

Poor splendid wings so frayed and soiled and torn!
  Poor kind wild eyes so dashed with light quick.
    tears!
Poor perfect voice, most blithe when most forlorn,

That rings athwart the sea whence no man steers
  Like joy-bells crossed with death-bells in our ears!
What far delight has cooled the fierce desire
That like some ravenous bird was strong to tire
  On that frail flesh and soul consumed with flame,
But left more sweet than roses to respire,
  Villon, our sad bad glad mad brother's name?

ENVOI

Prince of sweet songs made out of tears and fire,
A harlot was thy nurse, a God thy sire;
  Shame soiled thy song, and song assoiled thy shame.
But from thy feet now death has washed the mire,
Love reads out first at head of all our quire,
  Villon, our sad bad glad mad brother's name.

A VISION OF SPRING IN WINTER

I

O TENDER time that love thinks long to see,
  Sweet foot of spring that with her footfall sows
  Late snowlike flowery leavings of the snows,
Be not too long irresolute to be;
O mother-month, where have they hidden thee?
  Out of the pale time of the flowerless rose
I reach my heart out toward the springtime lands,
  I stretch my spirit forth to the fair hours,
      The purplest of the prime;
I lean my soul down over them, with hands
  Made wide to take the ghostly growths of flowers;
      I send my love back to the lovely time.

II

Where has the greenwood hid thy gracious head?
  Veiled with what visions while the grey world
      grieves,
  Or muffled with what shadows of green leaves,
What warm intangible green shadows spread
To sweeten the sweet twilight for thy bed?
  What sleep enchants thee? what delight deceives?
Where the deep dreamlike dew before the dawn
  Feels not the fingers of the sunlight yet
      Its silver web unweave,
Thy footless ghost on some unfooted lawn
  Whose air the unrisen sunbeams fear to fret
      Lives a ghost's life of daylong dawn and eve.

III

Sunrise it sees not, neither set of star,
  Large nightfall, nor imperial plenilune,
  Nor strong sweet shape of the full-breasted noon:
But where the silver-sandalled shadows are,
Too soft for arrows of the sun to mar,
  Moves with the mild gait of an ungrown moon:
Hard overhead the half-lit crescent swims,
  The tender-coloured night draws hardly breath,
      The light is listening;
They watch the dawn of slender-shapen limbs,
  Virginal, born again of doubtful death,
      Chill foster-father of the weanling spring.

IV

As sweet desire of day before the day,
  As dreams of love before the true love born,
  From the outer edge of winter overworn

The ghost arisen of May before the May
Takes through dim air her unawakened way,
   The gracious ghost of morning risen ere morn.
With little unblown breasts and child-eyed looks
   Following, the very maid, the girl-child spring,
      Lifts windward her bright brows,
Dips her light feet in warm and moving brooks,
   And kindles with her own mouth's colouring
      The fearful firstlings of the plumeless boughs.

                          V

I seek thee sleeping, and awhile I see,
   Fair face that art not, how thy maiden breath
   Shall put at last the deadly days to death
And fill the fields and fire the woods with thee
And seaward hollows where my feet would be
   When heaven shall hear the word that April saith
To change the cold heart of the weary time,
   To stir and soften all the time to tears,
      Tears joyfuller than mirth;
As even to May's clear height the young days climb
   With feet not swifter than those fair first years
      Whose flowers revive not with thy flowers on
         earth.

                          VI

I would not bid thee, though I might, give back
   One good thing youth has given and borne away;
   I crave not any comfort of the day
That is not, nor on time's retrodden track
Would turn to meet the white-robed hours or black
   That long since left me on their mortal way;

Nor light nor love that has been, nor the breath
  That comes with morning from the sun to be
    And sets light hope on fire;
No fruit, no flower thought once too fair for death,
  No flower nor hour once fallen from life's green tree,
    No leaf once plucked or once fulfilled desire.

VII

The morning song beneath the stars that fled
  With twilight through the moonless mountain air,
  While youth with burning lips and wreathless hair
Sang toward the sun that was to crown his head,
Rising; the hopes that triumphed and fell dead,
  The sweet swift eyes and songs of hours that were;
These may'st thou not give back for ever; these,
  As at the sea's heart all her wrecks lie waste,
    Lie deeper than the sea;
But flowers thou may'st, and winds, and hours of ease,
  And all its April to the world thou may'st
    Give back, and half my April back to me.

CHILD'S SONG

WHAT is gold worth, say,
Worth for work or play,
Worth to keep or pay,
Hide or throw away,
    Hope about or fear?
What is love worth, pray?
    Worth a tear?

Golden on the mould
Lie the dead leaves rolled
Of the wet woods old,
Yellow leaves and cold,
    Woods without a dove;
Gold is worth but gold;
    Love's worth love.

WINTER IN NORTHUMBERLAND

I

OUTSIDE the garden
The wet skies harden;
The gates are barred on
    The summer side:
'Shut out the flower-time,
Sunbeam and shower-time;
Make way for our time,'
    Wild winds have cried.
Green once and cheery,
The woods, worn weary,
Sigh as the dreary
    Weak sun goes home:
A great wind grapples
The wave, and dapples
The dead green floor of the sea with foam.

II

Through fell and moorland,
And salt-sea foreland,
Our noisy norland
    Resounds and rings;

Waste waves thereunder
Are blown in sunder,
And winds make thunder
　　With cloudwide wings;
Sea-drift makes dimmer
The beacon's glimmer;
Nor sail nor swimmer
　　Can try the tides;
And snowdrifts thicken
Where, when leaves quicken,
Under the heather the sundew hides.

III

Green land and red land,
Moorside and headland,
Are white as dead land,
　　Are all as one;
Nor honied heather,
Nor bells to gather,
Fair with fair weather
　　And faithful sun:
Fierce frost has eaten
All flowers that sweeten
The fells rain-beaten;
　　And winds their foes
Have made the snow's bed
Down in the rose-bed;
Deep in the snow's bed bury the rose.

IV

Bury her deeper
Than any sleeper;
Sweet dreams will keep her
　　All day, all night;

Though sleep benumb her
And time o'ercome her,
She dreams of summer,
    And takes delight,
Dreaming and sleeping,
In love's good keeping,
While rain is weeping
    And no leaves cling;
Winds will come bringing her
Comfort, and singing her
Stories and songs and good news of the spring.

V

Draw the white curtain
Close, and be certain
She takes no hurt in
    Her soft low bed;
She feels no colder,
And grows not older,
Though snows enfold her
    From foot to head;
She turns not chilly
Like weed and lily
In marsh and hilly
    High watershed,
Or green soft island
In lakes of highland;
She sleeps awhile, and she is not dead.

VI

For all the hours,
Come sun, come showers,
Are friends of flowers,
    And fairies all;

When frost entrapped her,
They came and lapped her
In leaves, and wrapped her
   With shroud and pall;
In red leaves wound her,
With dead leaves bound her
Dead brows, and round her
   A death-knell rang;
Rang the death-bell for her,
Sang, 'is it well for her,
Well, is it well with you, rose?' they sang.

VII

O what and where is
The rose now, fairies,
So shrill the air is,
   So wild the sky?
Poor last of roses,
Her worst of woes is
The noise she knows is
   The winter's cry;
His hunting hollo
Has scared the swallow;
Fain would she follow
   And fain would fly:
But wind unsettles
Her poor last petals;
Had she but wings, and she would not die.

VIII

Come, as you love her,
Come close and cover
Her white face over,
   And forth again

Ere sunset glances
On foam that dances,
Through lowering lances
    Of bright white rain;
And make your playtime
Of winter's daytime,
As if the Maytime
    Were here to sing;
As if the snowballs
Were soft like blowballs,
Blown in a mist from the stalk in the spring.

IX

Each reed that grows in
Our stream is frozen,
The fields it flows in
    Are hard and black;
The water-fairy
Waits wise and wary
Till time shall vary
    And thaws come back.
'O sister, water,'
The wind besought her,
'O twin-born daughter
    Of spring with me,
Stay with me, play with me,
    Take the warm way with me,
Straight for the summer and oversea.'

X

But winds will vary,
And wise and wary
The patient fairy
    Of water waits;

All shrunk and wizen,
In iron prison,
Till spring re-risen
  Unbar the gates;
Till, as with clamour
Of axe and hammer,
Chained streams that stammer
  And struggle in straits
Burst bonds that shiver,
And thaws deliver
The roaring river in stormy spates.

XI

In fierce March weather
White waves break tether,
And whirled together
  At either hand,
Like weeds uplifted,
The tree-trunks rifted
In spars are drifted,
  Like foam or sand,
Past swamp and sallow
And reed-beds callow,
Through pool and shallow,
  To wind and lee,
Till, no more tongue-tied,
Full flood and young tide
Roar down the rapids and storm the sea.

XII

As men's cheeks faded
On shores invaded,
When shorewards waded
  The lords of fight;

When churl and craven
Saw hard on haven
The wide-winged raven
    At mainmast height;
When monks affrighted
To windward sighted
The birds full-flighted
    Of swift sea-kings;
So earth turns paler
When Storm the sailor
Steers in with a roar in the race of his wings.

XIII

O strong sea-sailor,
Whose cheek turns paler
For wind or hail or
    For fear of thee?
O far sea-farer,
O thunder-bearer,
Thy songs are rarer
    Than soft songs be.
O fleet-foot stranger,
O north-sea ranger
Through days of danger
    And ways of fear,
Blow thy horn here for us,
Blow the sky clear for us,
Send us the song of the sea to hear.

XIV

Roll the strong stream of it
Up, till the scream of it
Wake from a dream of it
    Children that sleep,

Seamen that fare for them
Forth, with a prayer for them;
Shall not God care for them,
    Angels not keep?
Spare not the surges
Thy stormy scourges;
Spare us the dirges
    Of wives that weep.
Turn back the waves for us:
Dig no fresh graves for us,
Wind, in the manifold gulfs of the deep.

xv

O stout north-easter,
Sea-king, land-waster,
For all thine haste, or
    Thy stormy skill,
Yet hadst thou never,
For all endeavour,
Strength to dissever
    Or strength to spill,
Save of his giving
Who gave our living,
Whose hands are weaving
    What ours fulfil;
Whose feet tread under
The storms and thunder,
Who made our wonder to work his will.

xvi

His years and hours,
His world's blind powers,
His stars and flowers,
    His nights and days,

Sea-tide and river,
And waves that shiver,
Praise God, the giver
    Of tongues to praise.
Winds in their blowing,
And fruits in growing;
Time in its going,
    While time shall be;
In death and living,
With one thanksgiving,
Praise him whose hand is the strength of the sea.

FROM VILLON

BALLADE OF THE LORDS OF OLD TIME

After the former argument [1]

WHAT more? Where is the third Calixt,
    Last of that name now dead and gone,
Who held four years the Papalist?
    Alphonso king of Aragon,
    The gracious lord, duke of Bourbon,
And Arthur, duke of old Britaine?
    And Charles the Seventh, that worthy one?
Even with the good knight Charlemain.

The Scot too, king of mount and mist,
    With half his face vermilion,
Men tell us, like an amethyst
    From brow to chin that blazed and shone;
    The Cypriote king of old renown,
Alas! and that good king of Spain,
    Whose name I cannot think upon?
Even with the good knight Charlemain.

[1] i.e. of the *Ballad of the Ladies of Old Time*, left untranslated by A. C. S. as ' so incomparably rendered in the marvellous version of D. G. Rossetti '.

No more to say of them I list;
 'Tis all but vain, all dead and done:
For death may no man born resist,
 Nor make appeal when death comes on.
 I make yet one more question;
Where's Lancelot, king of far Bohain?
 Where's he whose grandson called him son?
Even with the good knight Charlemain.

Where is Guesclin, the good Breton?
 The lord of the eastern mountain-chain,
And the good late duke of Alençon?
 Even with the good knight Charlemain.

THE DISPUTE OF THE HEART AND BODY OF
FRANÇOIS VILLON

WHO is this I hear?—Lo, this is I, thine heart,
 That holds on merely now by a slender string.
Strength fails me, shape and sense are rent apart,
 The blood in me is turned to a bitter thing,
 Seeing thee skulk here like a dog shivering.—
Yea, and for what?—For that thy sense found sweet.—
What irks it thee?—I feel the sting of it.—
 Leave me at peace.—Why?—Nay now, leave me at
  peace;
I will repent when I grow ripe in wit.—
 I say no more.—I care not though thou cease.—

What art thou, trow?—A man worth praise, perfay.—
 This is thy thirtieth year of wayfaring.—
'Tis a mule's age,—Art thou a boy still?—Nay.—
 Is it hot lust that spurs thee with its sting,
 Grasping thy throat? Know'st thou not anything?—

Yea, black and white, when milk is specked with flies,
I can make out.—No more?—Nay, in no wise.
   Shall I begin again the count of these?—
Thou art undone.—I will make shift to rise.—
   I say no more.—I care not though thou cease.—

I have the sorrow of it, and thou the smart.
   Wert thou a poor mad fool or weak of wit,
Then might'st thou plead this pretext with thine
      heart;
   But if thou know not good from evil a whit,
   Either thy head is hard as stone to hit,
Or shame, not honour, gives thee most content.
What canst thou answer to this argument?—
   When I am dead I shall be well at ease.—
God!—what good hope!—Thou art over eloquent.—
   I say no more.—I care not though thou cease.—

Whence is this ill?—From sorrow and not from sin.
   When Saturn packed my wallet up for me
I well believe he put these ills therein.—
   Fool, wilt thou make thy servant lord of thee?
   Hear now the wise king's counsel; thus saith he:
All power upon the stars a wise man hath;
There is no planet that shall do him scathe.—
   Nay, as they made me I grow and I decrease.—
What say'st thou?—Truly this is all my faith.—
   I say no more.—I care not though thou cease.—

Wouldst thou live still?—God help me that I may!—
Then thou must—What? turn penitent and pray?—
Read always—What?—Grave words and good to say;
   Leave off the ways of fools, lest they displease.—
Good; I will do it.—Wilt thou remember?—Yea.—
Abide not till there come an evil day.
   I say no more.—I care not though thou cease.

THE EPITAPH IN FORM OF A BALLAD

*Which Villon made for himself and his comrades,
expecting to be hanged along with them*

MEN, brother men, that after us yet live,
  Let not your hearts too hard against us be;
For if some pity of us poor men ye give,
  The sooner God shall take of you pity.
  Here are we five or six strung up, you see,
And here the flesh that all too well we fed
Bit by bit eaten and rotten, rent and shred,
  And we the bones grow dust and ash withal;
Let no man laugh at us discomforted,
  But pray to God that he forgive us all.

If we call on you, brothers, to forgive,
  Ye should not hold our prayer in scorn, though we
Were slain by law; ye know that all alive
  Have not wit alway to walk righteously;
  Make therefore intercession heartily
With him that of a virgin's womb was bred,
That his grace be not as a dry well-head
  For us, nor let hell's thunder on us fall;
We are dead, let no man harry or vex us dead,
  But pray to God that he forgive us all.

The rain has washed and laundered us all five,
  And the sun dried and blackened; yea, perdie,
Ravens and pies with beaks that rend and rive
  Have dug our eyes out, and plucked off for fee
  Our beards and eyebrows; never are we free,
Not once, to rest; but here and there still sped,
Drive at its wild will by the wind's change led,

More pecked of birds than fruits on garden-wall;
Men, for God's love, let no gibe here be said,
But pray to God that he forgive us all.

Prince Jesus, that of all art lord and head,
Keep us, that hell be not our bitter bed;
We have nought to do in such a master's hall.
Be not ye therefore of our fellowhead,
But pray to God that he forgive us all.

TO A SEAMEW

WHEN I had wings, my brother,
    Such wings were mine as thine:
Such life my heart remembers
In all as wild Septembers
As this when life seems other,
    Though sweet, than once was mine;
When I had wings, my brother,
    Such wings were mine as thine.

Such life as thrills and quickens
    The silence of thy flight,
Or fills thy note's elation
With lordlier exultation
Than man's, whose faint heart sickens
    With hopes and fears that blight
Such life as thrills and quickens
    The silence of thy flight.

Thy cry from windward clanging
    Makes all the cliffs rejoice;
Though storm clothe seas with sorrow,
Thy call salutes the morrow;

While shades of pain seem hanging
   Round earth's most rapturous voice,
Thy cry from windward clanging
   Makes all the cliffs rejoice.

We, sons and sires of seamen,
   Whose home is all the sea,
What place man may, we claim it;
But thine—whose thought may name it?
Free birds live higher than freemen,
   And gladlier ye than we—
We, sons and sires of seamen,
   Whose home is all the sea.

For you the storm sounds only
   More notes of more delight
Than earth's in sunniest weather:
When heaven and sea together
Join strength against the lonely
   Lost bark borne down by night
For you the storm sounds only
   More notes of more delight.

With wider wing, and louder
   Long clarion-call of joy,
Thy tribe salutes the terror
Of darkness, wild as error,
But sure as truth, and prouder
   Than waves with man for toy;
With wider wing, and louder
   Long clarion-call of joy.

The wave's wing spreads and flutters,
   The wave's heart swells and breaks;
One moment's passion thrills it,
One pulse of power fulfils it

And ends the pride it utters
  When, loud with life that quakes,
The wave's wing spreads and flutters,
  The wave's heart swells and breaks.

But thine and thou, my brother,
  Keep heart and wing more high
Than ought may scare or sunder;
The waves whose throats are thunder
Fall hurtling each on other,
  And triumph as they die;
But thine and thou, my brother,
  Keep heart and wing more high.

More high than wrath or anguish,
  More strong than pride or fear,
The sense or soul half hidden
In thee, for us forbidden,
Bids thee nor change nor languish,
  But live thy life as here,
More high than wrath or anguish,
  More strong than pride or fear.

We are fallen, even we, whose passion
  On earth is nearest thine;
Who sing, and cease from flying;
Who live, and dream of dying:
Grey time, in time's grey fashion,
  Bids wingless creatures pine:
We are fallen, even we, whose passion
  On earth is nearest thine.

The lark knows no such rapture,
  Such joy no nightingale,
As sways the songless measure
Wherein thy wings take pleasure:

Thy love may no man capture,
  Thy pride may no man quail;
The lark knows no such rapture,
  Such joy no nightingale.

And we, whom dreams embolden,
  We can but creep and sing
And watch through heaven's waste hollow
The flight no sight may follow
To the utter bourne beholden
  Of none that lack thy wing:
And we, whom dreams embolden,
  We can but creep and sing.

Our dreams have wings that falter,
  Our hearts bear hopes that die;
For thee no dream could better
A life no fears may fetter,
A pride no care can alter,
  That wots not whence or why
Our dreams have wings that falter,
  Our hearts bear hopes that die.

With joy more fierce and sweeter
  Than joys we deem divine
Their lives, by time untarnished,
Are girt about and garnished,
Who match the wave's full metre
  And drink the wind's wild wine
With joy more fierce and sweeter
  Than joys we deem divine.

Ah, well were I for ever,
  Wouldst thou change lives with me,
And take my song's wild honey,
And give me back thy sunny

Wide eyes that weary never,
   And wings that search the sea;
Ah, well were I for ever,
   Wouldst thou change lives with me.

BEACHY HEAD: *September* 1886.

A RHYME

BABE, if rhyme be none
   For that sweet small word.
Babe, the sweetest one
    Ever heard,

Right it is and meet
   Rhyme should keep not true
Time with such a sweet
    Thing as you.

Meet it is that rhyme
   Should not gain such grace:
What is April's prime
    To your face?

What to yours is May's
   Rosiest smile? what sound
Like your laughter sways
    All hearts round?

None can tell in metre
   Fit for ears on earth
What sweet star grew sweeter
    At your birth.

Wisdom doubts what may be:
   Hope, with smile sublime,
Trusts: but neither, baby,
   Knows the rhyme.

Wisdom lies down lonely;
   Hope keeps watch from far;
None but one seer only
   Sees the star.

Love alone, with yearning
   Heart for astrolabe,
Takes the star's height, burning
   O'er the babe.

THALASSIUS

UPON the flowery forefront of the year,
One wandering by the grey-green April sea
Found on a reach of shingle and shallower sand
Inlaid with starrier glimmering jewellery
Left for the sun's love and the light wind's cheer
Along the foam-flowered strand
Breeze-brightened, something nearer sea than land
Though the last shoreward blossom-fringe was near,
A babe asleep with flower-soft face that gleamed
To sun and seaward as it laughed and dreamed,
Too sure of either love for either's fear,
Albeit so birdlike slight and light, it seemed
Nor man nor mortal child of man, but fair
As even its twin-born tenderer spray-flowers were,
That the wind scatters like an Oread's hair.

For when July strewed fire on earth and sea
The last time ere that year,
Out of the flame of morn Cymothoe
Beheld one brighter than the sunbright sphere
Move toward her from its fieriest heart, whence trod
The live sun's very God,
Across the foam-bright water-ways that are
As heavenlier heavens with star for answering star,
And on her eyes and hair and maiden mouth
Felt a kiss falling fierier than the South
And heard above afar
A noise of songs and wide-enamoured wings
And lutes and lyres of milder and mightier strings,
And round the resonant radiance of his car
Where depth is one with height,
Light heard as music, music seen as light.
And with that second moondawn of the spring's
That fosters the first rose,
A sun-child whiter than the sunlit snows
Was born out of the world of sunless things
That round the round earth flows and ebbs and flows.

But he that found the sea-flower by the sea
And took to foster like a graft of earth
Was born of man's most highest and heavenliest birth,
Free-born as winds and stars and waves are free;
A warrior grey with glories more than years,
Though more of years than change the quick to dead
Had rained their light and darkness on his head;
A singer that in time's and memory's ears
Should leave such words to sing as all his peers
Might praise with hallowing heat of rapturous tears
Till all the days of human flight were fled.
And at his knees his fosterling was fed

Not with man's wine and bread
Nor mortal mother-milk of hopes and fears,
But food of deep memorial days long sped;
For bread with wisdom and with song for wine
Clear as the full calm's emerald hyaline.
And from his grave glad lips the boy would gather
Fine honey of song-notes goldener than gold,
More sweet than bees make of the breathing heather,
That he, as glad and bold,
Might drink as they, and keep his spirit from cold.
And the boy loved his laurel-laden hair
As his own father's risen on the eastern air,
And that less white brow-binding bayleaf bloom
More than all flowers his father's eyes relume;
And those high songs he heard,
More than all notes of any landward bird,
More than all sounds less free
Than the wind's quiring to the choral sea.

   High things the high song taught him; how the
        breath
Too frail for life may be more strong than death;
And this poor flash of sense in life, that gleams
As a ghost's glory in dreams,
More stabile than the world's own heart's root seems,
By that strong faith of lordliest love which gives
To death's own sightless-seeming eyes a light
Clearer, to death's bare bones a verier might,
Than shines or strikes from any man that lives.
How he that loves life overmuch shall die
The dog's death, utterly:
And he that much less loves it than he hates
All wrongdoing that is done
Anywhere always underneath the sun

Shall live a mightier life than time's or fate's.
One fairer thing he shewed him, and in might
More strong than day and night
Whose strengths build up time's towering period:
Yea, one thing stronger and more high than God,
Which if man had not, then should God not be:
And that was Liberty.
And gladly should man die to gain, he said,
Freedom; and gladlier, having lost, lie dead.
For man's earth was not, nor the sweet sea-waves
His, nor his own land, nor its very graves,
Except they bred not, bore not, hid not slaves:
But all of all that is,
Were one man free in body and soul, were his.

And the song softened, even as heaven by night
Softens, from sunnier down to starrier light,
And with its moonbright breath
Blessed life for death's sake, and for life's sake death.
Till as the moon's own beam and breath confuse
In one clear hueless haze of glimmering hues
The sea's line and the land's line and the sky's,
And light for love of darkness almost dies,
As darkness only lives for light's dear love,
Whose hands the web of night is woven of,
So in that heaven of wondrous words were life
And death brought out of strife;
Yea, by that strong spell of serene increase
Brought out of strife to peace.

And the song lightened, as the wind at morn
Flashes, and even with lightning of the wind
Night's thick-spun web is thinned
And all its weft unwoven and overworn
Shrinks, as might love from scorn.

And as when wind and light on water and land
Leap as twin gods from heavenward hand in hand,
And with the sound and splendour of their leap
Strike darkness dead, and daunt the spirit of sleep,
And burn it up with fire;
So with the light that lightened from the lyre
Was all the bright heat in the child's heart stirred
And blown with blasts of music into flame
Till even his sense became
Fire, as the sense that fires the singing bird
Whose song calls night by name.
And in the soul within the sense began
The manlike passion of a godlike man,
And in the sense within the soul again
Thoughts that make men of gods and gods of men.

   For love the high song taught him: love that turns
God's heart toward man as man's to Godward; love
That life and death and life are fashioned of,
From the first breath that burns
Half kindled on the flowerlike yeanling's lip,
So light and faint that life seems like to slip,
To that yet weaklier drawn
When sunset dies of night's devouring dawn.
But the man dying not wholly as all men dies
If aught be left of his in live men's eyes
Out of the dawnless dark of death to rise;
If aught of deed or word
Be seen for all time or of all time heard.
Love, that though body and soul were overthrown
Should live for love's sake of itself alone,
Though spirit and flesh were one thing doomed and
      dead,
Not wholly annihilated.

Seeing even the hoariest ash-flake that the pyre
Drops, and forgets the thing was once afire
And gave its heart to feed the pile's full flame
Till its own heart its own heat overcame,
Outlives its own life, though by scarce a span,
As such men dying outlive themselves in man,
Outlive themselves for ever; if the heat
Outburn the heart that kindled it, the sweet
Outlast the flower whose soul it was, and flit
Forth of the body of it
Into some new shape of a strange perfume
More potent than its light live spirit of bloom,
How shall not something of that soul relive,
That only soul that had such gifts to give
As lighten something even of all men's doom
Even from the labouring womb
Even to the seal set on the unopening tomb?
And these the loving light of song and love
Shall wrap and lap round and impend above,
Imperishable; and all springs born illume
Their sleep with brighter thoughts than wake the dove
To music, when the hillside winds resume
The marriage-song of heather-flower and broom
And all the joy thereof.

   And hate the song too taught him: hate of all
That brings or holds in thrall
Of spirit or flesh, free-born ere God began,
The holy body and sacred soul of man.
And wheresoever a curse was or a chain,
A throne for torment or a crown for bane
Rose, moulded out of poor men's molten pain,
There, said he, should man's heaviest hate be set
Inexorably, to faint not or forget

Till the last warmth bled forth of the last vein
In flesh that none should call a king's again,
Seeing wolves and dogs and birds that plague-strike air
Leave the last bone of all the carrion bare.

　　And hope the high song taught him: hope whose
　　　　eyes
Can sound the seas unsoundable, the skies
Inaccessible of eyesight; that can see
What earth beholds not, hear what wind and sea
Hear not, and speak what all these crying in one
Can speak not to the sun.
For in her sovereign eyelight all things are
Clear as the closest seen and kindlier star
That marries morn and even and winter and spring
With one love's golden ring.
For she can see the days of man, the birth
Of good and death of evil things on earth
Inevitable and infinite, and sure
As present pain is, or herself is pure.
Yea, she can hear and see, beyond all things
That lighten from before Time's thunderous wings
Through the awful circle of wheel-winged periods,
The tempest of the twilight of all Gods:
And higher than all the circling course they ran
The sundawn of the spirit that was man.

　　And fear the song too taught him; fear to be
Worthless the dear love of the wind and sea
That bred him fearless, like a sea-mew reared
In rocks of man's foot feared,
Where nought of wingless life may sing or shine.
Fear to wax worthless of that heaven he had
When all the life in all his limbs was glad

And all the drops in all his veins were wine
And all the pulses music; when his heart,
Singing, bade heaven and wind and sea bear part
In one live song's reiterance, and they bore:
Fear to go crownless of the flower he wore
When the winds loved him and the waters knew,
The blithest life that clove their blithe life through
With living limbs exultant, or held strife
More amorous than all dalliance aye anew
With the bright breath and strength of their large life,
With all strong wrath of all sheer winds that blew,
All glories of all storms of the air that fell
Prone, ineluctable,
With roar from heaven of revel, and with hue
As of a heaven turned hell.
For when the red blast of their breath had made
All heaven aflush with light more dire than shade,
He felt it in his blood and eyes and hair
Burn as if all the fires of the earth and air
Had lain strong hold upon his flesh, and stung
The soul behind it as with serpent's tongue,
Forked like the loveliest lightnings: nor could bear
But hardly, half distraught with strong delight,
The joy that like a garment wrapped him round
And lapped him over and under
With raiment of great light
And rapture of great sound
At every loud leap earthward of the thunder
From heaven's most furthest bound:
So seemed all heaven in hearing and in sight,
Alive and mad with glory and angry joy,
That something of its marvellous mirth and might
Moved even to madness, fledged as even for flight,
The blood and spirit of one but mortal boy.

So, clothed with love and fear that love makes great,
And armed with hope and hate,
He set first foot upon the spring-flowered ways
That all feet pass and praise.
And one dim dawn between the winter and spring,
In the sharp harsh wind harrying heaven and earth
To put back April that had borne his birth
From sunward on her sunniest shower-struck wing,
With tears and laughter for the dew-dropt thing,
Slight as indeed a dew-drop, by the sea
One met him lovelier than all men may be,
God-featured, with god's eyes; and in their might
Somewhat that drew men's own to mar their sight,
Even of all eyes drawn toward him: and his mouth
Was as the very rose of all men's youth,
One rose of all the rose-beds in the world:
But round his brows the curls were snakes that curled,
And like his tongue a serpent's; and his voice
Speaks death, and bids rejoice.
Yet then he spake no word, seeming as dumb,
A dumb thing mild and hurtless; nor at first
From his bowed eyes seemed any light to come,
Nor his meek lips for blood or tears to thirst:
But as one blind and mute in mild sweet wise
Pleading for pity of piteous lips and eyes,
He strayed with faint bare lily-lovely feet
Helpless, and flowerlike sweet:
Nor might man see, not having word hereof,
That this of all gods was the great god Love.

And seeing him lovely and like a little child
That wellnigh wept for wonder that it smiled
And was so feeble and fearful, with soft speech
The youth bespake him softly; but there fell

From the sweet lips no sweet word audible
That ear or thought might reach:
No sound to make the dim cold silence glad,
No breath to thaw the hard harsh air with heat;
Only the saddest smile of all things sweet,
Only the sweetest smile of all things sad.

And so they went together one green way
Till April dying made free the world for May;
And on his guide suddenly Love's face turned,
And in his blind eyes burned
Hard light and heat of laughter; and like flame
That opens in a mountain's ravening mouth
To blear and sear the sunlight from the south,
His mute mouth opened, and his first word came:
'Knowest thou me now by name?'
And all his stature waxed immeasurable,
As of one shadowing heaven and lightening hell:
And statelier stood he than a tower that stands
And darkens with its darkness far-off sands
Whereon the sky leans red;
And with a voice that stilled the winds he said:
'I am he that was thy lord before thy birth,
I am he that is thy lord till thou turn earth:
I make the night more dark, and all the morrow
Dark as the night whose darkness was my breath:
O fool, my name is sorrow;
Thou fool, my name is death.'

And he that heard spake not, and looked right on
Again, and Love was gone.

Through many a night toward many a wearier day
His spirit bore his body down its way.
Through many a day toward many a wearier night
His soul sustained his sorrows in her sight.

And earth was bitter, and heaven, and even the sea
Sorrowful even as he.
And the wind helped not, and the sun was dumb;
And with too long strong stress of grief to be
His heart grew sere and numb.

And one bright eve ere summer in autumn sank
At stardawn standing on a grey sea-bank
He felt the wind fitfully shift and heave
As toward a stormier eve;
And all the wan wide sea shuddered; and earth
Shook underfoot as toward some timeless birth,
Intolerable and inevitable; and all
Heaven, darkling, trembled like a stricken thrall.
And far out of the quivering east, and far
From past the moonrise and its guiding star,
Began a noise of tempest and a light
That was not of the lightning; and a sound
Rang with it round and round
That was not of the thunder; and a flight
As of blown clouds by night,
That was not of them; and with songs and cries
That sang and shrieked their soul out at the skies
A shapeless earthly storm of shapes began
From all ways round to move in on the man,
Clamorous against him silent; and their feet
Were as the wind's are fleet,
And their shrill songs were as wild birds' are sweet.

And as when all the world of earth was wronged
And all the host of all men driven afoam
By the red hand of Rome,
Round some fierce amphitheatre overthronged
With fair clear faces full of bloodier lust
Than swells and stings the tiger when his mood

Is fieriest after blood
And drunk with trampling of the murderous must
That soaks and stains the tortuous close-coiled wood
Made monstrous with its myriad-mustering brood,
Face by fair face panted and gleamed and pressed,
And breast by passionate breast
Heaved hot with ravenous rapture, as they quaffed
The red ripe full fume of the deep live draught,
The sharp quick reek of keen fresh bloodshed, blown
Through the dense deep drift up to the emperor's
     throne
From the under steaming sands
With clamour of all-applausive throats and hands,
Mingling in mirthful time
With shrill blithe mockeries of the lithe-limbed mime:
So from somewhence far forth of the unbeholden,
Dreadfully driven from over and after and under,
Fierce, blown through fifes of brazen blast and golden,
With sound of chiming waves that drown the thunder
Or thunder that strikes dumb the sea's own chimes,
Began the bellowing of the bull-voiced mimes,
Terrible; firs bowed down as briars or palms
Even at the breathless blast as of a breeze
Fulfilled with clamour and clangour and storms of
     psalms;
Red hands rent up the roots of old-world trees,
Thick flames of torches tossed as tumbling seas
Made mad the moonless and infuriate air
That, ravening, revelled in the riotous hair
And raiment of the furred Bassarides.

So came all those in on him; and his heart,
As out of sleep suddenly struck astart,
Danced, and his flesh took fire of theirs, and grief

Was as a last year's leaf
Blown dead far down the wind's way; and he set
His pale mouth to the brightest mouth it met
That laughed for love against his lips, and bade
Follow; and in following all his blood grew glad
And as again a sea-bird's; for the wind
Took him to bathe him deep round breast and brow
Not as it takes a dead leaf drained and thinned,
But as the brightest bay-flower blown on bough,
Set springing toward it singing: and they rode
By many a vine-leafed, many a rose-hung road,
Exalt with exultation; many a night
Set all its stars upon them as for spies
On many a moon-bewildering mountain-height
Where he rode only by the fierier light
Of his dread lady's hot sweet hungering eyes.
For the moon wandered witless of her way,
Spell-stricken by strong magic in such wise
As wizards use to set the stars astray.
And in his ears the music that makes mad
Beat always; and what way the music bade,
That alway rode he; nor was any sleep
His, nor from height nor deep.
But heaven was as red iron, slumberless,
And had no heart to bless;
And earth lay sere and darkling as distraught,
And help in her was nought.

Then many a midnight, many a morn and even,
His mother, passing forth of her fair heaven,
With goodlier gifts than all save gods can give
From earth or from the heaven where sea-things live,
With shine of sea-flowers through the bay-leaf braid
Woven for a crown her foam-white hands had made

To crown him with land's laurel and sea-dew,
Sought the sea-bird that was her boy: but he
Sat panther-throned beside Erigone,
Riding the red ways of the revel through
Midmost of pale-mouthed passion's crownless crew.
Till on some winter's dawn of some dim year
He let the vine-bit on the panther's lip
Slide, and the green rein slip,
And set his eyes to seaward, nor gave ear
If sound from landward hailed him, dire or dear;
And passing forth of all those fair fierce ranks
Back to the grey sea-banks,
Against a sea-rock lying, aslant the steep,
Fell after many sleepless dreams on sleep.

And in his sleep the dun green light was shed
Heavily round his head
That through the veil of sea falls fathom-deep,
Blurred like a lamp's that when the night drops dead
Dies; and his eyes gat grace of sleep to see
The deep divine dark dayshine of the sea,
Dense water-walls and clear dusk water-ways,
Broad-based, or branching as a sea-flower sprays
That side or this dividing; and anew
The glory of all her glories that he knew.
And in sharp rapture of recovering tears
He woke on fire with yearnings of old years,
Pure as one purged of pain that passion bore,
Ill child of bitter mother; for his own
Looked laughing toward him from her midsea throne,
Up toward him there ashore.

Thence in his heart the great same joy began,
Of child that made him man:

And turned again from all hearts else on quest,
He communed with his own heart, and had rest.
And like sea-winds upon loud waters ran
His days and dreams together, till the joy
Burned in him of the boy.
Till the earth's great comfort and the sweet sea's
    breath
Breathed and blew life in where was heartless death,
Death spirit-stricken of soul-sick days, where strife
Of thought and flesh made mock of death and life.
And grace returned upon him of his birth
Where heaven was mixed with heavenlike sea and
    earth;
And song shot forth strong wings that took the sun
From inward, fledged with might of sorrow and mirth
And father's fire made mortal in his son.
Nor was not spirit of strength in blast and breeze
To exalt again the sun's child and the sea's;
For as wild mares in Thessaly grow great
With child of ravishing winds, that violate
Their leaping length of limb with manes like fire
And eyes outburning heaven's
With fires more violent than the lightning levin's
And breath drained out and desperate of desire,
Even so the spirit in him, when winds grew strong,
Grew great with child of song.
Nor less than when his veins first leapt for joy
To draw delight in such as burns a boy,
Now too the soul of all his senses felt
The passionate pride of deep sea-pulses dealt
Through nerve and jubilant vein
As from the love and largess of old time,
And with his heart again
The tidal throb of all the tides keep rhyme

And charm him from his own soul's separate sense
With infinite and invasive influence
That made strength sweet in him and sweetness
    strong,
Being now no more a singer, but a song.

Till one clear day when brighter sea-wind blew
And louder sea-shine lightened, for the waves
Were full of godhead and the light that saves,
His father's, and their spirit had pierced him through,
He felt strange breath and light all round him shed
That bowed him down with rapture; and he knew
His father's hand, hallowing his humbled head,
And the old great voice of the old good time, that said:

'Child of my sunlight and the sea, from birth
A fosterling and fugitive on earth;
Sleepless of soul as wind or wave or fire,
A manchild with an ungrown God's desire;
Because thou hast loved nought mortal more than me,
Thy father, and thy mother-hearted sea;
Because thou hast set thine heart to sing, and sold
Life and life's love for song, God's living gold;
Because thou hast given thy flower and fire of youth
To feed men's hearts with visions, truer than truth;
Because thou hast kept in those world-wandering eyes
The light that makes me music of the skies;
Because thou hast heard with world-unwearied ears
The music that puts light into the spheres;
Have therefore in thine heart and in thy mouth
The sound of song that mingles north and south,
The song of all the winds that sing of me,
And in thy soul the sense of all the sea.'

PRELUDE TO *SONGS BEFORE SUNRISE*

BETWEEN the green bud and the red
Youth sat and sang by Time, and shed
   From eyes and tresses flowers and tears,
   From heart and spirit hopes and fears,
Upon the hollow stream whose bed
   Is channelled by the foamless years;
And with the white the gold-haired head
   Mixed running locks, and in Time's ears
Youth's dreams hung singing, and Time's truth
Was half not harsh in the ears of Youth.

Between the bud and the blown flower
Youth talked with joy and grief an hour,
   With footless joy and wingless grief
   And twin-born faith and disbelief
Who share the seasons to devour;
   And long ere these made up their sheaf
Felt the winds round him shake and shower
   The rose-red and the blood-red leaf,
Delight whose germ grew never grain,
And passion dyed in its own pain.

Then he stood up, and trod to dust
Fear and desire, mistrust and trust,
   And dreams of bitter sleep and sweet,
   And bound for sandals on his feet
Knowledge and patience of what must
   And what things may be, in the heat
And cold of years that rot and rust
   And alter; and his spirit's meat
Was freedom, and his staff was wrought
Of strength, and his cloak woven of thought.

For what has he whose will sees clear
To do with doubt and faith and fear,
   Swift hopes and slow despondencies?
   His heart is equal with the sea's
And with the sea-wind's, and his ear
   Is level to the speech of these,
And his soul communes and takes cheer
   With the actual earth's equalities,
Air, light, and night, hills, winds, and streams,
And seeks not strength from strengthless dreams.

His soul is even with the sun
Whose spirit and whose eye are one,
   Who seeks not stars by day, nor light
   And heavy heat of day by night.
Him can no God cast down, whom none
   Can lift in hope beyond the height
Of fate and nature and things done
   By the calm rule of might and right
That bids men be and bear and do,
And die beneath blind skies or blue.

To him the lights of even and morn
Speak no vain things of love or scorn,
   Fancies and passions miscreate
   By man in things dispassionate.
Nor holds he fellowship forlorn
   With souls that pray and hope and hate,
And doubt they had better not been born,
   And fain would lure or scare off fate
And charm their doomsman from their doom
And make fear dig its own false tomb.

He builds not half of doubts and half
Of dreams his own soul's cenotaph,

Whence hopes and fears with helpless eyes,
  Wrapt loose in cast-off cerecloths, rise
And dance and wring their hands and laugh,
  And weep thin tears and sigh light sighs,
And without living lips would quaff
  The living spring in man that lies,
And drain his soul of faith and strength
It might have lived on a life's length.

He hath given himself and hath not sold
To God for heaven or man for gold,
  Or grief for comfort that it gives,
  Or joy for grief's restoratives.
He hath given himself to time, whose fold
  Shuts in the mortal flock that lives
On its plain pasture's heat and cold
  And the equal year's alternatives.
Earth, heaven, and time, death, life, and he,
Endure while they shall be to be.

'Yet between death and life are hours
To flush with love and hide in flowers;
  What profit save in these?' men cry:
'Ah, see, between soft earth and sky,
What only good things here are ours!'
  They say, 'what better wouldst thou try,
What sweeter sing of? or what powers
  Serve, that will give thee ere thou die
More joy to sing and be less sad,
More heart to play and grow more glad?'

Play then and sing; we too have played,
We likewise, in that subtle shade.
  We too have twisted through our hair
  Such tendrils as the wild Loves wear,

And heard what mirth the Mænads made,
   Till the wind blew our garlands bare
And left their roses disarrayed,
   And smote the summer with strange air,
And disengirdled and discrowned
The limbs and locks that vine-wreaths bound.

We too have tracked by star-proof trees
The tempest of the Thyiades
   Scare the loud night on hills that hid
   The blood-feasts of the Bassarid,
Heard their song's iron cadences
   Fright the wolf hungering from the kid,
Outroar the lion-throated seas,
   Outchide the north-wind if it chid,
And hush the torrent-tongued ravines
With thunders of their tambourines.

But the fierce flute whose notes acclaim
Dim goddesses of fiery fame,
   Cymbal and clamorous kettledrum,
   Timbrels and tabrets, all are dumb
That turned the high chill air to flame;
   The singing tongues of fire are numb
That called on Cotys by her name
   Edonian, till they felt her come
And maddened, and her mystic face
Lightened along the streams of Thrace.

For Pleasure slumberless and pale,
And Passion with rejected veil,
   Pass, and the tempest-footed throng
   Of hours that follow them with song
Till their feet flag and voices fail,
   And lips that were so loud so long

Learn silence, or a wearier wail;
  So keen is change, and time so strong,
To weave the robes of life and rend
And weave again till life have end.

But weak is change, but strengthless time,
To take the light from heaven, or climb
  The hills of heaven with wasting feet.
  Songs they can stop that earth found meet,
But the stars keep their ageless rhyme;
  Flowers they can slay that spring thought sweet,
But the stars keep their spring sublime;
  Passions and pleasures can defeat,
Actions and agonies control,
And life and death, but not the soul.

Because man's soul is man's God still,
What wind soever waft his will
  Across the waves of day and night
  To port or shipwreck, left or right,
By shores and shoals of good and ill;
  And still its flame at mainmast height
Through the rent air that foam-flakes fill
  Sustains the indomitable light
Whence only man hath strength to steer
Or helm to handle without fear.

Save his own soul's light overhead,
None leads him, and none ever led,
  Across birth's hidden harbour-bar,
  Past youth where shoreward shallows are,
Through age that drives on toward the red
  Vast void of sunset hailed from far,
To the equal waters of the dead;
  Save his own soul he hath no star,

And sinks, except his own soul guide,
Helmless in middle turn of tide.

No blast of air or fire of sun
Puts out the light whereby we run
  With girded loins our lamplit race,
  And each from each takes heart of grace
And spirit till his turn be done,
  And light of face from each man's face
In whom the light of trust is one;
  Since only souls that keep their place
By their own light, and watch things roll,
And stand, have light for any soul.

A little time we gain from time
To set our seasons in some chime,
  For harsh or sweet or loud or low,
  With seasons played out long ago
And souls that in their time and prime
  Took part with summer or with snow,
Lived abject lives out or sublime,
  And had their chance of seed to sow
For service or disservice done
To those days dead and this their son.

A little time that we may fill
Or with such good works or such ill
  As loose the bonds or make them strong
  Wherein all manhood suffers wrong.
By rose-hung river and light-foot rill
  There are who rest not; who think long
Till they discern as from a hill
  At the sun's hour of morning song,
Known of souls only, and those souls free,
The sacred places of the sea.

SUPER FLUMINA BABYLONIS

By the waters of Babylon we sat down and wept,
    Remembering thee,
That for ages of agony hast endured, and slept,
    And wouldst not see.

By the waters of Babylon we stood up and sang,
    Considering thee,
That a blast of deliverance in the darkness rang,
    To set thee free.

And with trumpets and thunderings and with morning
    song
        Came up the light;
And thy spirit uplifted thee to forget thy wrong
        As day doth night.

And thy sons were dejected not any more, as then
        When thou wast shamed;
When thy lovers went heavily without heart, as men
        Whose life was maimed.

In the desolate distances, with a great desire,
        For thy love's sake,
With our hearts going back to thee, they were filled
    with fire,
        Were nigh to break.

It was said to us: 'Verily ye are great of heart,
        But ye shall bend;
Ye are bondmen and bondwomen, to be scourged and
    smart,
        To toil and tend.'

And with harrows men harrowed us, and subdued
    with spears,
        And crushed with shame;
And the summer and winter was, and the length of
    years,
        And no change came.

By the rivers of Italy, by the sacred streams,
        By town, by tower,
There was feasting with revelling, there was sleep
    with dreams,
        Until thine hour.

And they slept and they rioted on their rose-hung
    beds,
        With mouths on flame,
And with love-locks vine-chapleted, and with rose-
    crowned heads
        And robes of shame.

And they knew not their forefathers, nor the hills and
    streams
        And words of power,
Nor the gods that were good to them, but with songs
    and dreams
        Filled up their hour.

By the rivers of Italy, by the dry streams' beds,
        When thy time came,
There was casting of crowns from them, from their
    young men's heads,
        The crowns of shame.

By the horn of Eridanus, by the Tiber mouth,
      As thy day rose,
They arose up and girded them to the north and
    south,
      By seas, by snows.

As a water in January the frost confines,
      Thy kings bound thee;
As a water in April is, in the new-blown vines,
      Thy sons made free.

And thy lovers that looked for thee, and that mourned
    from far,
      For thy sake dead,
We rejoiced in the light of thee, in the signal star
      Above thine head.

In thy grief had we followed thee, in thy passion
    loved,
      Loved in thy loss;
In thy shame we stood fast to thee, with thy pangs
    were moved,
      Clung to thy cross.

By the hillside of Calvary we beheld thy blood,
      Thy bloodred tears,
As a mother's in bitterness, an unebbing flood,
      Years upon years.

And the north was Gethsemane, without leaf or
    bloom,
      A garden sealed;
And the south was Aceldama, for a sanguine fume
      Hid all the field.

By the stone of the sepulchre we returned to weep,
     From far, from prison;
And the guards by it keeping it we beheld asleep,
     But thou wast risen.

And an angel's similitude by the unsealed grave,
     And by the stone:
And the voice was angelical, to whose words God gave
     Strength like his own.

'Lo, the graveclothes of Italy that are folded up
     In the grave's gloom!
And the guards as men wrought upon with a charmèd
     cup,
          By the open tomb.

'And her body most beautiful, and her shining head,
     These are not here;
For your mother, for Italy, is not surely dead:
     Have ye no fear.

'As of old time she spake to you, and you hardly
     heard,
          Hardly took heed,
So now also she saith to you, yet another word,
     Who is risen indeed.

'By my saying she saith to you, in your ears she saith,
     Who hear these things,
Put no trust in men's royalties, nor in great men's
     breath,
          Nor words of kings.

'For the life of them vanishes and is no more seen,
     Nor no more known;
Nor shall any remember him if a crown hath been,
     Or where a throne.

'Unto each man his handiwork, unto each his crown,
      The just Fate gives;
Whoso takes the world's life on him and his own lays
   down,
      He, dying so, lives.

'Whoso bears the whole heaviness of the wronged
   world's weight
      And puts it by,
It is well with him suffering, though he face man's fate;
      How should he die?

'Seeing death has no part in him any more, no power
      Upon his head;
He has bought his eternity with a little hour,
      And is not dead.

'For an hour, if ye look for him, he is no more found,
      For one hour's space;
Then ye lift up your eyes to him and behold him
   crowned,
      A deathless face.

'On the mountains of memory, by the world's well-
   springs,
      In all men's eyes,
Where the light of the life of him is on all past things,
      Death only dies.

'Not the light that was quenched for us, nor the deeds
   that were,
      Nor the ancient days,
Nor the sorrows not sorrowful, nor the face most fair
      Of perfect praise.'

So the angel of Italy's resurrection said,
     So yet he saith;
So the son of her suffering, that from breasts nigh dead
     Drew life, not death.

That the pavement of Golgotha should be white as
   snow,
     Not red, but white;
That the waters of Babylon should no longer flow,
     And men see light.

HERTHA

I AM that which began;
   Out of me the years roll;
Out of me God and man;
   I am equal and whole;
God changes, and man, and the form of them bodily;
   I am the soul.

Before ever land was,
   Before ever the sea,
Or soft hair of the grass,
   Or fair limbs of the tree,
Or the flesh-coloured fruit of my branches, I was, and
  thy soul was in me.

First life on my sources
   First drifted and swam;
Out of me are the forces
   That save it or damn;
Out of me man and woman, and wild-beast and bird;
  before God was, I am.

Beside or above me
    Nought is there to go;
Love or unlove me,
    Unknow me or know,
I am that which unloves me and loves; I am stricken,
    and I am the blow.

I the mark that is missed
    And the arrows that miss,
I the mouth that is kissed
    And the breath in the kiss,
The search, and the sought, and the seeker, the soul
    and the body that is.

I am that thing which blesses
    My spirit elate;
That which caresses
    With hands uncreate
My limbs unbegotten that measure the length of the
    measure of fate.

But what thing dost thou now,
    Looking Godward to cry,
'I am I, thou art thou,
    I am low, thou art high'?
I am thou, whom thou seekest to find him; find thou
    but thyself, thou art I.

I the grain and the furrow,
    The plough-cloven clod
And the ploughshare drawn thorough,
    The germ and the sod,
The deed and the doer, the seed and the sower, the
    dust which is God.

Hast thou known how I fashioned thee,
   Child, underground?
Fire that impassioned thee,
   Iron that bound,
Dim changes of water, what thing of all these hast
   thou known of or found?

Canst thou say in thine heart
   Thou hast seen with thine eyes
With what cunning of art
   Thou wast wrought in what wise,
By what force of what stuff thou wast shapen, and
   shown on my breast to the skies?

Who hath given, who hath sold it thee,
   Knowledge of me?
Hath the wilderness told it thee?
   Hast thou learnt of the sea?
Hast thou communed in spirit with night? have the
   winds taken counsel with thee?

Have I set such a star
   To show light on thy brow
That thou sawest from afar
   What I show to thee now?
Have ye spoken as brethren together, the sun and the
   mountains and thou?

What is here, dost thou know it?
   What was, hast thou known?
Prophet or poet
   Nor tripod nor throne
Nor spirit nor flesh can make answer, but only thy
   mother alone.

Mother, not maker,
　Born, and not made;
Though her children forsake her,
　Allured or afraid,
Praying prayers to the God of their fashion, she stirs
　not for all that have prayed.

A creed is a rod,
　And a crown is of night;
But this thing is God,
　To be man with thy might,
To grow straight in the strength of thy spirit, and live
　out thy life as the light.

I am in thee to save thee,
　As my soul in thee saith;
Give thou as I gave thee,
　Thy life-blood and breath,
Green leaves of thy labour, white flowers of thy
　thought, and red fruit of thy death.

Be the ways of thy giving
　As mine were to thee;
The free life of thy living,
　Be the gift of it free;
Not as servant to lord, nor as master to slave, shalt
　thou give thee to me.

O children of banishment,
　Souls overcast,
Were the lights ye see vanish meant
　Alway to last,
Ye would know not the sun overshining the shadows
　and stars overpast.

I that saw where ye trod
    The dim paths of the night
Set the shadow called God
    In your skies to give light;
But the morning of manhood is risen, and the shadow-
    less soul is in sight.

The tree many-rooted
    That swells to the sky
With frondage red-fruited,
    The life-tree am I;
In the buds of your lives is the sap of my leaves: ye
    shall live and not die.

But the Gods of your fashion
    That take and that give,
In their pity and passion
    That scourge and forgive,
They are worms that are bred in the bark that falls
    off; they shall die and not live.

My own blood is what stanches
    The wounds in my bark;
Stars caught in my branches
    Make day of the dark,
And are worshipped as suns till the sunrise shall tread
    out their fires as a spark.

Where dead ages hide under
    The live roots of the tree,
In my darkness the thunder
    Makes utterance of me;
In the clash of my boughs with each other ye hear the
    waves sound of the sea.

That noise is of Time,
As his feathers are spread
And his feet set to climb
Through the boughs overhead,
And my foliage rings round him and rustles, and
branches are bent with his tread.

The storm-winds of ages
Blow through me and cease,
The war-wind that rages,
The spring-wind of peace,
Ere the breath of them roughen my tresses, ere one of
my blossoms increase.

All sounds of all changes,
All shadows and lights
On the world's mountain-ranges
And stream-riven heights,
Whose tongue is the wind's tongue and language of
storm-clouds on earth-shaking nights;

All forms and all faces,
All works of all hands
In unsearchable places
Of time-stricken lands,
All death and all life, and all reigns and all ruins, drop
through me as sands.

Though sore be my burden
And more than ye know,
And my growth have no guerdon
But only to grow,
Yet I fail not of growing for lightnings above me or
deathworms below.

These too have their part in me,
　　As I too in these;
Such fire is at heart in me,
　　Such sap is this tree's,
Which hath in it sounds and all secrets of infinite lands
　　and of seas.

In the spring-coloured hours
　　When my mind was as May's,
There brake forth of me flowers
　　By centuries of days,
Strong blossoms with perfume of manhood, shot out
　　from my spirit as rays.

And the sound of them springing
　　And smell of their shoots
Were as warmth and sweet singing
　　And strength to my roots;
And the lives of my children made perfect with free-
　　dom of soul were my fruits.

I bid you but be;
　　I have need not of prayer;
I have need of you free
　　As your mouths of mine air;
That my heart may be greater within me, beholding
　　the fruits of me fair.

More fair than strange fruit is
　　Of faiths ye espouse;
In me only the root is
　　That blooms in your boughs;
Behold now your God that ye made you, to feed him
　　with faith of your vows.

In the darkening and whitening
   Abysses adored,
With dayspring and lightning
   For lamp and for sword,
God thunders in heaven, and his angels are red with
   the wrath of the Lord.

O my sons, O too dutiful
   Toward Gods not of me,
Was not I enough beautiful?
   Was it hard to be free?
For behold, I am with you, am in you and of you;
   look forth now and see.

Lo, winged with world's wonders,
   With miracles shod,
With the fires of his thunders
   For raiment and rod,
God trembles in heaven, and his angels are white with
   the terror of God.

For his twilight is come on him,
   His anguish is here;
And his spirits gaze dumb on him,
   Grown grey from his fear;
And his hour taketh hold on him stricken, the last of
   his infinite year.

Thought made him and breaks him,
   Truth slays and forgives;
But to you, as time takes him,
   This new thing it gives,
Even love, the beloved Republic, that feeds upon
   freedom and lives.

For truth only is living,
    Truth only is whole,
And the love of his giving
    Man's polestar and pole;
Man, pulse of my centre, and fruit of my body, and
    seed of my soul.

One birth of my bosom;
    One beam of mine eye;
One topmost blossom
    That scales the sky;
Man, equal and one with me, man that is made of me,
    man that is I.

BEFORE A CRUCIFIX

HERE, down between the dusty trees,
    At this lank edge of haggard wood,
Women with labour-loosened knees,
    With gaunt backs bowed by servitude,
Stop, shift their loads, and pray, and fare
Forth with souls easier for the prayer.

The suns have branded black, the rains
    Striped grey this piteous God of theirs;
The face is full of prayers and pains,
    To which they bring their pains and prayers;
Lean limbs that shew the labouring bones,
And ghastly mouth that gapes and groans.

God of this grievous people, wrought
    After the likeness of their race,
By faces like thine own besought,
    Thine own blind helpless eyeless face,
I too, that have nor tongue nor knee
For prayer, I have a word to thee.

It was for this then, that thy speech
  Was blown about the world in flame
And men's souls shot up out of reach
  Of fear or lust or thwarting shame—
That thy faith over souls should pass
As sea-winds burning the grey grass?

It was for this, that prayers like these
  Should spend themselves about thy feet,
And with hard overlaboured knees
  Kneeling, these slaves of men should beat
Bosoms too lean to suckle sons
And fruitless as their orisons?

It was for this, that men should make
  Thy name a fetter on men's necks,
Poor men's made poorer for thy sake,
  And women's withered out of sex?
It was for this, that slaves should be,
Thy word was passed to set men free?

The nineteenth wave of the ages rolls
  Now deathward since thy death and birth.
Hast thou fed full men's starved-out souls?
  Hast thou brought freedom upon earth?
Or are there less oppressions done
In this wild world under the sun?

Nay, if indeed thou be not dead,
  Before thy terrene shrine be shaken,
Look down, turn usward, bow thine head;
  O thou that wast of God forsaken,
Look on thine household here, and see
These that have not forsaken thee.

Thy faith is fire upon their lips,
   Thy kingdom golden in their hands;
They scourge us with thy words for whips,
   They brand us with thy words for brands;
The thirst that made thy dry throat shrink
To their moist mouths commends the drink.

The toothèd thorns that bit thy brows
   Lighten the weight of gold on theirs;
Thy nakedness enrobes thy spouse
   With the soft sanguine stuff she wears
Whose old limbs use for ointment yet
Thine agony and bloody sweat.

The blinding buffets on thine head
   On their crowned heads confirm the crown;
Thy scourging dyes their raiment red,
   And with thy bands they fasten down
For burial in the blood-bought field
The nations by thy stripes unhealed.

With iron for thy linen bands
   And unclean cloths for winding-sheet
They bind the people's nail-pierced hands,
   They hide the people's nail-pierced feet;
And what man or what angel known
Shall roll back the sepulchral stone?

But these have not the rich man's grave
   To sleep in when their pain is done.
These were not fit for God to save.
   As naked hell-fire is the sun
In their eyes living, and when dead
These have not where to lay their head.

They have no tomb to dig, and hide;
  Earth is not theirs, that they should sleep.
On all these tombless crucified
  No lover's eyes have time to weep.
So still, for all man's tears and creeds,
The sacred body hangs and bleeds.

Through the left hand a nail is driven,
  Faith, and another through the right,
Forged in the fires of hell and heaven,
  Fear that puts out the eye of light:
And the feet soiled and scarred and pale
Are pierced with falsehood for a nail.

And priests against the mouth divine
  Push their sponge full of poison yet
And bitter blood for myrrh and wine,
  And on the same reed is it set
Wherewith before they buffeted
The people's disanointed head.

O sacred head, O desecrate,
  O labour-wounded feet and hands,
O blood poured forth in pledge to fate
  Of nameless lives in divers lands,
O slain and spent and sacrificed
People, the grey-grown speechless Christ!

Is there a gospel in the red
  Old witness of thy wide-mouthed wounds?
From thy blind stricken tongueless head
  What desolate evangel sounds
A hopeless note of hope deferred?
What word, if there be any word?

O son of man, beneath man's feet
　　Cast down, O common face of man
Whereon all blows and buffets meet,
　　O royal, O republican
Face of the people bruised and dumb
And longing till thy kingdom come!

The soldiers and the high priests part
　　Thy vesture: all thy days are priced,
And all the nights that eat thine heart.
　　And that one seamless coat of Christ,
The freedom of the natural soul,
They cast their lots for to keep whole.

No fragment of it save the name
　　They leave thee for a crown of scorns
Wherewith to mock thy naked shame
　　And forehead bitten through with thorns
And, marked with sanguine sweat and tears,
The stripes of eighteen hundred years.

And we seek yet if God or man
　　Can loosen thee as Lazarus,
Bid thee rise up republican
　　And save thyself and all of us;
But no disciple's tongue can say
When thou shalt take our sins away.

And mouldering now and hoar with moss
　　Between us and the sunlight swings
The phantom of a Christless cross
　　Shadowing the sheltered heads of kings
And making with its moving shade
The souls of harmless men afraid.

It creaks and rocks to left and right
   Consumed of rottenness and rust,
Worm-eaten of the worms of night,
   Dead as their spirits who put trust,
Round its base muttering as they sit,
In the time-cankered name of it.

Thou, in the day that breaks thy prison,
   People, though these men take thy name,
And hail and hymn thee rearisen,
   Who made songs erewhile of thy shame,
Give thou not ear; for these are they
Whose good day was thine evil day.

Set not thine hand unto their cross.
   Give not thy soul up sacrificed.
Change not the gold of faith for dross
   Of Christian creeds that spit on Christ.
Let not thy tree of freedom be
Regrafted from that rotting tree.

This dead God here against my face
   Hath help for no man; who hath seen
The good works of it, or such grace
   As thy grace in it, Nazarene,
As that from thy live lips which ran
For man's sake, O thou son of man?

The tree of faith ingraffed by priests
   Puts its foul foliage out above thee,
And round it feed man-eating beasts
   Because of whom we dare not love thee;
Though hearts reach back and memories ache,
We cannot praise thee for their sake.

O hidden face of man, whereover
   The years have woven a viewless veil,
If thou wast verily man's lover,
   What did thy love or blood avail?
Thy blood the priests make poison of,
And in gold shekels coin thy love.

So when our souls look back to thee
   They sicken, seeing against thy side,
Too foul to speak of or to see,
   The leprous likeness of a bride,
Whose kissing lips through his lips grown
Leave their God rotten to the bone.

When we would see thee man, and know
   What heart thou hadst toward men indeed,
Lo, thy blood-blackened altars; lo,
   The lips of priests that pray and feed
While their own hell's worm curls and licks
The poison of the crucifix.

Thou bad'st let children come to thee;
   What children now but curses come?
What manhood in that God can be
   Who sees their worship, and is dumb?
No soul that lived, loved, wrought, and died,
Is this their carrion crucified.

Nay, if their God and thou be one,
   If thou and this thing be the same,
Thou shouldst not look upon the sun;
   The sun grows haggard at thy name.
Come down, be done with, cease, give o'er;
Hide thyself, strive not, be no more.

CHRISTMAS ANTIPHONES

I

IN CHURCH

Thou whose birth on earth
  Angels sang to men,
While thy stars made mirth,
Saviour at thy birth,
  This day born again;

As this night was bright
  With thy cradle-ray,
Very light of light,
Turn the wild world's night
  To thy perfect day.

God whose feet made sweet
  Those wild ways they trod,
From thy fragrant feet
Staining field and street
  With the blood of God;

God whose breast is rest
  In the time of strife,
In thy secret breast
Sheltering souls opprest
  From the heat of life;

God whose eyes are skies
  Love-lit as with spheres
By the lights that rise
To thy watching eyes,
  Orbèd lights of tears;

God whose heart hath part
    In all grief that is,
Was not man's the dart
That went through thine heart,
    And the wound not his?

Where the pale souls wail,
    Held in bonds of death,
Where all spirits quail,
Came thy Godhead pale
    Still from human breath—

Pale from life and strife,
    Wan with manhood, came
Forth of mortal life,
Pierced as with a knife,
    Scarred as with a flame.

Thou the word and Lord
    In all time and space
Heard, beheld, adored,
With all ages poured
    Forth before thy face,

Lord, what worth in earth
    Drew thee down to die?
What therein was worth,
Lord, thy death and birth?
    What beneath thy sky?

Light above all love
    By thy love was lit,
And brought down the Dove
Feathered from above
    With the wings of it.

From the height of night,
  Was not thine the star
That led forth with might
By no worldly light
  Wise men from afar?

Yet the wise men's eyes
  Saw thee not more clear
Than they saw thee rise
Who in shepherd's guise
  Drew as poor men near.

Yet thy poor endure,
  And are with us yet;
Be thy name a sure
Refuge for thy poor
  Whom men's eyes forget.

Thou whose ways we praise,
  Clear alike and dark,
Keep our works and ways
This and all thy days
  Safe inside thine ark.

Who shall keep thy sheep,
  Lord, and lose not one?
Who save one shall keep,
Lest the shepherds sleep?
  Who beside the Son?

From the grave-deep wave,
  From the sword and flame,
Thou, even thou, shalt save
Souls of king and slave
  Only by thy Name.

Light not born with morn
  Or her fires above,
Jesus virgin-born,
Held of men in scorn,
  Turn their scorn to love.

Thou whose face gives grace
  As the sun's doth heat,
Let thy sunbright face
Lighten time and space
  Here beneath thy feet.

Bid our peace increase,
  Thou that madest morn;
Bid oppressions cease;
Bid the night be peace;
  Bid the day be born.

II

OUTSIDE CHURCH

WE whose days and ways
  All the night makes dark,
What day shall we praise
Of these weary days
  That our life-drops mark?

We whose mind is blind,
  Fed with hope of nought;
Wastes of worn mankind,
Without heart or mind,
  Without meat or thought;

We with strife of life
  Worn till all life cease,
Want, a whetted knife,
Sharpening strife on strife,
  How should we love peace?

Ye whose meat is sweet
  And your wine-cup red,
Us beneath your feet
Hunger grinds as wheat,
  Grinds to make you bread.

Ye whose night is bright
  With soft rest and heat,
Clothed like day with light,
Us the naked night
  Slays from street to street.

Hath your God no rod,
  That ye tread so light?
Man on us as God,
God as man hath trod,
  Trod us down with might.

We that one by one
  Bleed from either's rod.
What for us hath done
Man beneath the sun,
  What for us hath God?

We whose blood is food
  Given your wealth to feed,
From the Christless rood
Red with no God's blood,
  But with man's indeed;

How shall we that see
  Night-long overhead
Life, the flowerless tree,
Nailed whereon as we
  Were our fathers dead—

We whose ear can hear,
  Not whose tongue can name,
Famine, ignorance, fear,
Bleeding tear by tear
  Year by year of shame,

Till the dry life die
  Out of bloodless breast,
Out of beamless eye,
Out of mouths that cry
  Till death feed with rest—

How shall we as ye,
  Though ye bid us, pray?
Though ye call, can we
Hear you call, or see,
  Though ye show us day?

We whose name is shame,
  We whose souls walk bare,
Shall we call the same
God as ye by name,
  Teach our lips your prayer?

God, forgive and give,
  For His sake who died?
Nay, for ours who live,
How shall we forgive
  Thee, then, on our side?

We whose right to light
  Heaven's high noon denies,
Whom the blind beams smite
That for you shine bright,
  And but burn our eyes,

With what dreams of beams
  Shall we build up day,
At what sourceless streams
Seek to drink in dreams
  Ere they pass away?

In what street shall meet,
  At what market-place,
Your feet and our feet,
With one goal to greet,
  Having run one race?

What one hope shall ope
  For us all as one
One same horoscope,
Where the soul sees hope
  That outburns the sun?

At what shrine what wine,
  At what board what bread,
Salt as blood or brine,
Shall we share in sign
  How we poor were fed?

In what hour what power
  Shall we pray for morn,
If your perfect hour,
When all day bears flower,
  Not for us is born?

III

BEYOND CHURCH

Ye that weep in sleep,
  Souls and bodies bound,
Ye that all night keep
Watch for change, and weep
  That no change is found;

Ye that cry and die,
  And the world goes on
Without ear or eye,
And the days go by
  Till all days are gone.

Man shall do for you,
  Men the sons of man,
What no God would do
That they sought unto
  While the blind years ran.

Brotherhood of good,
  Equal laws and rights,
Freedom, whose sweet food
Feeds the multitude
  All their days and nights

With the bread full-fed
  Of her body blest
And the soul's wine shed
From her table spread
  Where the world is guest,

Mingling me and thee,
  When like light of eyes
Flashed through thee and me
Truth shall make us free,
  Liberty make wise;

These are they whom day
  Follows and gives light
Whence they see to slay
Night, and burn away
  All the seed of night.

What of thine and mine,
  What of want and wealth,
When one faith is wine
For my heart and thine
  And one draught is health?

For no sect elect
  Is the soul's wine poured
And her table decked;
Whom should man reject
  From man's common board?

Gods refuse and choose,
  Grudge and sell and spare;
None shall man refuse,
None of all men lose,
  None leave out of care.

No man's might of sight
  Knows that hour before;
No man's hand hath might
To put back that light
  For one hour the more.

Not though all men call,
  Kneeling with void hands,
Shall they see light fall
Till it come for all
  Tribes of men and lands.

No desire brings fire
   Down from heaven by prayer,
Though man's vain desire
Hang faith's wind-struck lyre
   Out in tuneless air.

One hath breath and saith
   What the tune shall be—
Time, who puts his breath
Into life and death,
   Into earth and sea.

To and fro years flow,
   Fill their tides and ebb,
As his fingers go
Weaving to and fro
   One unfinished web.

All the range of change
   Hath its bounds therein,
All the lives that range
All the byways strange
   Named of death or sin.

Star from far to star
   Speaks, and white moons wake,
Watchful from afar
What the night's ways are
   For the morning's sake.

Many names and flames
   Pass and flash and fall,
Night-begotten names,
And the night reclaims,
   As she bare them, all.

But the sun is one,
   And the sun's name Right;
And when light is none
Saving of the sun,
   All men shall have light.

All shall see and be
   Parcel of the morn;
Ay, though blind were we,
None shall choose but see
   When that day is born.

COR CORDIUM

O HEART of hearts, the chalice of love's fire,
   Hid round with flowers and all the bounty of bloom;
   O wonderful and perfect heart, for whom
The lyrist liberty made life a lyre;
O heavenly heart, at whose most dear desire
   Dead love, living and singing, cleft his tomb,
   And with him risen and regent in death's room
All day thy choral pulses rang full choir;
O heart whose beating blood was running song,
   O sole thing sweeter than thine own songs were,
      Help us for thy free love's sake to be free,
True for thy truth's sake, for thy strength's sake
      strong,
   Till very liberty make clean and fair
      The nursing earth as the sepulchral sea.

THE OBLATION

Ask nothing more of me, sweet;
  All I can give you I give.
    Heart of my heart, were it more,
More would be laid at your feet:
  Love that should help you to live,
    Song that should spur you to soar.

All things were nothing to give
  Once to have sense of you more,
    Touch you and taste of you sweet,
Think you and breathe you and live,
  Swept of your wings as they soar,
    Trodden by chance of your feet.

I that have love and no more
  Give you but love of you, sweet:
    He that hath more, let him give;
He that hath wings, let him soar;
  Mine is the heart at your feet
    Here, that must love you to live.

A DEAD KING

[Ferdinand II entered Malebolge May 22nd, 1859.]

Go down to hell. This end is good to see;
  The breath is lightened and the sense at ease
  Because thou art not; sense nor breath there is
In what thy body was, whose soul shall be
Chief nerve of hell's pained heart eternally.
  Thou art abolished from the midst of these
  That are what thou wast: Pius from his knees
Blows off the dust that flecked them, bowed for thee.

Yea, now the long-tongued slack-lipped litanies
   Fail, and the priest has no more prayer to sell—
Now the last Jesuit found about thee is
   The beast that made thy fouler flesh his cell—
Time lays his finger on thee, saying, 'Cease;
   Here is no room for thee; go down to hell.'

A COUNSEL

O STRONG Republic of the nobler years
   Whose white feet shine beside time's fairer flood
   That shall flow on the clearer for our blood
Now shed, and the less brackish for our tears;
When time and truth have put out hopes and fears
   With certitude, and love has burst the bud,
   If these whose powers then down the wind shall scud
Still live to feel thee smite their eyes and ears,
When thy foot's tread hath crushed their crowns and
      creeds,
Care thou not then to crush the beast that bleeds,
   The snake whose belly cleaveth to the sod,
Nor set thine heel on men as on their deeds;
   But let the worm Napoleon crawl untrod,
   Nor grant Mastai the gallows of his God.
1869.

APOLOGIA

IF wrath embitter the sweet mouth of song,
   And make the sunlight fire before those eyes
   That would drink draughts of peace from the un-
      soiled skies,
The wrongdoing is not ours, but ours the wrong,

Who hear too loud on earth and see too long
  The grief that dies not with the groan that dies,
  Till the strong bitterness of pity cries
Within us, that our anger should be strong.
For chill is known by heat and heat by chill,
And the desire that hope makes love to still
  By the fear flying beside it or above,
  A falcon fledged to follow a fledgeling dove,
And by the fume and flame of hate of ill
  The exuberant light and burning bloom of love.

DEDICATORY SONNET TO TRISTRAM
OF LYONESSE

Spring speaks again, and all our woods are stirred,
  And all our wide glad wastes aflower around,
  That twice have heard keen April's clarion sound
Since here we first together saw and heard
Spring's light reverberate and reiterate word
  Shine forth and speak in season. Life stands crowned
  Here with the best one thing it ever found,
As of my soul's best birthdays dawns the third.

There is a friend that as the wise man saith
  Cleaves closer than a brother: nor to me
    Hath time not shown, through days like waves at
      strife,
This truth more sure than all things else but death,
  This pearl most perfect found in all the sea
    That washes toward your feet these waifs of life.

The Pines: *April* 1882.

TRISTRAM OF LYONESSE

Prelude

LOVE, that is first and last of all things made,
The light that has the living world for shade,
The spirit that for temporal veil has on
The souls of all men woven in unison,
One fiery raiment with all lives inwrought.
And lights of sunny and starry deed and thought,
And alway through new act and passion new
Shines the divine same body and beauty through,
The body spiritual of fire and light
That is to worldly noon as noon to night;
Love, that is flesh upon the spirit of man
And spirit within the flesh whence breath began;
Love, that keeps all the choir of lives in chime;
Love, that is blood within the veins of time;
That wrought the whole world without stroke of hand,
Shaping the breadth of sea, the length of land,
And with the pulse and motion of his breath
Through the great heart of the earth strikes life and
  death,
The sweet twain chords that make the sweet tune live
Through day and night of things alternative,
Through silence and through sound of stress and
  strife,
And ebb and flow of dying death and life;
Love, that sounds loud or light in all men's ears,
Whence all men's eyes take fire from sparks of tears,
That binds on all men's feet or chains or wings;
Love, that is root and fruit of terrene things;
Love, that the whole world's waters shall not drown,
The whole world's fiery forces not burn down;

Love, that what time his own hands guard his head
The whole world's wrath and strength shall not
      strike dead;
Love, that if once his own hands make his grave
The whole world's pity and sorrow shall not save;
Love, that for very life shall not be sold,
Nor bought nor bound with iron nor with gold;
So strong that heaven, could love bid heaven farewell,
Would turn to fruitless and unflowering hell;
So sweet that hell, to hell could love be given,
Would turn to splendid and sonorous heaven;
Love that is fire within thee and light above,
And lives by grace of nothing but of love;
Through many and lovely thoughts and much desire
Led these twain to the life of tears and fire;
Through many and lovely days and much delight
Led these twain to the lifeless life of night.

  Yea, but what then? albeit all this were thus,
And soul smote soul and left it ruinous,
And love led love as eyeless men lead men,
Through chance by chance to deathward—Ah, what
      then?
Hath love not likewise led them further yet,
Out through the years where memories rise and set,
Some large as suns, some moon-like warm and pale,
Some starry-sighted, some through clouds that sail
Seen as red flame through spectral float of fume,
Each with the blush of its own special bloom
On the fair face of its own coloured light,
Distinguishable in all the host of night,
Divisible from all the radiant rest
And separable in splendour? Hath the best
Light of love's all, of all that burn and move,
A better heaven than heaven is? Hath not love

Made for all these their sweet particular air
To shine in, their own beams and names to bear,
Their ways to wander and their wards to keep,
Till story and song and glory and all things sleep?
Hath he not plucked from death of lovers dead
Their musical soft memories, and kept red
The rose of their remembrance in men's eyes,
The sunsets of their stories in his skies,
The blush of their dead blood in lips that speak
Of their dead lives, and in the listener's cheek
That trembles with the kindling pity lit
In gracious hearts for some sweet fever-fit,
A fiery pity enkindled of pure thought
By tales that make their honey out of nought,
The faithless faith that lives without belief
Its light life through, the griefless ghost of grief?
Yea, as warm night refashions the sere blood
In storm-struck petal or in sun-struck bud,
With tender hours and tempering dew to cure
The hunger and thirst of day's distemperature
And ravin of the dry discolouring hours,
Hath he not bid relume their flameless flowers
With summer fire and heat of lamping song,
And bid the short-lived things, long dead, live long,
And thought remake their wan funereal fames,
And the sweet shining signs of women's names
That mark the months out and the weeks anew
He moves in changeless change of seasons through
To fill the days up of his dateless year
Flame from Queen Helen to Queen Guenevere?
For first of all the sphery signs whereby
Love severs light from darkness, and most high,
In the white front of January there glows
The rose-red sign of Helen like a rose:

And gold-eyed as the shore-flower shelterless
Whereon the sharp-breathed sea blows bitterness,
A storm-star that the seafarers of love
Strain their wind-wearied eyes for glimpses of,
Shoots keen through February's grey frost and damp
The lamplike star of Hero for a lamp;
The star that Marlowe sang into our skies
With mouth of gold, and morning in his eyes;
And in clear March across the rough blue sea
The signal sapphire of Alcyone
Makes bright the blown brows of the wind-foot year;
And shining like a sunbeam-smitten tear
Full ere it fall, the fair next sign in sight
Burns opal-wise with April-coloured light
When air is quick with song and rain and flame,
My birth-month star that in love's heaven hath name
Iseult, a light of blossom and beam and shower,
My singing sign that makes the song-tree flower;
Next like a pale and burning pearl beyond
The rose-white sphere of flower-named Rosamond
Signs the sweet head of Maytime; and for June
Flares like an angered and storm-reddening moon
Her signal sphere, whose Carthaginian pyre
Shadowed her traitor's flying sail with fire;
Next, glittering as the wine-bright jacinth-stone,
A star south-risen that first to music shone,
The keen girl-star of golden Juliet bears
Light northward to the month whose forehead wears
Her name for flower upon it, and his trees
Mix their deep English song with Veronese;
And like an awful sovereign chrysolite
Burning, the supreme fire that blinds the night,
The hot gold head of Venus kissed by Mars,
A sun-flower among small sphered flowers of stars,

The light of Cleopatra fills and burns
The hollow of heaven whence ardent August yearns;
And fixed and shining as the sister-shed
Sweet tears for Phaethon disorbed and dead,
The pale bright autumn's amber-coloured sphere,
That through September sees the saddening year
As love sees change through sorrow, hath to name
Francesca's; and the star that watches flame
The embers of the harvest overgone
Is Thisbe's, slain of love in Babylon,
Set in the golden girdle of sweet signs
A blood-bright ruby; last save one light shines
An eastern wonder of sphery chrysopras,
The star that made men mad, Angelica's;
And latest named and lordliest, with a sound
Of swords and harps in heaven that ring it round,
Last love-light and last love-song of the year's,
Gleams like a glorious emerald Guenevere's.
These are the signs wherethrough the year sees move,
Full of the sun, the sun-god which is love,
A fiery body blood-red from the heart
Outward, with fire-white wings made wide apart,
That close not and unclose not, but upright
Steered without wind by their own light and might
Sweep through the flameless fire of air that rings
From heaven to heaven with thunder of wheels and
      wings
And antiphones of motion-moulded rhyme
Through spaces out of space and timeless time.
   So shine above dead chance and conquered change
The spherèd signs, and leave without their range
Doubt and desire, and hope with fear for wife,
Pale pains, and pleasures long worn out of life.
Yea, even the shadows of them spiritless,

Through the dim door of sleep that seem to press,
Forms without form, a piteous people and blind,
Men and no men, whose lamentable kind
The shadow of death and shadow of life compel
Through semblances of heaven and false-faced hell,
Through dreams of light and dreams of darkness tost
On waves innavigable, are these so lost?
Shapes that wax pale and shift in swift strange wise,
Void faces with unspeculative eyes,
Dim things that gaze and glare, dead mouths that
    move,
Featureless heads discrowned of hate and love,
Mockeries and masks of motion and mute breath,
Leavings of life, the superflux of death—
If these things and no more than these things be
Left when man ends or changes, who can see?
Or who can say with what more subtle sense
Their subtler natures taste in air less dense
A life less thick and palpable than ours,
Warmed with faint fires and sweetened with dead
    flowers
And measured by low music? how time fares
In that wan time-forgotten world of theirs,
Their pale poor world too deep for sun or star
To live in, where the eyes of Helen are,
And hers who made as God's own eyes to shine
The eyes that met them of the Florentine,
Wherein the godhead thence transfigured lit
All time for all men with the shadow of it?
Ah, and these too felt on them as God's grace
The pity and glory of this man's breathing face;
For these too, these my lovers, these my twain,
Saw Dante, saw God visible by pain,
With lips that thundered and with feet that trod

Before men's eyes incognisable God;
Saw love and wrath and light and night and fire
Live with one life and at one mouth respire,
And in one golden sound their whole soul heard
Sounding, one sweet immitigable word.
    They have the night, who had like us the day;
We, whom day binds, shall have the night as they.
We, from the fetters of the light unbound,
Healed of our wound of living, shall sleep sound.
All gifts but one the jealous God may keep
From our soul's longing, one he cannot—sleep.
This, though he grudge all other grace to prayer,
This grace his closed hand cannot choose but
    spare.
This, though his ear be sealed to all that live,
Be it lightly given or lothly, God must give.
We, as the men whose name on earth is none,
We too shall surely pass out of the sun;
Out of the sound and eyeless light of things,
Wide as the stretch of life's time-wandering wings,
Wide as the naked world and shadowless,
And long-lived as the world's own weariness.
Us too, when all the fires of time are cold,
The heights shall hide us and the depths shall hold.
Us too, when all the tears of time are dry,
The night shall lighten from her tearless eye.
Blind is the day and eyeless all its light,
But the large unbewildered eye of night
Hath sense and speculation; and the sheer
Limitless length of lifeless life and clear,
The timeless space wherein the brief worlds move
Clothed with light life and fruitful with light love,
With hopes that threaten, and with fears that cease,
Past fear and hope, hath in it only peace.

Yet of these lives inlaid with hopes and fears,
Spun fine as fire and jewelled thick with tears,
These lives made out of loves that long since were,
Lives wrought as ours of earth and burning air,
Fugitive flame, and water of secret springs,
And clothed with joys and sorrows as with wings,
Some yet are good, if aught be good, to save
Some while from washing wreck and wrecking wave.
Was such not theirs, the twain I take, and give
Out of my life to make their dead life live
Some days of mine, and blow my living breath
Between dead lips forgotten even of death?
So many and many of old have given my twain
Love and live song and honey-hearted pain,
Whose root is sweetness and whose fruit is sweet,
So many and with such joy have tracked their feet,
What should I do to follow? yet I too,
I have the heart to follow, many or few
Be the feet gone before me; for the way,
Rose-red with remnant roses of the day
Westward, and eastward white with stars that break,
Between the green and foam is fair to take
For any sail the sea-wind steers for me
From morning into morning, sea to sea.

Book I

THE SAILING OF THE SWALLOW

About the middle music of the spring
Came from the castled shore of Ireland's king
A fair ship stoutly sailing, eastward bound
And south by Wales and all its wonders round
To the loud rocks and ringing reaches home
That take the wild wrath of the Cornish foam,
Past Lyonesse unswallowed of the tides

And high Carlion that now the steep sea hides
To the wind-hollowed heights and gusty bays
Of sheer Tintagel, fair with famous days.
Above the stem a gilded swallow shone,
Wrought with straight wings and eyes of glittering
    stone
As flying sunward oversea, to bear
Green summer with it through the singing air.
And on the deck between the rowers at dawn,
As the bright sail with brightening wind was drawn,
Sat with full face against the strengthening light
Iseult, more fair than foam or dawn was white.
Her gaze was glad past love's own singing of,
And her face lovely past desire of love.
Past thought and speech her maiden motions were,
And a more golden sunrise was her hair.
The very veil of her bright flesh was made
As of light woven and moonbeam-coloured shade
More fine than moonbeams; white her eyelids shone
As snow sun-stricken that endures the sun,
And through their curled and coloured clouds of deep
Luminous lashes thick as dreams in sleep
Shone as the sea's depth swallowing up the sky's
The springs of unimaginable eyes.
As the wave's subtler emerald is pierced through
With the utmost heaven's inextricable blue,
And both are woven and molten in one sleight
Of amorous colour and implicated light
Under the golden guard and gaze of noon,
So glowed their aweless amorous plenilune,
Azure and gold and ardent grey, made strange
With fiery difference and deep interchange
Inexplicable of glories multiform;
Now as the sullen sapphire swells toward storm

Foamless, their bitter beauty grew acold,
And now afire with ardour of fine gold.
Her flower-soft lips were meek and passionate,
For love upon them like a shadow sate
Patient, a foreseen vision of sweet things,
A dream with eyes fast shut and plumeless wings
That knew not what man's love or life should be,
Nor had it sight nor heart to hope or see
What thing should come, but childlike satisfied
Watched out its virgin vigil in soft pride
And unkissed expectation; and the glad
Clear cheeks and throat and tender temples had
Such maiden heat as if a rose's blood
Beat in the live heart of a lily-bud.
Between the small round breasts a white way led
Heavenward, and from slight foot to slender head
The whole fair body flower-like swayed and shone
Moving, and what her light hand leant upon
Grew blossom-scented: her warm arms began
To round and ripen for delight of man
That they should clasp and circle: her fresh hands,
Like regent lilies of reflowering lands
Whose vassal firstlings, crown and star and plume,
Bow down to the empire of that sovereign bloom,
Shone sceptreless, and from her face there went
A silent light as of a God content;
Save when, more swift and keen than love or shame,
Some flash of blood, light as the laugh of flame,
Broke it with sudden beam and shining speech,
As dream by dream shot through her eyes, and each
Outshone the last that lightened, and not one
Showed her such things as should be borne and done.
Though hard against her shone the sunlike face
That in all change and wreck of time and place

Should be the star of her sweet living soul.
Nor had love made it as his written scroll
For evil will and good to read in yet;
But smooth and mighty, without scar or fret,
Fresh and high-lifted was the helmless brow
As the oak-tree flower that tops the topmost bough,
Ere it drop off before the perfect leaf;
And nothing save his name he had of grief,
The name his mother, dying as he was born,
Made out of sorrow in very sorrow's scorn,
And set it on him smiling in her sight,
Tristram; who now, clothed with sweet youth and
    might,
As a glad witness wore that bitter name,
The second symbol of the world for fame.
Famous and full of fortune was his youth
Ere the beard's bloom had left his cheek unsmooth,
And in his face a lordship of strong joy
And height of heart no chance could curb or cloy
Lightened, and all that warmed them at his eyes
Loved them as larks that kindle as they rise
Toward light they turn to music love the blue strong
    skies.
So like the morning through the morning moved
Tristram, a light to look on and be loved.
Song sprang between his lips and hands, and shone
Singing, and strengthened and sank down thereon
As a bird settles to the second flight,
Then from beneath his harping hands with might
Leapt, and made way and had its fill and died,
And all whose hearts were fed upon it sighed
Silent, and in them all the fire of tears
Burned as wine drunken not with lips but ears.
And gazing on his fervent hands that made

The might of music all their souls obeyed
With trembling strong subservience of delight
Full many a maid that had him once in sight
Thought in the secret rapture of her heart
In how dark onset had these hands borne part
How oft, and were so young and sweet of skill;
And those red lips whereon the song burned still,
What words and cries of battle had they flung
Athwart the swing and shriek of swords, so young;
And eyes as glad as summer, what strange youth
Fed them so full of happy heart and truth,
That had seen sway from side to sundering side
The steel flow of that terrible springtide
That the moon rules not, but the fire and light
Of men's hearts mixed in the mid mirth of fight.
Therefore the joy and love of him they had
Made thought more amorous in them and more glad
For his fame's sake remembered, and his youth
Gave his fame flowerlike fragrance and soft growth
As of a rose requickening, when he stood
Fair in their eye, a flower of faultless blood.
And that sad queen to whom his life was death,
A rose plucked forth of summer in mid breath,
A star fall'n out of season in mid throe
Of that life's joy that makes the star's life glow,
Made their love sadder toward him and more strong.
And in mid change of time and fight and song
Chance cast him westward on the low sweet strand
Where songs are sung of the old green Irish land,
And the sky loves it, and the sea loves best,
And as a bird is taken to man's breast
The sweet-souled land where sorrow sweetest sings
Is wrapt round with them as with hands and wings
And taken to the sea's heart as a flower.

There in the luck and light of his good hour
Came to the king's court like a noteless man
Tristram, and while some half a season ran
Abode before him harping in his hall,
And taught sweet craft of new things musical
To the dear maiden mouth and innocent hands
That for his sake are famous in all lands.
Yet was not love between them, for their fate
Lay wrapt in its appointed hour at wait,
And had no flower to show yet, and no sting.
But once being vexed with some past wound the king
Bade him give comfort of sweet baths, and then
Should Iseult watch him as his handmaiden,
For his more honour in men's sight, and ease
The hurts he had with holy remedies
Made by her mother's magic in strange hours
Out of live roots and life-compelling flowers.
And finding by the wound's shape in his side
This was the knight by whom their strength had died
And all their might in one man overthrown
Had left their shame in sight of all men shown,
She would have slain him swordless with his sword;
Yet seemed he to her so great and fair a lord
She heaved up hand and smote not; then said he,
Laughing—'What comfort shall this dead man be,
Damsel? what hurt is for my blood to heal?
But set your hand not near the toothèd steel
Lest the fang strike it.'—'Yea, the fang,' she said,
'Should it not sting the very serpent dead
That stung mine uncle? for his slayer art thou,
And half my mother's heart is bloodless now
Through thee, that mad'st the veins of all her kin
Bleed in his wounds whose veins through thee ran
    thin.'

Yet thought she how their hot chief's violent heart
Had flung the fierce word forth upon their part
Which bade to battle the best knight that stood
On Arthur's, and so dying of his wild mood
Had set upon his conqueror's flesh the seal
Of his mishallowed and anointed steel,
Whereof the venom and enchanted might
Made the sign burn here branded in her sight.
These things she stood recasting, and her soul
Subsiding till its wound of wrath were whole
Grew smooth again, as thought still softening stole
Through all its tempered passion; nor might hate
Keep high the fire against him lit of late;
But softly from his smiling sight she passed.
And peace thereafter made between them fast
Made peace between two kingdoms, when he went
Home with hands reconciled and heart content,
To bring fair truce 'twixt Cornwall's wild bright
    strand
And the long wrangling wars of that loud land.
And when full peace was struck betwixt them twain
Forth must he fare by those green straits again,
And bring back Iseult for a plighted bride
And set to reign at Mark his uncle's side.
So now with feast made and all triumphs done
They sailed between the moonfall and the sun
Under the spent stars eastward; but the queen
Out of wise heart and subtle love had seen
Such things as might be, dark as in a glass,
And lest some doom of these should come to pass
Bethought her with her secret soul alone
To work some charm for marriage unison
And strike the heart of Iseult to her lord
With power compulsive more than stroke of sword.

Therefore with marvellous herbs and spells she wrought
To win the very wonder of her thought,
And brewed it with her secret hands and blest
And drew and gave out of her secret breast
To one her chosen and Iseult's handmaiden,
Brangwain, and bade her hide from sight of men
This marvel covered in a golden cup,
So covering in her heart the counsel up
As in the gold the wondrous wine lay close;
And when the last shout with the last cup rose
About the bride and bridegroom bound to bed,
Then should this one word of her will be said
To her new-married maiden child, that she
Should drink with Mark this draught in unity,
And no lip touch it for her sake but theirs:
For with long love and consecrating prayers
The wine was hallowed for their mouths to pledge;
And if a drop fell from the beaker's edge
That drop should Iseult hold as dear as blood
Shed from her mother's heart to do her good.
And having drunk they twain should be one heart
Who were one flesh till fleshly death should part—
Death, who parts all. So Brangwain swore, and kept
The hid thing by her while she waked or slept.
And now they sat to see the sun again
Whose light of eye had looked on no such twain
Since Galahault in the rose-time of the year
Brought Launcelot first to sight of Guenevere.

And Tristram caught her changing eyes and said:
'As this day raises daylight from the dead
Might not this face the life of a dead man?'

And Iseult, gazing where the sea was wan
Out of the sun's way, said: 'I pray you not
Praise me, but tell me there in Camelot,

Saving the queen, who hath most name of fair?
I would I were a man and dwelling there,
That I might win me better praise than yours,
Even such as you have; for your praise endures,
That with great deeds ye wring from mouths of men,
But ours—for shame, where is it? Tell me then,
Since woman may not wear a better here,
Who of this praise hath most save Guenevere?'
    And Tristram, lightening with a laugh held in—
'Surely a little praise is this to win,
A poor praise and a little! but of these
Hapless, whom love serves only with bowed knees,
Of such poor women fairer face hath none
That lifts her eyes alive against the sun
Than Arthur's sister, whom the north seas call
Mistress of isles; so yet majestical
Above the crowns on younger heads she moves,
Outlightening with her eyes our late-born loves.'
    'Ah,' said Iseult, 'is she more tall than I?
Look, I am tall;' and struck the mast hard by,
With utmost upward reach of her bright hand;
'And look, fair lord, now, when I rise and stand,
How high with feet unlifted I can touch
Standing straight up; could this queen do thus much?
Nay, over tall she must be then, like me;
Less fair than lesser women. May this be,
That still she stands the second stateliest there,
So more than many so much younger fair,
She, born when yet the king your lord was not,
And has the third knight after Launcelot
And after you to serve her? nay, sir, then
God made her for a godlike sign to men.'
    'Ay,' Tristram answered, 'for a sign, a sign—
Would God it were not! for no planets shine

With half such fearful forecast of men's fate
As a fair face so more unfortunate.'
   Then with a smile that lit not on her brows
But moved upon her red mouth tremulous
Light as a sea-bird's motion oversea,
'Yea,' quoth Iseult, 'the happier hap for me,
With no such face to bring men no such fate.
Yet her might all we women born too late
Praise for good hap, who so enskied above
Not more in age excels us than man's love.'
   There came a glooming light on Tristram's face
Answering: 'God keep you better in his grace
Than to sit down beside her in men's sight.
For if men be not blind whom God gives light
And lie not in whose lips he bids truth live,
Great grief shall she be given, and greater give.
For Merlin witnessed of her years ago
That she should work woe and should suffer woe
Beyond the race of women: and in truth
Her face, a spell that knows nor age nor youth,
Like youth being soft, and subtler-eyed than age,
With lips that mock the doom her eyes presage,
Hath on it such a light of cloud and fire,
With charm and change of keen or dim desire,
And over all a fearless look of fear
Hung like a veil across its changing cheer,
Made up of fierce foreknowledge and sharp scorn,
That it were better she had not been born.
For not love's self can help a face which hath
Such insubmissive anguish of wan wrath,
Blind prescience and self-contemptuous hate
Of her own soul and heavy-footed fate,
Writ broad upon its beauty: none the less
Its fire of bright and burning bitterness

Takes with as quick a flame the sense of men
As any sunbeam, nor is quenched again
With any drop of dewfall; yea, I think
No herb of force or blood-compelling drink
Would heal a heart that ever it made hot.
Ay, and men too that greatly love her not,
Seeing the great love of her and Lamoracke,
Make no great marvel, nor look strangely back
When with his gaze about her she goes by
Pale as a breathless and star-quickening sky
Between moonrise and sunset, and moves out
Clothed with the passion of his eyes about
As night with all her stars, yet night is black;
And she, clothed warm with love of Lamoracke,
Girt with his worship as with girdling gold,
Seems all at heart anhungered and acold,
Seems sad at heart and loveless of the light,
As night, star-clothed or naked, is but night.'
    And with her sweet eyes sunken, and the mirth
Dead in their look as earth lies dead in earth
That reigned on earth and triumphed, Iseult said:
'Is it her shame of something done and dead
Or fear of something to be born and done
That so in her soul's eye puts out the sun?'
    And Tristram answered: 'Surely, as I think,
This gives her soul such bitterness to drink,
The sin born blind, the sightless sin unknown,
Wrought when the summer in her blood was blown
But scarce aflower, and spring first flushed her will
With bloom of dreams no fruitage should fulfil,
When out of vision and desire was wrought
The sudden sin that from the living thought
Leaps a live deed and died not: then there came
On that blind sin swift eyesight like a flame

Touching the dark to death, and made her mad
With helpless knowledge that too late forbade
What was before the bidding: and she knew
How sore a life dead love should lead her through
To what sure end how fearful; and though yet
Nor with her blood nor tears her way be wet
And she look bravely with set face on fate,
Yet she knows well the serpent hour at wait
Somewhere to sting and spare not; ay, and he,
Arthur'——

       'The king,' quoth Iseult suddenly,
'Doth the king too live so in sight of fear?
They say sin touches not a man so near
As shame a woman; yet he too should be
Part of the penance, being more deep than she
Set in the sin.'

       'Nay,' Tristram said, 'for thus
It fell by wicked hap and hazardous,
That wittingly he sinned no more than youth
May sin and be assoiled of God and truth,
Repenting; since in his first year of reign
As he stood splendid with his foemen slain
And light of new-blown battles, flushed and hot
With hope and life, came greeting from King Lot
Out of his wind-worn islands oversea,
And homage to my king and fealty
Of those north seas wherein the strange shapes swim,
As from his man; and Arthur greeted him
As his good lord and courteously, and bade
To his high feast; who coming with him had
This Queen Morgause of Orkney, his fair wife,
In the green middle Maytime of her life,
And scarce in April was our king's as then,
And goodliest was he of all flowering men,

And of what graft as yet himself knew not;
But cold as rains in autumn was King Lot
And grey-grown out of season: so there sprang
Swift love between them, and all spring through sang
Light in their joyous hearing; for none knew
The bitter bond of blood between them two,
Twain fathers but one mother, till too late
The sacred mouth of Merlin set forth fate
And brake the secret seal on Arthur's birth,
And showed his ruin and his rule on earth
Inextricable, and light on lives to be.
For surely, though time slay us, yet shall we
Have such high name and lordship of good days
As shall sustain us living, and men's praise
Shall burn a beacon lit above us dead.
And of the king how shall not this be said
When any of us from any mouth has praise,
That such were men in only this king's days,
In Arthur's? yea, come shine or shade, no less
His name shall be one name with knightliness,
His fame one light with sunlight. Yet in sooth
His age shall bear the burdens of his youth
And bleed from his own bloodshed; for indeed
Blind to him blind his sister brought forth seed,
And of the child between them shall be born
Destruction: so shall God not suffer scorn,
Nor in men's souls and lives his law lie dead.'
    And as one moved and marvelling Iseult said:
'Great pity it is and strange it seems to me
God could not do them so much right as we,
Who slay not men for witless evil done;
And these the noblest under God's glad sun
For sin they knew not he that knew shall slay,
And smite blind men for stumbling in fair day.

What good is it to God that such should die?
Shall the sun's light grow sunnier in the sky
Because their light of spirit is clean put out?'
   And sighing, she looked from wave to cloud about,
And even with that the full-grown feet of day
Sprang upright on the quivering water-way,
And his face burned against her meeting face
Most like a lover's thrilled with great love's grace
Whose glance takes fire and gives; the quick sea shone
And shivered like spread wings of angels blown
By the sun's breath before him; and a low
Sweet gale shook all the foam-flowers of thin snow
As into rainfall of sea-roses shed
Leaf by wild leaf on that green garden-bed
Which tempests till and sea-winds turn and plough;
For rosy and fiery round the running prow
Fluttered the flakes and feathers of the spray,
And bloomed like blossoms cast by God away
To waste on the ardent water; swift the moon
Withered to westward as a face in swoon
Death-stricken by glad tidings: and the height
Throbbed and the centre quivered with delight
And the depth quailed with passion as of love,
Till like the heart of some new-mated dove
Air, light, and wave seemed full of burning rest,
With motion as of one God's beating breast.
   And her heart sprang in Iseult, and she drew
With all her spirit and life the sunrise through,
And through her lips the keen triumphant air
Sea-scented, sweeter than land-roses were,
And through her eyes the whole rejoicing east
Sun-satisfied, and all the heaven at feast
Spread for the morning; and the imperious mirth
Of wind and light that moved upon the earth,

Making the spring, and all the fruitful might
And strong regeneration of delight
That swells the seedling leaf and sapling man,
Since the first life in the first world began
To burn and burgeon through void limbs and veins,
And the first love with sharp sweet procreant pains
To pierce and bring forth roses; yea, she felt
Through her own soul the sovereign morning melt,
And all the sacred passion of the sun;
And as the young clouds flamed and were undone
About him coming, touched and burnt away
In rosy ruin and yellow spoil of day,
The sweet veil of her body and corporal sense
Felt the dawn also cleave it, and incense
With light from inward and with effluent heat
The kindling soul through fleshly hands and feet.
And as the august great blossom of the dawn
Burst, and the full sun scarce from sea withdrawn
Seemed on the fiery water a flower afloat,
So as a fire the mighty morning smote
Throughout her, and incensed with the influent hour
Her whole soul's one great mystical red flower
Burst, and the bud of her sweet spirit broke
Rose-fashion, and the strong spring at a stroke
Thrilled, and was cloven, and from the full sheath came
The whole rose of the woman red as flame:
And all her Mayday blood as from a swoon
Flushed, and May rose up in her and was June.
So for a space her heart as heavenward burned:
Then with half summer in her eyes she turned,
And on her lips was April yet, and smiled,
As though the spirit and sense unreconciled
Shrank laughing back, and would not ere its hour
Let life put forth the irrevocable flower.

And the soft speech between them grew again
With questionings and records of what men
Rose mightiest, and what names for love or fight
Shone starriest overhead of queen or knight.
There Tristram spake of many a noble thing,
High feast and storm of tournay round the king,
Strange quest by perilous lands of marsh and
    brake
And circling woods branch-knotted like a snake
And places pale with sins that they had seen,
Where was no life of red fruit or of green
But all was as a dead face wan and dun;
And bowers of evil builders whence the sun
Turns silent, and the moon holds hardly light
Above them through the sick and star-crossed night;
And of their hands through whom such holds lay
    waste,
And all their strengths dishevelled and defaced
Fell ruinous, and were not from north to south:
And of the might of Merlin's ancient mouth,
The son of no man's loins, begot by doom
In speechless sleep out of a spotless womb;
For sleeping among graves where none had rest
And ominous houses of dead bones unblest
Among the grey grass rough as old rent hair
And wicked herbage whitening like despair
And blown upon with blasts of dolorous breath
From gaunt rare gaps and hollow doors of death,
A maid unspotted, senseless of the spell,
Felt not about her breathe some thing of hell
Whose child and hers was Merlin; and to him
Great light from God gave sight of all things dim
And wisdom of all wondrous things, to say
What root should bear what fruit of night or day,

And sovereign speech and counsel higher than man;
Wherefore his youth like age was wise and wan,
And his age sorrowful and fain to sleep;
Yet should sleep never, neither laugh nor weep,
Till in some depth of deep sweet land or sea
The heavenly hands of holier Nimue,
That was the nurse of Launcelot, and most sweet
Of all that move with magical soft feet
Among us, being of lovelier blood and breath,
Should shut him in with sleep as kind as death:
For she could pass between the quick and dead:
And of her love towards Pelleas, for whose head
Love-wounded and world-wearied she had won
A place beyond all pain in Avalon;
And of the fire that wasted afterward
The loveless eyes and bosom of Ettarde,
In whose false love his faultless heart had burned;
And now being rapt from her, her lost heart yearned
To seek him, and passed hungering out of life:
And after all the thunder-hours of strife
That roared between King Claudas and King Ban
How Nimue's mighty nursling waxed to man,
And how from his first field such grace he got
That all men's hearts bowed down to Launcelot,
And how the high prince Galahault held him dear
And led him even to love of Guenevere
And to that kiss which made break forth as fire
The laugh that was the flower of his desire,
The laugh that lightened at her lips for bliss
To win from Love so great a lover's kiss:
And of the toil of Balen all his days
To reap but thorns for fruit and tears for praise,
Whose hap was evil as his heart was good,
And all his works and ways by wold and wood

Led through much pain to one last labouring day
When blood for tears washed grief with life away:
And of the kin of Arthur, and their might;
The misborn head of Mordred, sad as night,
With cold waste cheeks and eyes as keen as pain,
And the close angry lips of Agravaine;
And gracious Gawain, scattering words as flowers,
The kindliest head of worldly paramours;
And the fair hand of Gareth, found in fight
Strong as a sea-beast's tushes and as white;
And of the king's self, glorious yet and glad
For all the toil and doubt of doom he had,
Clothed with men's loves and full of kingly days.

    Then Iseult said: 'Let each knight have his praise
And each good man good witness of his worth;
But when men laud the second name on earth,
Whom would they praise to have no worldly peer
Save him whose love makes glorious Guenevere?'

    'Nay,' Tristram said, 'such man as he is none.'

    'What,' said she, 'there is none such under sun
Of all the large earth's living? yet I deemed
Men spake of one—but maybe men that dreamed,
Fools and tongue-stricken, witless, babbler's breed—
That for all high things was his peer indeed
Save this one highest, to be so loved and love.'

    And Tristram: 'Little wit had these thereof;
For there is none such in the world as this.'

    'Ay, upon land,' quoth Iseult, 'none such is,
I doubt not, nor where fighting folk may be;
But were there none such between sky and sea,
The world's whole worth were poorer than I wist.'

    And Tristram took her flower-white hand and kissed,
Laughing; and through his fair face as in shame
The light blood lightened. 'Hear they no such name?

She said; and he, 'If there be such a word,
I wot the queen's poor harper hath not heard.'
Then as the fuller-feathered hours grew long,
He holp to speed their warm slow feet with song.

'Love, is it morning risen or night deceased
That makes the mirth of this triumphant east?
　　Is it bliss given or bitterness put by
That makes most glad men's hearts at love's high feast?
　　Grief smiles, joy weeps, that day should live and die.

'Is it with soul's thirst or with body's drouth
That summer yearns out sunward to the south,
　　With all the flowers that when thy birth drew nigh
Were molten in one rose to make thy mouth?
　　O love, what care though day should live and die?

'Is the sun glad of all the love on earth,
The spirit and sense and work of things and worth?
　　Is the moon sad because the month must fly
And bring her death that can but bring back birth?
　　For all these things as day must live and die.

'Love, is it day that makes thee thy delight
Or thou that seest day made out of thy light?
　　Love, as the sun and sea are thou and I,
Sea without sun dark, sun without sea bright;
　　The sun is one though day should live and die.

'O which is elder, night or light, who knows?
And life or love, which first of these twain grows?
　　For life is born of love to wail and cry,
And love is born of life to heal his woes,
　　And light of night, that day should live and die.

'O sun of heaven above the worldly sea,
O very love, what light is this of thee!
　　My sea of soul is deep as thou art high,
But all thy light is shed through all of me,
　　As love's through love, while day shall live and die.

'Nay,' said Iseult, 'your song is hard to read.'
'Ay?' said he: 'or too light a song to heed,

Too slight to follow, it may be? Who shall sing
Of love but as a churl before a king
If by love's worth men rate his worthiness?
Yet as the poor churl's worth to sing is less,
Surely the more shall be the great king's grace
To show for churlish love a kindlier face.'

'No churl,' she said, 'but one in soothsayer's wise
Who tells but truths that help no more than lies.
I have heard men sing of love a simpler way
Than these wrought riddles made of night and day,
Like jewelled reins whereon the rhyme-bells hang.'

And Tristram smiled and changed his song and
sang.

'The breath between my lips of lips not mine,
Like spirit in sense that makes pure sense divine,
    Is as life in them from the living sky
That entering fills my heart with blood of thine
    And thee with me, while day shall live and die.

'Thy soul is shed into me with thy breath,
And in my heart each heartbeat of thee saith
    How in thy life the lifesprings of me lie,
Even one life to be gathered of one death
    In me and thee, though day may live and die.

'Ah, who knows now if in my veins it be
My blood that feels life sweet, or blood of thee,
    And this thine eyesight kindled in mine eye
That shows me in thy flesh the soul of me,
    For thine made mine, while day may live and die?

'Ah, who knows yet if one be twain or one,
And sunlight separable again from sun,
    And I from thee with all my lifesprings dry,
And thou from me with all thine heartbeats done,
    Dead separate souls while day shall live and die?

'I see my soul within thine eyes, and hear
My spirit in all thy pulses thrill with fear,
    And in my lips the passion of thee sigh,

And music of me made in mine own ear;
　　Am I not thou while day shall live and die?

'Art thou not I as I thy love am thou?
So let all things pass from us; we are now,
　　For all that was and will be, who knows why?
And all that is and is not, who knows how?
　　Who knows? God knows why day should live and die.'

And Iseult mused and spake no word, but sought
Through all the hushed ways of her tongueless thought
What face or covered likeness of a face
In what veiled hour or dream-determined place
She seeing might take for love's face, and believe
This was the spirit to whom all spirits cleave.
For what sweet wonder of the twain made one
And each one twain, incorporate sun with sun,
Star with star molten, soul with soul imbued,
And all the soul's works, all their multitude,
Made one thought and one vision and one song,
Love—this thing, this, laid hand on her so strong
She could not choose but yearn till she should see.
So went she musing down her thoughts; but he,
Sweet-hearted as a bird that takes the sun
With clear strong eyes and feels the glad god run
Bright through his blood and wide rejoicing wings,
And opens all himself to heaven and sings,
Made her mind light and full of noble mirth
With words and songs the gladdest grown on earth,
Till she was blithe and high of heart as he.
So swam the Swallow through the springing sea.

　　And while they sat at speech as at a feast,
Came a light wind fast hardening forth of the east
And blackening till its might had marred the skies;
And the sea thrilled as with heart-sundering sighs
One after one drawn, with each breath it drew,

And the green hardened into iron blue,
And the soft light went out of all its face.
Then Tristram girt him for an oarsman's place
And took his oar and smote, and toiled with might
In the east wind's full face and the strong sea's spite
Labouring; and all the rowers rowed hard, but he
More mightily than any wearier three.
And Iseult watched him rowing with sinless eyes
That loved him but in holy girlish wise
For noble joy in his fair manliness
And trust and tender wonder; none the less
She thought if God had given her grace to be
Man, and make war on danger of earth and sea,
Even such a man she would be; for his stroke
Was mightiest as the mightier water broke,
And in sheer measure like strong music drave
Clean through the wet weight of the wallowing wave;
And as a tune before a great king played
For triumph was the tune their strong strokes made,
And sped the ship through with smooth strife of oars
Over the mid sea's grey foam-paven floors,
For all the loud breach of the waves at will.
So for an hour they fought the storm out still,
And the shorn foam spun from the blades, and high
The keel sprang from the wave-ridge, and the sky
Glared at them for a breath's space through the rain;
Then the bows with a sharp shock plunged again
Down, and the sea clashed on them, and so rose
The bright stem like one panting from swift blows,
And as a swimmer's joyous beaten head
Rears itself laughing, so in that sharp stead
The light ship lifted her long quivering bows
As might the man his buffeted strong brows
Out of the wave-breach; for with one stroke yet

Went all men's oars together, strongly set
As to loud music, and with hearts uplift
They smote their strong way through the drench and
    drift:
Till the keen hour had chafed itself to death
And the east wind fell fitfully, breath by breath,
Tired; and across the thin and slackening rain
Sprang the face southward of the sun again.
Then all they rested and were eased at heart;
And Iseult rose up where she sat apart,
And with her sweet soul deepening her deep eyes
Cast the furs from her and subtle embroideries
That wrapt her from the storming rain and spray,
And shining like all April in one day,
Hair, face, and throat dashed with the straying
    showers,
She stood the first of all the whole world's flowers,
And laughed on Tristram with her eyes, and said,
'I too have heart then, I was not afraid.'
And answering some light courteous word of grace
He saw her clear face lighten on his face
Unwittingly, with unenamoured eyes,
For the last time. A live man in such wise
Looks in the deadly face of his fixed hour
And laughs with lips wherein he hath no power
To keep the life yet some five minutes' space.
So Tristram looked on Iseult face to face
And knew not, and she knew not. The last time—
The last that should be told in any rhyme
Heard anywhere on mouths of singing men
That ever should sing praise of them again;
The last hour of their hurtless hearts at rest,
The last that peace should touch them, breast to breast,
The last that sorrow far from them should sit,

This last was with them, and they knew not it.
   For Tristram being athirst with toil now spake,
Saying, 'Iseult, for all dear love's labour's sake
Give me to drink, and give me for a pledge
The touch of four lips on the beaker's edge.'
And Iseult sought and would not wake Brangwain
Who slept as one half dead with fear and pain,
Being tender-natured; so with hushed light feet
Went Iseult round her, with soft looks and sweet
Pitying her pain; so sweet a spirited thing
She was, and daughter of a kindly king.
And spying what strange bright secret charge was kept
Fast in that maid's white bosom while she slept,
She sought and drew the gold cup forth and smiled
Marvelling, with such light wonder as a child
That hears of glad sad life in magic lands;
And bare it back to Tristram with pure hands
Holding the love-draught that should be for flame
To burn out of them fear and faith and shame,
And lighten all their life up in men's sight,
And make them sad for ever. Then the knight
Bowed toward her and craved whence had she this
      strange thing
That might be spoil of some dim Asian king,
By starlight stolen from some waste place of sands,
And a maid bore it here in harmless hands.
And Iseult, laughing—'Other lords that be
Feast, and their men feast after them; but we,
Our men must keep the best wine back to feast
Till they be full and we of all men least
Feed after them and fain to fare so well:
So with mine handmaid and your squire it fell
That hid this bright thing from us in a wile:'
And with light lips yet full of their swift smile,

And hands that wist not though they dug a grave,
Undid the hasps of gold, and drank, and gave,
And he drank after, a deep glad kingly draught:
And all their life changed in them, for they quaffed
Death; if it be death so to drink, and fare
As men who change and are what these twain were.
And shuddering with eyes full of fear and fire
And heart-stung with a serpentine desire
He turned and saw the terror in her eyes
That yearned upon him shining in such wise
As a star midway in the midnight fixed.

Their Galahault was the cup, and she that mixed;
Nor other hand there needed, nor sweet speech
To lure their lips together; each on each
Hung with strange eyes and hovered as a bird
Wounded, and each mouth trembled for a word;
Their heads neared, and their hands were drawn in one,
And they saw dark, though still the unsunken sun
Far through fine rain shot fire into the south;
And their four lips became one burning mouth.

Book IX

THE SAILING OF THE SWAN

FATE, that was born ere spirit and flesh were made,
The fire that fills man's life with light and shade;
The power beyond all godhead which puts on
All forms of multitudinous unison,
A raiment of eternal change inwrought
With shapes and hues more subtly spun than thought,
Where all things old bear fruit of all things new
And one deep chord throbs all the music through,
The chord of change unchanging, shadow and light
Inseparable as reverberate day from night;

Fate, that of all things save the soul of man
Is lord and God since body and soul began;
Fate, that keeps all the tune of things in chime;
Fate, that breathes power upon the lips of time;
That smites and soothes with heavy and healing hand
All joys and sorrows born in life's dim land,
Till joy be found a shadow and sorrow a breath
And life no discord in the tune with death,
But all things fain alike to die and live
In pulse and lapse of tides alternative,
Through silence and through sound of peace and strife,
Till birth and death be one in sight of life;
Fate, heard and seen of no man's eyes or ears,
To no man shown through light of smiles or tears,
And moved of no man's prayer to fold its wings;
Fate, that is night and light on worldly things;
Fate, that is fire to burn and sea to drown,
Strength to build up and thunder to cast down;
Fate, shield and screen for each man's lifelong head,
And sword at last or dart that strikes it dead;
Fate, higher than heaven and deeper than the grave,
That saves and spares not, spares and doth not save;
Fate, that in gods' wise is not bought and sold
For prayer or price of penitence or gold;
Whose law shall live when life bids earth farewell,
Whose justice hath for shadows heaven and hell:
Whose judgement into no god's hand is given,
Nor is its doom not more than hell or heaven:
Fate, that is pure of love and clean of hate,
Being equal-eyed as naught may be but fate;
Through many and weary days of foiled desire
Leads life to rest where tears no more take fire;
Through many and weary dreams of quenched delight
Leads life through death past sense of day and night.

Nor shall they feel or fear, whose date is done,
Aught that made once more dark the living sun
And bitterer in their breathing lips the breath
Than the dark dawn and bitter dust of death.
For all the light, with fragrance as of flowers,
That clothes the lithe live limbs of separate hours,
More sweet to savour and more clear to sight
Dawns on the soul death's undivided night.
No vigils has that perfect night to keep,
No fever-fits of vision shake that sleep.
Nor if they wake, and any place there be
Wherein the soul may feel her wings beat free
Through air too clear and still for sound or strife;
If life were haply death, and death be life;
If love with yet some lovelier laugh revive,
And song relume the light it bore alive,
And friendship, found of all earth's gifts most good,
Stand perfect in perpetual brotherhood;
If aught indeed at all of all this be,
Though none might say nor any man might see,
Might he that sees the shade thereof not say
This dream were trustier than the truth of day.
Nor haply may not hope, with heart more clear,
Burn deathward, and the doubtful soul take cheer,
Seeing through the channelled darkness yearn a star
Whose eyebeams are not as the morning's are,
Transient, and subjugate of lordlier light,
But all unconquerable by noon or night,
Being kindled only of life's own inmost fire,
Truth, stablished and made sure by strong desire.
Fountain of all things living, source and seed,
Force that perforce transfigures dream to deed.
God that begets on time, the body of death,
Eternity: nor may man's darkening breath,

Albeit it stain, disfigure or destroy
The glass wherein the soul sees life and joy
Only, with strength renewed and spirit of youth,
And brighter than the sun's the body of Truth
Eternal, unimaginable of man,
Whose very face not Thought's own eyes may scan,
But see far off his radiant feet at least,
Trampling the head of Fear, the false high priest,
Whose broken chalice foams with blood no more,
And prostrate on that high priest's chancel floor,
Bruised, overthrown, blind, maimed, with bloodless
    rod,
The miscreation of his miscreant God.
That sovereign shadow cast of souls that dwell
In darkness and the prison-house of hell
Whose walls are built of deadly dread, and bound
The gates thereof with dreams as iron round,
And all the bars therein and stanchions wrought
Of shadow forged like steel and tempered thought
And words like swords and thunder-clouded creeds
And faiths more dire than sin's most direful deeds:
That shade accursed and worshipped, which hath
    made
The soul of man that brought it forth a shade
Black as the womb of darkness, void and vain,
A throne for fear, a pasturage for pain,
Impotent, abject, clothed upon with lies,
A foul blind fume of words and prayers that rise,
Aghast and harsh, abhorrent and abhorred,
Fierce as its God, blood-saturate as its Lord;
With loves and mercies on its lips that hiss
Comfort, and kill compassion with a kiss,
And strike the world black with their blasting breath;
That ghost whose core of life is very death

And all its light of heaven a shadow of hell,
Fades, falls, wanes, withers by none other spell
But theirs whose eyes and ears have seen and heard
Not the face naked, not the perfect word,
But the bright sound and feature felt from far
Of life which feeds the spirit and the star,
Thrills the live light of all the suns that roll,
And stirs the still sealed springs of every soul.
   Three dim days through, three slumberless nights
     long,
Perplexed at dawn, oppressed at evensong,
The strong man's soul now sealed indeed with pain
And all its springs half dried with drought, had lain
Prisoner within the fleshly dungeon-dress
Sore chafed and wasted with its weariness.
And fain it would have found the star, and fain
Made this funereal prison-house of pain
A watch-tower whence its eyes might sweep, and see
If any place for any hope might be
Beyond the hells and heavens of sleep and strife,
Or any light at all of any life
Beyond the dense false darkness woven above,
And could not, lacking grace to look on love,
And in the third night's dying hour he spake,
Seeing scarce the seals that bound the dayspring
     break
And scarce the daystar burn above the sea:
'O Ganhardine, my brother true to me,
I charge thee by those nights and days we knew
No great while since in England, by the dew
That bathed those nights with blessing, and the fire
That thrilled those days as music thrills a lyre,
Do now for me perchance the last good deed
That ever love may crave or life may need

Ere love lay life in ashes: take to thee
My ship that shows aloft against the sea
Carved on her stem the semblance of a swan,
And ere the waves at even again wax wan
Pass, if it may be, to my lady's land,
And give this ring into her secret hand,
And bid her think how hard on death I lie,
And fain would look upon her face and die.
But as a merchant's laden be the bark
With royal ware for fraughtage, that King Mark
May take for toll thereof some costly thing;
And when this gift finds grace before the king,
Choose forth a cup, and put therein my ring
Where sureliest only of one it may be seen,
And bid her handmaid bear it to the queen
For earnest of thine homage: then shall she
Fear, and take counsel privily with thee,
To know what errand there is thine from me
And what my need in secret of her sight.
But make thee two sails, one like sea-foam white
To spread for signal if thou bring her back,
And if she come not see the sail be black,
That I may know or ever thou take land
If these my lips may die upon her hand
Or hers may never more be mixed with mine.'
    And his heart quailed for grief in Ganhardine,
Hearing; and all his brother bade he swore
Surely to do, and straight fare forth from shore.
But the white-handed Iseult hearkening heard
All, and her heart waxed hot, and every word
Thereon seemed graven and printed in her thought
As lines with fire and molten iron wrought.
And hard within her heavy heart she cursed
Both, and her life was turned to fiery thirst,

And all her soul was hunger, and its breath
Of hope and life a blast of raging death.
For only in hope of evil was her life.
So bitter burned within the unchilded wife
A virgin lust for vengeance, and such hate
Wrought in her now the fervent work of fate.

   Then with a south-west wind the Swan set forth,
And over wintering waters bore to north,
And round the wild land's windy westward end
Up the blown channel bade her bright way bend
East on toward high Tintagel: where at dark
Landing, fair welcome found they of King Mark,
And Ganhardine with Brangwain as of old
Spake, and she took the cup of chiselled gold
Wherein lay secret Tristram's trothplight ring,
And bare it unbeholden of the king
Even to her lady's hand, which hardly took
A gift whereon a queen's eyes well might look,
With grace forlorn of weary gentleness.
But, seeing, her life leapt in her, keen to guess
The secret of the symbol: and her face
Flashed bright with blood whence all its grief-worn
      grace
Took fire and kindled to the quivering hair.
And in the dark soft hour of starriest air
Thrilled through with sense of midnight, when the
      world
Feels the wide wings of sleep about it furled,
Down stole the queen, deep-muffled to her wan
Mute restless lips, and came where yet the Swan
Swung fast at anchor: whence by starlight she
Hoised snowbright sails, and took the glimmering sea.

   But all the long night long more keen and sore
His wound's grief waxed in Tristram evermore,

And heavier always hung his heart asway
Between dim fear and clouded hope of day.
And still with face and heart at silent strife
Beside him watched the maiden called his wife,
Patient, and spake not save when scarce he spake,
Murmuring with sense distraught and spirit awake
Speech bitterer than the words thereof were sweet:
And hatred thrilled her to the hands and feet,
Listening: for alway back reiterate came
The passionate faint burden of her name.
Nor ever through the labouring lips astir
Came any word of any thought of her.
But the soul wandering struggled and clung hard
Only to dreams of joy in Joyous Gard
Or wildwood nights beside the Cornish strand,
Or Merlin's holier sleep here hard at hand
Wrapped round with deep soft spells in dim Broce-
     liande.
And with such thirst as joy's drained wine-cup leaves
When fear to hope as hope to memory cleaves
His soul desired the dewy sense of leaves,
The soft green smell of thickets drenched with dawn.
The faint slot kindling on the fiery lawn
As day's first hour made keen the spirit again
That lured and spurred on quest his hound Hodain,
The breeze, the bloom, the splendour and the sound,
That stung like fire the hunter and the hound.
The pulse of wind, the passion of the sea,
The rapture of the woodland: then would he
Sigh, and as one that fain would all be dead
Heavily turn his heavy-laden head
Back, and close eyes for comfort, finding none.
And fain he would have died or seen the sun,
Being sick at heart of darkness: yet afresh

Began the long strong strife of spirit and flesh
And branching pangs of thought whose branches bear
The bloodred fruit whose core is black, despair.
And the wind slackened and again grew great,
Palpitant as men's pulses palpitate
Between the flowing and ebbing tides of fate
That wash their lifelong waifs of weal and woe
Through night and light and twilight to and fro.
Now as a pulse of hope its heartbeat throbbed,
Now like one stricken shrank and sank and sobbed,
Then, yearning as with child of death, put forth
A wail that filled the night up south and north
With woful sound of waters: and he said,
'So might the wind wail if the world were dead
And its wings wandered over naught but sea.
I would I knew she would not come to me,
For surely she will come not: then should I,
Once knowing I shall not look upon her, die.
I knew not life could so long breathe such breath
As I do. Nay, what grief were this, if death,
The sole sure friend of whom the whole world saith
He lies not, nor hath ever this been said,
That death would heal not grief—if death were dead
And all ways closed whence grief might pass with life!'
    Then softly spake his watching virgin wife
Out of her heart, deep down below her breath:
'Fear not but death shall come—and after death
Judgment.' And he that heard not answered her,
Saying—'Ah, but one there was, if truth not err,
For true men's trustful tongues have said it—one
Whom these mine eyes knew living while the sun
Looked yet upon him, and mine own ears heard
The deep sweet sound once of his godlike word—
Who sleeps and dies not, but with soft live breath

Takes always all the deep delight of death,
Through love's gift of a woman: but for me
Love's hand is not the hand of Nimue,
Love's word no still smooth murmur of the dove,
No kiss of peace for me the kiss of love.
Nor, whatsoe'er thy life's love ever give,
Dear, shall it ever bid me sleep or live;
Nor from thy brows and lips and living breast
As his from Nimue's shall my soul take rest;
Not rest but unrest hath our long love given—
Unrest on earth that wins not rest in heaven.
What rest may we take ever? what have we
Had ever more of peace than has the sea?
Has not our life been as the wind that blows
Through lonelier lands than rear the wild white rose
That each year sees requickened, but for us
Time once and twice hath here or there done thus
And left the next year following empty and bare?
What rose hath our last year's rose left for heir,
What wine our last year's vintage? and to me
More were one fleet forbidden sense of thee,
One perfume of thy present grace, one thought
Made truth one hour, ere all mine hours be naught,
One very word, breath, look, sign, touch of hand,
Than all the green leaves in Broceliande
Full of sweet sound, full of sweet wind and sun;
O God, thou knowest I would no more but one,
I would no more but once more ere I die
Find thus much mercy. Nay, but then were I
Happier than he whom there thy grace hath found,
For thine it must be, this that wraps him round,
Thine only, albeit a fiend's force gave him birth,
Thine that has given him heritage on earth
Of slumber-sweet eternity to keep

Fast in soft hold of everliving sleep.
Happier were I, more sinful man, than he,
Whom one love-worthier then than Nimue
Should with a breath make blest among the dead.'
　　And the wan wedded maiden answering said,
Soft as hate speaks within itself apart:
'Surely ye shall not, ye that rent mine heart,
Being one in sin, in punishment be twain.'
And the great knight that heard not spake again
And sighed, but sweet thought of sweet things gone
　　　by
Kindled with fire of joy the very sigh
And touched it through with rapture: 'Ay, this were
How much more than the sun and sunbright air,
How much more than the springtide, how much more
Than sweet strong sea-wind quickening wave and
　　　shore
With one divine pulse of continuous breath,
If she might kiss me with the kiss of death,
And make the light of life by death's look dim!'
　　And the white wedded virgin answered him,
Inwardly, wan with hurt no herb makes whole:
'Yea surely, ye whose sin hath slain my soul,
Surely your own souls shall have peace in death
And pass with benediction in their breath
And blessing given of mine their sin hath slain.'
　　And Tristram with sore yearning spake again,
Saying: 'Yea, might this thing once be, how should I,
With all my soul made one thanksgiving, die,
And pass before what judgment-seat may be,
And cry, "Lord, now do all thou wilt with me,
Take all thy fill of justice, work thy will;
Though all thy heart of wrath have all its fill,
My heart of suffering shall endure, and say,

For that thou gavest me living yesterday
I bless thee though thou curse me." Ay, and well
Might one cast down into the gulf of hell,
Remembering this, take heart and thank his fate—
That God, whose doom now scourges him with hate,
Once, in the wild and whirling world above,
Bade mercy kiss his dying lips with love.
But if this come not, then he doth me wrong.
For what hath love done, all this long life long
That death should trample down his poor last prayer
Who prays not for forgiveness? Though love were
Sin dark as hate, have we not here that sinned
Suffered? has that been less than wintry wind
Wherewith our love lies blasted? O mine own,
O mine and no man's yet save mine alone,
Iseult! what ails thee that I lack so long
All of thee, all things thine for which I long?
For more than watersprings to shadeless sands,
More to me were the comfort of her hands
Touched once, and more than rays that set and rise
The glittering arrows of her glorious eyes,
More to my sense than fire to dead cold air
The wind and light and odour of her hair,
More to my soul than summer's to the south
The mute clear music of her amorous mouth,
And to my heart's heart more than heaven's great rest
The fullness of the fragrance of her breast.
Iseult, Iseult, what grace hath life to give
More than we twain have had of life, and live?
Iseult, Iseult, what grace may death not keep
As sweet for us to win of death, and sleep?
Come therefore, let us twain pass hence and try
If it be better not to live but die,
With love for lamp to light us out of life.'

And on that word his wedded maiden wife,
Pale as the moon in star-forsaken skies
Ere the sun fill them, rose with set strange eyes
And gazed on him that saw not: and her heart
Heaved as a man's death-smitten with a dart
That smites him sleeping, warm and full of life:
So toward her lord that was not looked his wife,
His wife that was not: and her heart within
Burnt bitter like an aftertaste of sin
To one whose memory drinks and loathes the lee
Of shame or sorrow deeper than the sea:
And no fear touched him of her eyes above
And ears that hoarded each poor word whence love
Made sweet the broken music of his breath.
'Iseult, my life that wast and art my death,
My life in life that hast been, and that art
Death in my death, sole wound that cleaves mine
      heart,
Mine heart that else, how spent soe'er, were whole,
Breath of my spirit and anguish of my soul,
How can this be that hence thou canst not hear,
Being but by space divided? One is here,
But one of twain I looked at once to see;
Shall death keep time and thou not keep with me?'
   And the white married maiden laughed at heart,
Hearing, and scarce with lips at all apart
Spake, and as fire between them was her breath;
'Yea, now thou liest not: yea, for I am death.'
   By this might eyes that watched without behold
Deep in the gulfs of aching air acold
The roses of the dawning heaven that strew
The low soft sun's way ere his power shine through
And burn them up with fire: but far to west
Had sunk the dead moon on the live sea's breast,

Slain as with bitter fear to see the sun:
And eastward was a strong bright wind begun
Between the clouds and waters: and he said,
Seeing hardly through dark dawn her doubtful head,
'Iseult?' and like a death-bell faint and clear
The virgin voice rang answer—'I am here.'
And his heart sprang, and sank again: and she
Spake, saying, 'What would my knightly lord with
    me?'
And Tristram: 'Hath my lady watched all night
Beside me, and I knew not? God requite
Her love for comfort shown a man nigh dead.'
  'Yea, God shall surely guerdon it,' she said,
'Who hath kept me all my days through to this hour.'
  And Tristram: 'God alone hath grace and power
To pay such grace toward one unworthier shown
Than ever durst, save only of God alone,
Crave pardon yet and comfort, as I would
Crave now for charity if my heart were good,
But as a coward's it fails me, even for shame.'
  Then seemed her face a pale funereal flame
That burns down slow by midnight, as she said:
'Speak, and albeit thy bidding spake me dead,
God's love renounce me if it were not done.'
  And Tristram: 'When the sea-line takes the sun
That now should be not far off sight from far,
Look if there come not with the morning star
My ship bound hither from the northward back,
And if the sail be white thereof or black.'
  And knowing the soothfast sense of his desire
So sore the heart within her raged like fire
She could not wring forth of her lips a word,
But bowing made sign how humbly had she heard.
And the sign given made light in his heart; and she

Set her face hard against the yearning sea
Now all athirst with trembling trust of hope
To see the sudden gates of sunrise ope;
But thirstier yearned the heart whose fiery gate
Lay wide that vengeance might come in to hate.
And Tristram lay at thankful rest, and thought
Now surely life nor death could grieve him aught,
Since past was now life's anguish as a breath,
And surely past the bitterness of death.
For seeing he had found at these her hands this grace,
It could not be but yet some breathing-space
Might leave him life to look again on love's own face.
'Since if for death's sake,' in his heart he said,
'Even she take pity upon me quick or dead,
How shall not even from God's hand be compassion
        shed?
For night bears dawn, how weak soe'er and wan,
And sweet ere death, men fable, sings the swan.
So seems the Swan my signal from the sea
To sound a song that sweetens death to me
Clasped round about with radiance from above
Of dawn, and closer clasped on earth by love.
Shall all things brighten, and this my sign be dark?'
    And high from heaven suddenly rang the lark,
Triumphant; and the far first refluent ray
Filled all the hollow darkness full with day.
And on the deep sky's verge a fluctuant light
Gleamed, grew, shone, strengthened into perfect
        sight,
As bowed and dipped and rose again the sail's clear
        white.
And swift and steadfast as a sea-mew's wing
It neared before the wind, as fain to bring
Comfort, and shorten yet its narrowing track.

And she that saw looked hardly toward him back,
Saying, 'Ay, the ship comes surely; but her sail is
    black.'
And fain he would have sprung upright, and seen,
And spoken: but strong death struck sheer between,
And darkness closed as iron round his head:
And smitten through the heart lay Tristram dead.
   And scarce the word had flown abroad, and wail
Risen, ere to shoreward came the snowbright sail,
And lightly forth leapt Ganhardine on land,
And led from ship with swift and reverent hand
Iseult: and round them up from all the crowd
Broke the great wail for Tristram out aloud.
And ere her ear might hear her heart had heard,
Nor sought she sign for witness of the word;
But came and stood above him newly dead,
And felt his death upon her: and her head
Bowed, as to reach the spring that slakes all drouth;
And their four lips became one silent mouth.

So came their hour on them that were in life
Tristram and Iseult: so from love and strife
The stroke of love's own hand felt last and best
Gave them deliverance to perpetual rest.
So, crownless of the wreaths that life had wound,
They slept, with flower of tenderer comfort crowned;
From bondage and the fear of time set free,
And all the yoke of space on earth and sea
Cast as a curb for ever: nor might now
Fear and desire bid soar their souls or bow,
Lift up their hearts or break them: doubt nor grief
More now might move them, dread nor disbelief
Touch them with shadowy cold or fiery sting,
Nor sleepless languor with its weary wing,

Nor harsh estrangement, born of time's vain breath,
Nor change, a darkness deeper far than death.
And round the sleep that fell around them then
Earth lies not wrapped, nor records wrought of men
Rise up for timeless token: but their sleep
Hath round it like a raiment all the deep;
No change or gleam or gloom of sun and rain,
But all time long the might of all the main
Spread round them as round earth soft heaven is
    spread,
And peace more strong than death round all the dead.
For death is of an hour, and after death
Peace: nor for aught that fear or fancy saith,
Nor even for very love's own sake, shall strife
Perplex again that perfect peace with life.
And if, as men that mourn may deem or dream,
Rest haply here than there might sweeter seem,
And sleep, that lays one hand on all, more good
By some sweet grave's grace given of wold or wood
Or clear high glen or sunbright wind-worn down
Than where life thunders through the trampling town
With daylong feet and nightlong overhead,
What grave may cast such grace round any dead,
What so sublime sweet sepulchre may be
For all that life leaves mortal, as the sea?
And these, rapt forth perforce from earthly ground,
These twain the deep sea guards, and girdles round
Their sleep more deep than any sea's gulf lies,
Though changeless with the change in shifting skies,
Nor mutable with seasons: for the grave
That held them once, being weaker than a wave,
The waves long since have buried: though their tomb
Was royal that by ruth's relenting doom
Men gave them in Tintagel: for the word

Took wing which thrilled all piteous hearts that heard
The word wherethrough their lifelong lot stood shown,
And when the long sealed springs of fate were known,
The blind bright innocence of lips that quaffed
Love, and the marvel of the mastering draught,
And all the fraughtage of the fateful bark,
Loud like a child upon them wept King Mark,
Seeing round the sword's hilt which long since had
    fought
For Cornwall's love a scroll of writing wrought,
A scripture writ of Tristram's hand, wherein
Lay bare the sinless source of all their sin,
No choice of will, but chance and sorcerous art,
With prayer of him for pardon: and his heart
Was molten in him, wailing as he kissed
Each with the kiss of kinship—'Had I wist,
Ye had never sinned nor died thus, nor had I
Borne in this doom that bade you sin and die
So sore a part of sorrow.' And the king
Built for their tomb a chapel bright like spring
With flower-soft wealth of branching tracery made
Fair as the frondage each fleet year sees fade,
That should not fall till many a year were done.
There slept they wedded under moon and sun
And change of stars: and through the casements came
Midnight and noon girt round with shadow and flame
To illume their grave or veil it: till at last
On these things too was doom as darkness cast:
For the strong sea hath swallowed wall and tower,
And where their limbs were laid in woful hour
For many a fathom gleams and moves and moans
The tide that sweeps above their coffined bones
In the wrecked chancel by the shivered shrine:
Nor where they sleep shall moon or sunlight shine

Nor man look down for ever: none shall say,
Here once, or here, Tristram and Iseult lay:
But peace they have that none may gain who live,
And rest about them that no love can give,
And over them, while death and life shall be,
The light and sound and darkness of the sea.

ATALANTA IN CALYDON

THE ARGUMENT

ALTHÆA, daughter of Thestius and Eurythemis, queen
of Calydon, being with child of Meleager her first-
born son, dreamed that she brought forth a brand
burning; and upon his birth came the three Fates and
prophesied of him three things, namely these; that
he should have great strength of his hands, and good
fortune in this life, and that he should live no longer
when the brand then in the fire were consumed:
wherefore his mother plucked it forth and kept it by
her. And the child being a man grown sailed with
Jason after the fleece of gold, and won himself great
praise of all men living; and when the tribes of the
north and west made war upon Ætolia, he fought
against their army and scattered it. But Artemis,
having at the first stirred up these tribes to war against
Œneus king of Calydon, because he had offered sacrifice to all the gods saving her alone, but her he had
forgotten to honour, was yet more wroth because of
the destruction of this army, and sent upon the land
of Calydon a wild boar which slew many and wasted
all their increase, but him could none slay, and many
went against him and perished. Then were all the
chief men of Greece gathered together, and among
them Atalanta daughter of Iasius the Arcadian, a
virgin; for whose sake Artemis let slay the boar, seeing
she favoured the maiden greatly; and Meleager
having despatched it gave the spoil thereof to Atalanta, as one beyond measure enamoured of her; but
the brethren of Althæa his mother, Toxeus and Plexippus, with such others as misliked that she only should

bear off the praise whereas many had borne the labour, laid wait for her to take away her spoil; but Meleager fought against them and slew them: whom when Althæa their sister beheld and knew to be slain of her son, she waxed for wrath and sorrow like as one mad, and taking the brand whereby the measure of her son's life was meted to him, she cast it upon a fire; and with the wasting thereof his life likewise wasted away, that being brought back to his father's house he died in a brief space; and his mother also endured not long after for very sorrow; and this was his end, and the end of that hunting.

THE PERSONS

CHIEF HUNTSMAN	TOXEUS
CHORUS	PLEXIPPUS
ALTHÆA	HERALD
MELEAGER	MESSENGER
ŒNEUS	SECOND MESSENGER
ATALANTA	

ἴστω δ' ὅστις οὐχ ὑπόπτερος
φροντίσιν δαεὶς,
τὰν ἁ παιδολυμὰς τάλαινα Θεστιὰς μήσατο
πυρδαῆ τινα πρόνοιαν,
καταίθουσα παιδὸς δαφοινὸν
δαλὸν ἥλικ', ἐπεὶ μολὼν
ματρόθεν κελάδησε;
σύμμετρόν τε διαὶ βίου
μοιρόκραντον ἐς ἁμαρ.

ÆSCH. *Cho.* 602–610

ATALANTA IN CALYDON

CHIEF HUNTSMAN

MAIDEN, and mistress of the months and stars
Now folded in the flowerless fields of heaven,
Goddess whom all gods love with threefold heart,
Being treble in thy divided deity,
A light for dead men and dark hours, a foot
Swift on the hills as morning, and a hand
To all things fierce and fleet that roar and range
Mortal, with gentler shafts than snow or sleep;
Hear now and help and lift no violent hand,
But favourable and fair as thine eye's beam
Hidden and shown in heaven; for I all night
Amid the king's hounds and the hunting men
Have wrought and worshipped toward thee; nor shall
    man
See goodlier hounds or deadlier edge of spears;
But for the end, that lies unreached at yet
Between the hands and on the knees of gods.
O fair-faced sun, killing the stars and dews
And dreams and desolation of the night!
Rise up, shine, stretch thine hand out, with thy bow
Touch the most dimmest height of trembling heaven,
And burn and break the dark about thy ways,
Shot through and through with arrows; let thine hair
Lighten as flame above that flameless shell
Which was the moon, and thine eyes fill the world
And thy lips kindle with swift beams; let earth
Laugh, and the long sea fiery from thy feet
Through all the roar and ripple of streaming springs
And foam in reddening flakes and flying flowers
Shaken from hands and blown from lips of nymphs
Whose hair or breast divides the wandering wave

With salt close tresses cleaving lock to lock,
All gold, or shuddering and unfurrowed snow;
And all the winds about thee with their wings,
And fountain-heads of all the watered world;
Each horn of Acheloüs, and the green
Euenus, wedded with the straitening sea.
For in fair time thou comest; come also thou,
Twin-born with him, and virgin, Artemis,
And give our spears their spoil, the wild boar's hide,
Sent in thine anger against us for sin done
And bloodless altars without wine or fire.
Him now consume thou; for thy sacrifice
With sanguine-shining steam divides the dawn,
And one, the maiden rose of all thy maids,
Arcadian Atalanta, snowy-souled,
Fair as the snow and footed as the wind,
From Ladon and well-wooded Mænalus
Over the firm hills and the fleeting sea
Hast thou drawn hither, and many an armèd king,
Heroes, the crown of men, like gods in fight.
Moreover out of all the Ætolian land,
From the full-flowered Lelantian pasturage
To what of fruitful field the son of Zeus
Won from the roaring river and labouring sea
When the wild god shrank in his horn and fled
And foamed and lessened through his wrathful fords,
Leaving clear lands that steamed with sudden sun,
These virgins with the lightening of the day
Bring thee fresh wreaths and their own sweeter hair,
Luxurious locks and flower-like mixed with flowers,
Clean offering, and chaste hymns; but me the time
Divides from these things; whom do thou not less
Help and give honour, and to mine hounds good speed,
And edge to spears, and luck to each man's hand.

CHORUS

When the hounds of spring are on winter's traces,
   The mother of months in meadow or plain
Fills the shadows and windy places
   With lisp of leaves and ripple of rain;
And the brown bright nightingale amorous
Is half assuaged for Itylus,
For the Thracian ships and the foreign faces,
   The tongueless vigil, and all the pain.

Come with bows bent and with emptying of quivers,
   Maiden most perfect, lady of light,
With a noise of winds and many rivers,
   With a clamour of waters, and with might;
Bind on thy sandals, O thou most fleet,
Over the splendour and speed of thy feet;
For the faint east quickens, the wan west shivers,
   Round the feet of the day and the feet of the night.

Where shall we find her, how shall we sing to her,
   Fold our hands round her knees, and cling?
O that man's heart were as fire and could spring to her,
   Fire, or the strength of the streams that spring!
For the stars and the winds are unto her
As raiment, as songs of the harp-player;
For the risen stars and the fallen cling to her,
   And the southwest-wind and the west-wind sing.

For winter's rains and ruins are over,
   And all the season of snows and sins;
The days dividing lover and lover,
   The light that loses, the night that wins;
And time remembered is grief forgotten,
And frosts are slain and flowers begotten,

And in green underwood and cover
   Blossom by blossom the spring begins.

The full streams feed on flower of rushes,
   Ripe grasses trammel a travelling foot,
The faint fresh flame of the young year flushes
   From leaf to flower and flower to fruit;
And fruit and leaf are as gold and fire,
And the oat is heard above the lyre,
And the hoofèd heel of a satyr crushes
   The chestnut-husk at the chestnut-root.

And Pan by noon and Bacchus by night,
   Fleeter of foot than the fleet-foot kid,
Follows with dancing and fills with delight
   The Mænad and the Bassarid;
And soft as lips that laugh and hide
The laughing leaves of the trees divide,
And screen from seeing and leave in sight
   The god pursuing, the maiden hid.

The ivy falls with the Bacchanal's hair
   Over her eyebrows hiding her eyes;
The wild vine slipping down leaves bare
   Her bright breast shortening into sighs;
The wild vine slips with the weight of its leaves,
But the berried ivy catches and cleaves
To the limbs that glitter, the feet that scare
   The wolf that follows, the fawn that flies.

ALTHÆA

What do ye singing? what is this ye sing?

CHORUS

Flowers bring we, and pure lips that please the gods,
And raiment meet for service: lest the day
Turn sharp with all its honey in our lips.

ALTHÆA

Night, a black hound, follows the white fawn day,
Swifter than dreams the white flown feet of sleep;
Will ye pray back the night with any prayers?
And though the spring put back a little while
Winter, and snows that plague all men for sin,
And the iron time of cursing, yet I know
Spring shall be ruined with the rain, and storm
Eat up like fire the ashen autumn days.
I marvel what men do with prayers awake
Who dream and die with dreaming; any god,
Yea the least god of all things called divine,
Is more than sleep and waking; yet we say,
Perchance by praying a man shall match his god.
For if sleep have no mercy, and man's dreams
Bite to the blood and burn into the bone,
What shall this man do waking? By the gods,
He shall not pray to dream sweet things to-night,
Having dreamt once more bitter things than death.

CHORUS

Queen, but what is it that hath burnt thine heart?
For thy speech flickers like a blown-out flame.

ALTHÆA

Look, ye say well, and know not what ye say;
For all my sleep is turned into a fire,
And all my dreams to stuff that kindles it.

CHORUS

Yet one doth well being patient of the gods.

ALTHÆA

Yea, lest they smite us with some four-foot plague.

CHORUS

But when time spreads find out some herb for it.

ALTHÆA

And with their healing herbs infect our blood.

CHORUS

What ails thee to be jealous of their ways?

ALTHÆA

What if they give us poisonous drinks for wine?

CHORUS

They have their will; much talking mends it not.

ALTHÆA

And gall for milk, and cursing for a prayer?

CHORUS

Have they not given life, and the end of life?

ALTHÆA

Lo, where they heal, they help not; thus they do,
They mock us with a little piteousness,
And we say prayers, and weep; but at the last,
Sparing awhile, they smite and spare no whit.

CHORUS

Small praise man gets dispraising the high gods:
What have they done that thou dishonourest them?

ALTHÆA

First Artemis for all this harried land
I praise not, and for wasting of the boar
That mars with tooth and tusk and fiery feet
Green pasturage and the grace of standing corn
And meadow and marsh with springs and unblown
      leaves,
Flocks and swift herds and all that bite sweet grass,
I praise her not; what things are these to praise?

CHORUS

But when the king did sacrifice, and gave
Each god fair dues of wheat and blood and wine,
Her not with bloodshed nor burnt-offering
Revered he, nor with salt or cloven cake;
Wherefore being wroth she plagued the land; but now
Takes off from us fate and her heavy things.
Which deed of these twain were not good to praise?
For a just deed looks always either way
With blameless eyes, and mercy is no fault.

ALTHÆA

Yea, but a curse she hath sent above all these
To hurt us where she healed us; and hath lit
Fire where the old fire went out, and where the wind
Slackened, hath blown on us with deadlier air.

CHORUS

What storm is this that tightens all our sail?

ALTHÆA

Love, a thwart sea-wind full of rain and foam.

CHORUS

Whence blown, and born under what stormier star?

ALTHÆA

Southward across Euenus from the sea.

CHORUS

Thy speech turns toward Arcadia like blown wind.

ALTHÆA

Sharp as the north sets when the snows are out.

CHORUS

Nay, for this maiden hath no touch of love.

ALTHÆA

I would she had sought in some cold gulf of sea
Love, or in dens where strange beasts lurk, or fire,
Or snows on the extreme hills, or iron land
Where no spring is; I would she had sought therein
And found, or ever love had found her here.

CHORUS

She is holier than all holy days or things,
The sprinkled water or fume of perfect fire;
Chaste, dedicated to pure prayers, and filled
With higher thoughts than heaven; a maiden clean,
Pure iron, fashioned for a sword; and man
She loves not; what should one such do with love?

ALTHÆA

Look you, I speak not as one light of wit,
But as a queen speaks, being heart-vexed; for oft
I hear my brothers wrangling in mid hall,
And am not moved; and my son chiding them,
And these things nowise move me, but I know
Foolish and wise men must be to the end,

And feed myself with patience; but this most,
This moves me, that for wise men as for fools
Love is one thing, an evil thing, and turns
Choice words and wisdom into fire and air.
And in the end shall no joy come, but grief,
Sharp words and soul's division and fresh tears
Flower-wise upon the old root of tears brought forth,
Fruit-wise upon the old flower of tears sprung up,
Pitiful sighs, and much regrafted pain.
These things are in my presage, and myself
Am part of them and know not; but in dreams
The gods are heavy on me, and all the fates
Shed fire across my eyelids mixed with night,
And burn me blind, and disilluminate
My sense of seeing, and my perspicuous soul
Darken with vision; seeing I see not, hear
And hearing am not holpen, but mine eyes
Stain many tender broideries in the bed
Drawn up about my face that I may weep
And the king wake not; and my brows and lips
Tremble and sob in sleeping, like swift flames
That tremble, or water when it sobs with heat
Kindled from under; and my tears fill my breast
And speck the fair dyed pillows round the king
With barren showers and salter than the sea,
Such dreams divide me dreaming; for long since
I dreamed that out of this my womb had sprung
Fire and a firebrand; this was ere my son,
Meleager, a goodly flower in fields of fight,
Felt the light touch him coming forth, and wailed
Childlike; but yet he was not; and in time
I bare him, and my heart was great; for yet
So royally was never strong man born,
Nor queen so nobly bore as noble a thing

As this my son was: such a birth God sent
And such a grace to bear it. Then came in
Three weaving women, and span each a thread,
Saying This for strength and That for luck, and one
Saying Till the brand upon the hearth burn down,
So long shall this man see good days and live.
And I with gathered raiment from the bed
Sprang, and drew forth the brand, and cast on it
Water, and trod the flame bare-foot, and crushed
With naked hand spark beaten out of spark
And blew against and quenched it; for I said,
These are the most high Fates that dwell with us,
And we find favour a little in their sight,
A little, and more we miss of, and much time
Foils us; howbeit they have pitied me, O son,
And thee most piteous, thee a tenderer thing
Than any flower of fleshly seed alive.
Wherefore I kissed and hid him with my hands,
And covered under arms and hair, and wept,
And feared to touch him with my tears, and laughed;
So light a thing was this man, grown so great
Men cast their heads back, seeing against the sun
Blaze the armed man carven on his shield, and hear
The laughter of little bells along the brace
Ring, as birds singing or flutes blown, and watch,
High up, the cloven shadow of either plume
Divide the bright light of the brass, and make
His helmet as a windy and wintering moon
Seen through blown cloud and plume-like drift, when
    ships
Drive, and men strive with all the sea, and oars
Break, and the beaks dip under, drinking death;
Yet was he then but a span long, and moaned
With inarticulate mouth inseparate words,

And with blind lips and fingers wrung my breast
Hard, and thrust out with foolish hands and feet,
Murmuring; but those grey women with bound hair
Who fright the gods frighted not him; he laughed
Seeing them, and pushed out hands to feel and haul
Distaff and thread, intangible; but they
Passed, and I hid the brand, and in my heart
Laughed likewise, having all my will of heaven.
But now I know not if to left or right
The gods have drawn us hither; for again
I dreamt, and saw the black brand burst on fire
As a branch bursts in flower, and saw the flame
Fade flower-wise, and Death came and with dry lips
Blew the charred ash into my breast; and Love
Trampled the ember and crushed it with swift feet.
This I have also at heart; that not for me,
Not for me only or son of mine, O girls,
The gods have wrought life, and desire of life,
Heart's love and heart's division; but for all
There shines one sun and one wind blows till night.
And when night comes the wind sinks and the sun,
And there is no light after, and no storm,
But sleep and much forgetfulness of things.
In such wise I gat knowledge of the gods
Years hence, and heard high sayings of one most wise,
Eurythemis my mother, who beheld
With eyes alive and spake with lips of these
As one on earth disfleshed and disallied
From breath or blood corruptible; such gifts
Time gave her, and an equal soul to these
And equal face to all things; thus she said.
But whatsoever intolerable or glad
The swift hours weave and unweave, I go hence
Full of mine own soul, perfect of myself,

Toward mine and me sufficient; and what chance
The gods cast lots for and shake out on us,
That shall we take, and that much bear withal.
And now, before these gather to the hunt,
I will go arm my son and bring him forth,
Lest love or some man's anger work him harm.

CHORUS

Before the beginning of years
   There came to the making of man
Time, with a gift of tears;
   Grief, with a glass that ran;
Pleasure, with pain for leaven;
   Summer, with flowers that fell;
Remembrance fallen from heaven,
   And madness risen from hell;
Strength without hands to smite;
   Love that endures for a breath:
Night, the shadow of light,
   And life, the shadow of death.
And the high gods took in hand
   Fire, and the falling of tears,
And a measure of sliding sand
   From under the feet of the years;
And froth and drift of the sea;
   And dust of the labouring earth;
And bodies of things to be
   In the houses of death and of birth;
And wrought with weeping and laughter,
   And fashioned with loathing and love
With life before and after
   And death beneath and above,
For a day and a night and a morrow,
   That his strength might endure for a span

With travail and heavy sorrow,
  The holy spirit of man.

From the winds of the north and the south
  They gathered as unto strife;
They breathed upon his mouth,
  They filled his body with life;
Eyesight and speech they wrought
  For the veils of the soul therein,
A time for labour and thought,
  A time to serve and to sin;
They gave him light in his ways,
  And love, and a space for delight,
And beauty and length of days,
  And night, and sleep in the night.
His speech is a burning fire;
  With his lips he travaileth;
In his heart is a blind desire,
  In his eyes foreknowledge of death;
He weaves, and is clothed with derision;
  Sows, and he shall not reap;
His life is a watch or a vision
  Between a sleep and a sleep.

MELEAGER

O sweet new heaven and air without a star,
Fair day, be fair and welcome, as to men
With deeds to do and praise to pluck from thee.
Come forth a child, born with clear sound and light,
With laughter and swift limbs and prosperous looks;
That this great hunt with heroes for the hounds
May leave thee memorable and us well sped.

ALTHÆA

Son, first I praise thy prayer, then bid thee speed;
But the gods hear men's hands before their lips,
And heed beyond all crying and sacrifice
Light of things done and noise of labouring men.
But thou, being armed and perfect for the deed,
Abide; for like rain-flakes in a wind they grow,
The men thy fellows, and the choice of the world,
Bound to root out the tuskèd plague, and leave
Thanks and safe days and peace in Calydon.

MELEAGER

For the whole city and all the low-lying land
Flames, and the soft air sounds with them that come;
The gods give all these fruit of all their works.

ALTHÆA

Set thine eye thither and fix thy spirit and say
Whom there thou knowest; for sharp mixed shadow
        and wind
Blown up between the morning and the mist,
With steam of steeds and flash of bridle or wheel,
And fire, and parcels of the broken dawn,
And dust divided by hard light, and spears
That shine and shift as the edge of wild beasts' eyes,
Smite upon mine; so fiery their blind edge
Burns, and bright points break up and baffle day.

MELEAGER

The first, for many I know not, being far off,
Peleus the Larissæan, couched with whom
Sleeps the white sea-bred wife and silver-shod,
Fair as fled foam, a goddess; and their son

Most swift and splendid of men's children born,
Most like a god, full of the future fame.

ALTHÆA

Who are these shining like one sundered star?

MELEAGER

Thy sister's sons, a double flower of men.

ALTHÆA

O sweetest kin to me in all the world,
O twin-born blood of Leda, gracious heads
Like kindled lights in untempestuous heaven,
Fair flower-like stars on the iron foam of fight,
With what glad heart and kindliness of soul,
Even to the staining of both eyes with tears
And kindling of warm eyelids with desire,
A great way off I greet you, and rejoice
Seeing you so fair, and moulded like as gods.
Far off ye come, and least in years of these,
But lordliest, but worth love to look upon.

MELEAGER

Even such (for sailing hither I saw far hence,
And where Eurotas hollows his moist rock
Nigh Sparta with a strenuous-hearted stream)
Even such I saw their sisters; one swan-white,
The little Helen, and less fair than she
Fair Clytæmnestra, grave as pasturing fawns
Who feed and fear some arrow; but at whiles,
As one smitten with love or wrung with joy,
She laughs and lightens with her eyes, and then
Weeps; whereat Helen, having laughed, weeps too,

And the other chides her, and she being chid speaks
    naught,
But cheeks and lips and eyelids kisses her,
Laughing; so fare they, as in their bloomless bud
And full of unblown life, the blood of gods.

ALTHÆA

Sweet days befall them and good loves and lords,
And tender and temperate honours of the hearth,
Peace, and a perfect life and blameless bed.
But who shows next an eagle wrought in gold,
That flames and beats broad wings against the sun
And with void mouth gapes after emptier prey?

MELEAGER

Know by that sign the reign of Telamon
Between the fierce mouths of the encountering brine
On the strait reefs of twice-washed Salamis.

ALTHÆA

For like one great of hand he bears himself,
Vine-chapleted, with savours of the sea,
Glittering as wine and moving as a wave.
But who girt round there roughly follows him?

MELEAGER

Ancæus, great of hand, an iron bulk,
Two-edged for fight as the axe against his arm,
Who drives against the surge of stormy spears
Full-sailed; him Cepheus follows, his twin-born,
Chief name next his of all Arcadian men.

ALTHÆA

Praise be with men abroad; chaste lives with us,
Home-keeping days and household reverences.

MELEAGER

Next by the left unsandalled foot know thou
The sail and oar of this Ætolian land,
Thy brethren, Toxeus and the violent-souled
Plexippus, over-swift with hand and tongue;
For hands are fruitful, but the ignorant mouth
Blows and corrupts their work with barren breath.

ALTHÆA

Speech too bears fruit, being worthy; and air blows
   down
Things poisonous, and high-seated violences,
And with charmed words and songs have men put out
Wild evil, and the fire of tyrannies.

MELEAGER

Yea, all things have they, save the gods and love.

ALTHÆA

Love thou the law and cleave to things ordained.

MELEAGER

Law lives upon their lips whom these applaud.

ALTHÆA

How sayest thou these? what god applauds new
   things?

MELEAGER

Zeus, who hath fear and custom under foot.

ALTHÆA

But loves not laws thrown down and lives awry.

MELEAGER

Yet is not less himself than his own law.

ALTHÆA

Nor shifts and shuffles old things up and down.

MELEAGER

But what he will remoulds and discreates.

ALTHÆA

Much, but not this, that each thing live its life.

MELEAGER

Nor only live, but lighten and lift up higher.

ALTHÆA

Pride breaks itself, and too much gained is gone.

MELEAGER

Things gained are gone, but great things done endure.

ALTHÆA

Child, if a man serve law through all his life
And with his whole heart worship, him all gods
Praise; but who loves it only with his lips,
And not in heart and deed desiring it
Hides a perverse will with obsequious words,
Him heaven infatuates and his twin-born fate
Tracks, and gains on him, scenting sins far off,
And the swift hounds of violent death devour.
Be man at one with equal-minded gods,
So shall he prosper; not through laws torn up,
Violated rule and a new face of things.
A woman armed makes war upon herself,

Unwomanlike, and treads down use and wont
And the sweet common honour that she hath,
Love, and the cry of children, and the hand
Trothplight and mutual mouth of marriages.
This doth she, being unloved; whom if one love,
Not fire nor iron and the wide-mouthed wars
Are deadlier than her lips or braided hair.
For of the one comes poison, and a curse
Falls from the other and burns the lives of men.
But thou, son, be not filled with evil dreams,
Nor with desire of these things; for with time
Blind love burns out; but if one feed it full
Till some discolouring stain dyes all his life,
He shall keep nothing praiseworthy, nor die
The sweet wise death of old men honourable,
Who have lived out all the length of all their years
Blameless, and seen well-pleased the face of gods,
And without shame and without fear have wrought
Things memorable, and while their days held out
In sight of all men and the sun's great light
Have gat them glory and given of their own praise
To the earth that bare them and the day that bred,
Home friends and far-off hospitalities,
And filled with gracious and memorial fame
Lands loved of summer or washed by violent seas,
Towns populous and many unfooted ways,
And alien lips and native with their own.
But when white age and venerable death
Mow down the strength and life within their limbs,
Drain out the blood and darken their clear eyes,
Immortal honour is on them, having past
Through splendid life and death desirable
To the clear seat and remote throne of souls,
Lands indiscoverable in the unheard-of west,

Round which the strong stream of a sacred sea
Rolls without wind for ever, and the snow
There shows not her white wings and windy feet,
Nor thunder nor swift rain saith anything,
Nor the sun burns, but all things rest and thrive;
And these, filled full of days, divine and dead,
Sages and singers fiery from the god,
And such as loved their land and all things good
And, best beloved of best men, liberty,
Free lives and lips, free hands of men free-born,
And whatsoever on earth was honourable
And whosoever of all the ephemeral seed,
Live there a life no liker to the gods
But nearer than their life of terrene days.
Love thou such life and look for such a death.
But from the light and fiery dreams of love
Spring heavy sorrows and a sleepless life,
Visions not dreams, whose lids no charm shall close
Nor song assuage them waking; and swift death
Crushes with sterile feet the unripening ear,
Treads out the timeless vintage; whom do thou
Eschewing embrace the luck of this thy life,
Not without honour; and it shall bear to thee
Such fruit as men reap from spent hours and wear,
Few men, but happy; of whom be thou, O son,
Happiest, if thou submit thy soul to fate,
And set thine eyes and heart on hopes high-born
And divine deeds and abstinence divine.
So shalt thou be toward all men all thy days
As light and might communicable, and burn
From heaven among the stars above the hours,
And break not as a man breaks nor burn down:
For to whom other of all heroic names
Have the gods given his life in hand as thine?

And gloriously hast thou lived, and made thy life
To me that bare thee and to all men born
Thankworthy, a praise for ever; and hast won fame
When wild wars broke all round thy father's house,
And the mad people of windy mountain ways
Laid spears against us like a sea, and all
Ætolia thundered with Thessalian hoofs;
Yet these, as wind baffles the foam, and beats
Straight back the relaxed ripple, didst thou break
And loosen all their lances, till undone
And man from man they fell; for ye twain stood
God against god, Ares and Artemis,
And thou the mightier; wherefore she unleashed
A sharp-toothed curse thou too shalt overcome;
For in the greener blossom of thy life
Ere the full blade caught flower, and when time gave
Respite, thou didst not slacken soul nor sleep,
But with great hand and heart seek praise of men
Out of sharp straits, and many a grievous thing,
Seeing the strange foam of undivided seas
On channels never sailed in, and by shores
Where the old winds cease not blowing, and all the
     night
Thunders, and day is no delight to men.

CHORUS

Meleager, a noble wisdom and fair words
The gods have given this woman; hear thou these.

MELEAGER

O mother, I am not fain to strive in speech
Nor set my mouth against thee, who art wise
Even as they say and full of sacred words.
But one thing I know surely, and cleave to this;

That though I be not subtle of wit as thou
Nor womanlike to weave sweet words, and melt
Mutable minds of wise men as with fire,
I too, doing justly and reverencing the gods,
Shall not want wit to see what things be right.
For whom they love and whom reject, being gods,
There is no man but seeth, and in good time
Submits himself, refraining all his heart.
And I too as thou sayest have seen great things;
Seen otherwhere, but chiefly when the sail
First caught between stretched ropes the roaring west,
And all our oars smote eastward, and the wind
First flung round faces of seafaring men
White splendid snow-flakes of the sundering foam,
And the first furrow in virginal green sea
Followed the plunging ploughshare of hewn pine,
And closed, as when deep sleep subdues man's breath
Lips close and heart subsides; and closing, shone
Sunlike with many a Nereid's hair, and moved
Round many a trembling mouth of doubtful gods,
Risen out of sunless and sonorous gulfs
Through waning water and into shallow light,
That watched us; and when flying the dove was
    snared
As with men's hands, but we shot after and sped
Clear through the irremeable Symplegades;
And chiefliest when hoar beach and herbless cliff
Stood out ahead from Colchis, and we heard
Clefts hoarse with wind, and saw through narrowing
    reefs
The lightning of the intolerable wave
Flash, and the white wet flame of breakers burn
Far under a kindling south-wind, as a lamp
Burns and bends all its blowing flame one way;

Wild heights untravelled of the wind, and vales
Cloven seaward by their violent streams, and white
With bitter flowers and bright salt scurf of brine;
Heard sweep their sharp swift gales, and bowing bird-
    wise
Shriek with birds' voices, and with furious feet
Tread loose the long skirts of a storm; and saw
The whole white Euxine clash together and fall
Full-mouthed, and thunderous from a thousand
    throats:
Yet we drew thither and won the fleece and won
Medea, deadlier than the sea; but there
Seeing many a wonder and fearful things to men
I saw not one thing like this one seen here,
Most fair and fearful, feminine, a god,
Faultless; whom I that love not, being unlike,
Fear, and give honour, and choose from all the gods.

ŒNEUS

Lady, the daughter of Thestius, and thou, son,
Not ignorant of your strife nor light of wit,
Scared with vain dreams and fluttering like spent fire,
I come to judge between you, but a king
Full of past days and wise from years endured.
Nor thee I praise, who art fain to undo things done:
Nor thee, who art swift to esteem them overmuch.
For what the hours have given is given, and this
Changeless; howbeit these change, and in good time
Devise new things and good, not one thing still.
Us have they sent now at our need for help
Among men armed a woman, foreign born,
Virgin, not like the natural flower of things
That grows and bears and brings forth fruit and dies;
Unlovable, no light for a husband's house,

Espoused; a glory among unwedded girls,
And chosen of gods who reverence maidenhood.
These too we honour in honouring her; but thou,
Abstain thy feet from following, and thine eyes
From amorous touch; nor set toward hers thine heart,
Son, lest hate bear no deadlier fruit than love.

ALTHÆA

O king, thou art wise, but wisdom halts; and just,
But the gods love not justice more than fate,
And smite the righteous and the violent mouth,
And mix with insolent blood the reverent man's,
And bruise the holier as the lying lips.
Enough; for wise words fail me, and my heart
Takes fire and trembles flamewise, O my son,
O child, for thine head's sake; mine eyes wax thick,
Turning toward thee, so goodly a weaponed man,
So glorious; and for love of thine own eyes
They are darkened, and tears burn them, fierce as
    fire,
And my lips pause and my soul sinks with love.
But by thine hand, by thy sweet life and eyes,
By thy great heart and these clasped knees, O son,
I pray thee that thou slay me not with thee.
For there was never a mother woman-born
Loved her sons better; and never a queen of men
More perfect in her heart toward whom she loved.
For what lies light on many and they forget,
Small things and transitory as a wind o' the sea,
I forget never; I have seen thee all thine years
A man in arms, strong and a joy to men
Seeing thine head glitter and thine hand burn its way
Through a heavy and iron furrow of sundering spears;
But always also a flower of three suns old,

The small one thing that lying drew down my life
To lie with thee and feed thee; a child and weak,
Mine, a delight to no man, sweet to me.
Who then sought to thee? who gat help? who knew
If thou wert goodly? nay, no man at all.
Or what sea saw thee, or sounded with thine oar,
Child? or what strange land shone with war through
    thee?
But fair for me thou wert, O little life,
Fruitless, the fruit of mine own flesh, and blind,
More than much gold, ungrown, a foolish flower.
For silver nor bright snow nor feather of foam
Was whiter, and no gold yellower than thine hair,
O child, my child; and now thou art lordlier grown,
Not lovelier, nor a new thing in mine eyes,
I charge thee by thy soul and this my breast,
Fear thou the gods and me and thine own heart,
Lest all these turn against thee; for who knows
What wind upon what wave of altering time
Shall speak a storm and blow calamity?
And there is nothing stabile in the world
But the gods break it; yet not less, fair son,
If but one thing be stronger, if one endure,
Surely the bitter and the rooted love
That burns between us, going from me to thee,
Shall more endure than all things. What dost thou,
Following strange loves? why wilt thou kill mine
    heart?
Lo, I talk wild and windy words, and fall
From my clear wits, and seem of mine own self
Dethroned, dispraised, disseated; and my mind,
That was my crown, breaks, and mine heart is gone,
And I am naked of my soul, and stand
Ashamed, as a mean woman; take thou thought:

Live if thou wilt, and if thou wilt not, look,
The gods have given thee life to lose or keep,
Thou shalt not die as men die, but thine end
Fallen upon thee shall break me unaware.

MELEAGER

Queen, my whole heart is molten with thy tears,
And my limbs yearn with pity of thee, and love
Compels with grief mine eyes and labouring breath;
For what thou art I know thee, and this thy breast
And thy fair eyes I worship, and am bound
Toward thee in spirit and love thee in all my soul.
For there is nothing terribler to men
Than the sweet face of mothers, and the might.
But what shall be let be; for us the day
Once only lives a little, and is not found.
Time and the fruitful hour are more than we,
And these lay hold upon us; but thou, God,
Zeus, the sole steersman of the helm of things,
Father, be swift to see us, and as thou wilt
Help: or if adverse, as thou wilt, refrain.

CHORUS

We have seen thee, O Love, thou art fair; thou art
    goodly, O Love;
Thy wings make light in the air as the wings of a dove.
Thy feet are as winds that divide the stream of the sea;
Earth is thy covering to hide thee, the garment of thee.
Thou art swift and subtle and blind as a flame of fire;
Before thee the laughter, behind thee the tears of
    desire;
And twain go forth beside thee, a man with a maid;
Her eyes are the eyes of a bride whom delight makes
    afraid;

As the breath in the buds that stir is her bridal
    breath:
But Fate is the name of her; and his name is Death.

    For an evil blossom was born
        Of sea-foam and the frothing of blood,
            Blood-red and bitter of fruit,
                And the seed of it laughter and tears,
        And the leaves of it madness and scorn;
            A bitter flower from the bud,
                Sprung of the sea without root,
                    Sprung without graft from the years.

    The weft of the world was untorn
        That is woven of the day on the night,
        The hair of the hours was not white
    Nor the raiment of time overworn,
        When a wonder, a world's delight,
    A perilous goddess was born;
        And the waves of the sea as she came
    Clove, and the foam at her feet,
            Fawning, rejoiced to bring forth
        A fleshly blossom, a flame
    Filling the heavens with heat
            To the cold white ends of the north.

    And in air the clamorous birds,
        And men upon earth that hear
    Sweet articulate words
            Sweetly divided apart,
        And in shallow and channel and mere
    The rapid and footless herds,
            Rejoiced, being foolish of heart.

For all they said upon earth,
   She is fair, she is white like a dove,
     And the life of the world in her breath
Breathes, and is born at her birth;
   For they knew thee for mother of love,
     And knew thee not mother of death.

What hadst thou to do being born,
   Mother, when winds were at ease,
As a flower of the springtime of corn,
   A flower of the foam of the seas?
For bitter thou wast from thy birth,
   Aphrodite, a mother of strife;
For before thee some rest was on earth,
     A little respite from tears,
   A little pleasure of life;
For life was not then as thou art,
     But as one that waxeth in years
   Sweet-spoken, a fruitful wife;
     Earth had no thorn, and desire
No sting, neither death any dart;
   What hadst thou to do amongst these,
     Thou, clothed with a burning fire,
Thou, girt with sorrow of heart,
   Thou, sprung of the seed of the seas
As an ear from a seed of corn,
     As a brand plucked forth of a pyre,
As a ray shed forth of the morn,
   For division of soul and disease,
For a dart and a sting and a thorn?
What ailed thee then to be born?

Was there not evil enough,
   Mother, and anguish on earth

Born with a man at his birth,
Wastes underfoot, and above
    Storm out of heaven, and dearth
Shaken down from the shining thereof,
        Wrecks from afar overseas
    And peril of shallow and firth,
        And tears that spring and increase
    In the barren places of mirth,
That thou, having wings as a dove,
    Being girt with desire for a girth,
        That thou must come after these,
That thou must lay on him love?

Thou shouldst not so have been born:
    But death should have risen with thee,
        Mother, and visible fear,
            Grief, and the wringing of hands,
And noise of many that mourn;
    The smitten bosom, the knee
        Bowed, and in each man's ear
            A cry as of perishing lands,
A moan as of people in prison,
    A tumult of infinite griefs;
        And a thunder of storm on the sands,
    And wailing of wives on the shore;
And under thee newly arisen
    Loud shoals and shipwrecking reefs,
        Fierce air and violent light;
    Sail rent and sundering oar,
        Darkness, and noises of night;
Clashing of streams in the sea,
    Wave against wave as a sword,
        Clamour of currents, and foam;
        Rains making ruin on earth,

Winds that wax ravenous and roam
As wolves in a wolfish horde;
Fruits growing faint in the tree,
    And blind things dead in their birth;
    Famine, and blighting of corn,
    When thy time was come to be born.

All these we know of; but thee
    Who shall discern or declare?
In the uttermost ends of the sea
    The light of thine eyelids and hair,
        The light of thy bosom as fire
            Between the wheel of the sun
    And the flying flames of the air?
        Wilt thou turn thee not yet nor have pity,
But abide with despair and desire
    And the crying of armies undone,
        Lamentation of one with another
    And breaking of city by city;
The dividing of friend against friend,
        The severing of brother and brother;
Wilt thou utterly bring to an end?
        Have mercy, mother!

For against all men from of old
    Thou hast set thine hand as a curse,
        And cast out gods from their places.
        These things are spoken of thee.
Strong kings and goodly with gold
    Thou hast found out arrows to pierce,
        And made their kingdoms and races
            As dust and surf of the sea.
All these, overburdened with woes
    And with length of their days waxen weak,

Thou slewest; and sentest moreover
Upon Tyro an evil thing,
Rent hair and a fetter and blows
Making bloody the flower of the cheek,
Though she lay by a god as a lover,
Though fair, and the seed of a king.

For of old, being full of thy fire,
She endured not longer to wear
On her bosom a saffron vest,
On her shoulder an ashwood quiver;
Being mixed and made one through desire
With Enipeus, and all her hair
Made moist with his mouth, and her breast
Filled full of the foam of the river.

ATALANTA

Sun, and clear light among green hills, and day
Late risen and long sought after, and you just gods
Whose hands divide anguish and recompense,
But first the sun's white sister, a maid in heaven,
On earth of all maids worshipped—hail, and hear,
And witness with me if not without sign sent,
Not without rule and reverence, I a maid
Hallowed, and huntress holy as whom I serve,
Here in your sight and eyeshot of these men
Stand, girt as they toward hunting, and my shafts
Drawn; wherefore all ye stand up on my side,
If I be pure and all ye righteous gods,
Lest one revile me, a woman, yet no wife,
That bear a spear for a spindle, and this bow strung
For a web woven; and with pure lips salute
Heaven, and the face of all the gods, and dawn
Filling with maiden flames and maiden flowers
The starless fold o' the stars, and making sweet

The warm wan heights of the air, moon-trodden ways
And breathless gates and extreme hills of heaven.
Whom, having offered water and bloodless gifts,
Flowers, and a golden circlet of pure hair,
Next Artemis I bid be favourable
And make this day all golden, hers and ours,
Gracious and good and white to the unblamed end.
But thou, O well-beloved, of all my days
Bid it be fruitful, and a crown for all,
To bring forth leaves and bind round all my hair
With perfect chaplets woven for thine of thee.
For not without the word of thy chaste mouth,
For not without law given and clean command,
Across the white straits of the running sea
From Elis even to the Acheloïan horn,
I with clear winds came hither and gentle gods,
Far off my father's house, and left uncheered
Iasius, and uncheered the Arcadian hills
And all their green-haired waters, and all woods
Disconsolate, to hear no horn of mine
Blown, and behold no flash of swift white feet.

MELEAGER

For thy name's sake and awe toward thy chaste head,
O holiest Atalanta, no man dares
Praise thee, though fairer than whom all men praise,
And godlike for thy grace of hallowed hair
And holy habit of thine eyes, and feet
That make the blown foam neither swift nor white
Though the wind winnow and whirl it; yet we praise
Gods, found because of thee adorable
And for thy sake praiseworthiest from all men:
Thee therefore we praise also, thee as these,
Pure, and a light lit at the hands of gods.

TOXEUS

How long will ye whet spears with eloquence,
Fight, and kill beasts dry-handed with sweet words?
Cease, or talk still and slay thy boars at home.

PLEXIPPUS

Why, if she ride among us for a man,
Sit thou for her and spin; a man grown girl
Is worth a woman weaponed; sit thou here.

MELEAGER

Peace, and be wise; no gods love idle speech.

PLEXIPPUS

Nor any man a man's mouth woman-tongued.

MELEAGER

For my lips bite not sharper than mine hands.

PLEXIPPUS

Nay, both bite soft, but no whit softly mine.

MELEAGER

Keep thine hands clean; they have time enough to
    stain.

PLEXIPPUS

For thine shall rest and wax not red to-day.

MELEAGER

Have all thy will of words; talk out thine heart.

ALTHÆA

Refrain your lips, O brethren, and my son,
Lest words turn snakes and bite you uttering them.

TOXEUS

Except she give her blood before the gods,
What profit shall a maid be among men?

PLEXIPPUS

Let her come crowned and stretch her throat for a
    knife,
Bleat out her spirit and die, and so shall men
Through her too prosper and through prosperous
    gods,
But nowise through her living; shall she live
A flower-bud of the flower-bed, or sweet fruit
For kisses and the honey-making mouth,
And play the shield for strong men and the spear?
Then shall the heifer and her mate lock horns,
And the bride overbear the groom, and men
Gods; for no less division sunders these;
Since all things made are seasonable in time,
But if one alter unseasonable are all.
But thou, O Zeus, hear me that I may slay
This beast before thee and no man halve with me
Nor woman, lest these mock thee, though a god,
Who hast made men strong, and thou being wise be
    held
Foolish; for wise is that thing which endures.

ATALANTA

Men, and the chosen of all this people, and thou,
King, I beseech you a little bear with me.
For if my life be shameful that I live,
Let the gods witness and their wrath; but these
Cast no such word against me. Thou, O mine,
O holy, O happy goddess, if I sin
Changing the words of women and the works

For spears and strange men's faces, hast not thou
One shaft of all thy sudden seven that pierced
Seven through the bosom or shining throat or side,
All couched about one mother's loosening knees,
All holy born, engraffed of Tantalus?
But if toward any of you I am overbold
That take thus much upon me, let him think
How I, for all my forest holiness,
Fame, and this armed and iron maidenhood,
Pay thus much also; I shall have no man's love
For ever, and no face of children born
Or feeding lips upon me or fastening eyes
For ever, nor being dead shall kings my sons
Mourn me and bury, and tears on daughters' cheeks
Burn; but a cold and sacred life, but strange,
But far from dances and the back-blowing torch,
Far off from flowers or any bed of man,
Shall my life be for ever: me the snows
That face the first o' the morning, and cold hills
Full of the land-wind and sea-travelling storms
And many a wandering wing of noisy nights
That know the thunder and hear the thickening
    wolves—
Me the utmost pine and footless frost of woods
That talk with many winds and gods, the hours
Re-risen, and white divisions of the dawn,
Springs thousand-tongued with the intermitting reed
And streams that murmur of the mother snow—
Me these allure, and know me; but no man
Knows, and my goddess only. Lo now, see
If one of all you these things vex at all.
Would God that any of you had all the praise
And I no manner of memory when I die,
So might I show before her perfect eyes

Pure, whom I follow, a maiden to my death.
But for the rest let all have all they will;
For is it a grief to you that I have part,
Being woman merely, in your male might and deeds
Done by main strength? yet in my body is throned
As great a heart, and in my spirit, O men,
I have not less of godlike. Evil it were
That one a coward should mix with you, one hand
Fearful, one eye abase itself; and these
Well might ye hate and well revile, not me.
For not the difference of the several flesh
Being vile or noble or beautiful or base
Makes praiseworthy, but purer spirit and heart
Higher than these meaner mouths and limbs, that
      feed,
Rise, rest, and are and are not; and for me,
What should I say? but by the gods of the world
And this my maiden body, by all oaths
That bind the tongue of men and the evil will,
I am not mighty-minded, nor desire
Crowns, nor the spoil of slain things nor the fame;
Feed ye on these, eat and wax fat; cry out,
Laugh, having eaten, and leap without a lyre,
Sing, mix the wind with clamour, smite and shake
Sonorous timbrels and tumultuous hair,
And fill the dance up with tempestuous feet,
For I will none; but having prayed my prayers
And made thank-offering for prosperities,
I shall go hence and no man see me more.
What thing is this for you to shout me down,
What, for a man to grudge me this my life
As it were envious of all yours, and I
A thief of reputations? nay, for now,
If there be any highest in heaven, a god

Above all thrones and thunders of the gods
Throned, and the wheel of the world roll under him,
Judge he between me and all of you, and see
If I transgress at all: but ye, refrain
Transgressing hands and reinless mouths, and keep
Silence, lest by much foam of violent words
And proper poison of your lips ye die.

ŒNEUS

O flower of Tegea, maiden, fleetest foot
And holiest head of women, have good cheer
Of thy good words: but ye, depart with her
In peace and reverence, each with blameless eye
Following his fate; exalt your hands and hearts,
Strike, cease not, arrow on arrow and wound on
　　wound,
And go with gods and with the gods return.

CHORUS

Who hath given man speech? or who hath set therein
A thorn for peril and a snare for sin?
For in the word his life is and his breath,
　　And in the word his death,
That madness and the infatuate heart may breed
　　From the word's womb the deed
And life bring one thing forth ere all pass by,
Even one thing which is ours yet cannot die—
Death. Hast thou seen him ever anywhere,
Time's twin-born brother, imperishable as he
Is perishable and plaintive, clothed with care
　　And mutable as sand,
But death is strong and full of blood and fair

And perdurable and like a lord of land?
Nay, time thou seest not, death thou wilt not see
Till life's right hand be loosened from thine hand
   And thy life-days from thee.

For the gods very subtly fashion
   Madness with sadness upon earth:
Not knowing in any wise compassion,
   Nor holding pity of any worth;
And many things they have given and taken,
   And wrought and ruined many things;
The firm land have they loosed and shaken,
   And sealed the sea with all her springs;
They have wearied time with heavy burdens
   And vexed the lips of life with breath:
Set men to labour and given them guerdons,
   Death, and great darkness after death:
Put moans into the bridal measure
   And on the bridal wools a stain;
And circled pain about with pleasure,
   And girdled pleasure about with pain;
And strewed one marriage-bed with tears and fire
For extreme loathing and supreme desire.

What shall be done with all these tears of ours?
   Shall they make watersprings in the fair heaven
To bathe the brows of morning? or like flowers
Be shed and shine before the starriest hours,
   Or made the raiment of the weeping Seven?
Or rather, O our masters, shall they be
Food for the famine of the grievous sea,
   A great well-head of lamentation
Satiating the sad gods? or fall and flow
Among the years and seasons to and fro,
   And wash their feet with tribulation

And fill them full with grieving ere they go?
  Alas, our lords, and yet alas again,
Seeing all your iron heaven is gilt as gold
  But all we smite thereat in vain;

Smite the gates barred with groanings manifold,
  But all the floors are paven with our pain.
Yea, and with weariness of lips and eyes,
With breaking of the bosom, and with sighs,
  We labour, and are clad and fed with grief
And filled with days we would not fain behold
And nights we would not hear of; we wax old,
  All we wax old and wither like a leaf.
We are outcast, strayed between bright sun and moon;
  Our light and darkness are as leaves of flowers,
Black flowers and white, that perish; and the noon
  As midnight, and the night as daylight hours.
  A little fruit a little while is ours,
     And the worm finds it soon.

But up in heaven the high gods one by one
  Lay hands upon the draught that quickeneth,
Fulfilled with all tears shed and all things done,
  And stir with soft imperishable breath
  The bubbling bitterness of life and death,
And hold it to our lips and laugh; but they
Preserve their lips from tasting night or day,
  Lest they too change and sleep, the fates that spun,
The lips that made us and the hands that slay;
  Lest all these change, and heaven bow down to
     none,
Change and be subject to the secular sway
  And terrene revolution of the sun.
Therefore they thrust it from them, putting time away.

I would the wine of time, made sharp and sweet
  With multitudinous days and nights and tears
  And many mixing savours of strange years,
Were no more trodden of them under feet,
  Cast out and spilt about their holy places:
That life were given them as a fruit to eat
And death to drink as water; that the light
Might ebb, drawn backward from their eyes, and night
  Hide for one hour the imperishable faces.
That they might rise up sad in heaven, and know
Sorrow and sleep, one paler than young snow,
  One cold as blight of dew and ruinous rain;
Rise up and rest and suffer a little, and be
Awhile as all things born with us and we,
  And grieve as men, and like slain men be slain.

For now we know not of them; but one saith
  The gods are gracious, praising God; and one,
When hast thou seen? or hast thou felt his breath
  Touch, nor consume thine eyelids as the sun,
Nor fill thee to the lips with fiery death?
  None hath beheld him, none
Seen above other gods and shapes of things,
Swift without feet and flying without wings,
Intolerable, not clad with death or life,
  Insatiable, not known of night or day,
The lord of love and loathing and of strife
  Who gives a star and takes a sun away;
Who shapes the soul, and makes her a barren wife
  To the earthly body and grievous growth of clay;
Who turns the large limbs to a little flame
  And binds the great sea with a little sand;
Who makes desire, and slays desire with shame;
  Who shakes the heaven as ashes in his hand;

Who, seeing the light and shadow for the same,
   Bids day waste night as fire devours a brand,
Smites without sword, and scourges without rod;
   The supreme evil, God.

Yea, with thine hate, O God, thou hast covered us,
   One saith, and hidden our eyes away from sight,
And made us transitory and hazardous,
   Light things and slight;
Yet have men praised thee, saying, He hath made
     man thus,
   And he doeth right.
Thou hast kissed us, and hast smitten; thou hast laid
Upon us with thy left hand life, and said,
Live: and again thou hast said, Yield up your breath,
And with thy right hand laid upon us death.
Thou hast sent us sleep, and stricken sleep with
     dreams,
   Saying, Joy is not, but love of joy shall be;
Thou hast made sweet springs for all the pleasant
     streams,
   In the end thou hast made them bitter with the sea.
Thou hast fed one rose with dust of many men;
   Thou hast marred one face with fire of many tears;
Thou hast taken love, and given us sorrow again;
   With pain thou hast filled us full to the eyes and
     ears.
Therefore because thou art strong, our father, and we
   Feeble; and thou art against us, and thine hand
Constrains us in the shallows of the sea
   And breaks us at the limits of the land;
Because thou hast bent thy lightnings as a bow,
   And loosed the hours like arrows; and let fall
Sins and wild words and many a wingèd woe

And wars among us, and one end of all;
Because thou hast made the thunder, and thy feet
   Are as a rushing water when the skies
Break, but thy face as an exceeding heat
   And flames of fire the eyelids of thine eyes;
Because thou art over all who are over us;
   Because thy name is life and our name death;
Because thou art cruel and men are piteous,
   And our hands labour and thine hand scattereth;
Lo, with hearts rent and knees made tremulous,
   Lo, with ephemeral lips and casual breath,
      At least we witness of thee ere we die
That these things are not otherwise, but thus;
   That each man in his heart sigheth, and saith,
      That all men even as I,
All we are against thee, against thee, O God most
      high.

   But ye, keep ye on earth
   Your lips from over-speech,
Loud words and longing are so little worth;
   And the end is hard to reach.
For silence after grievous things is good,
   And reverence, and the fear that makes men whole,
And shame, and righteous governance of blood,
   And lordship of the soul.
But from sharp words and wits men pluck no fruit,
And gathering thorns they shake the tree at root;
For words divide and rend;
But silence is most noble till the end.

ALTHÆA

I heard within the house a cry of news
And came forth eastward hither, where the dawn

Cheers first these warder gods that face the sun
And next our eyes unrisen; for unaware
Came clashes of swift hoofs and trampling feet
And through the windy pillared corridor
Light sharper than the frequent flames of day
That daily fill it from the fiery dawn;
Gleams, and a thunder of people that cried out,
And dust and hurrying horsemen; lo their chief,
That rode with Œneus rein by rein, returned.
What cheer, O herald of my lord the king?

HERALD

Lady, good cheer and great; the boar is slain.

CHORUS

Praised be all gods that look toward Calydon.

ALTHÆA

Good news and brief; but by whose happier hand?

HERALD

A maiden's and a prophet's and thy son's.

ALTHÆA

Well fare the spear that severed him and life.

HERALD

Thine own, and not an alien, hast thou blest.

ALTHÆA

Twice be thou too for my sake blest and his.

HERALD

At the king's word I rode afoam for thine.

ALTHÆA

Thou sayest he tarrieth till they bring the spoil?

HERALD

Hard by the quarry, where they breathe, O queen.

ALTHÆA

Speak thou their chance; but some bring flowers and
    crown
These gods and all the lintel, and shed wine,
Fetch sacrifice and slay; for heaven is good.

HERALD

Some furlongs northward where the brakes begin
West of that narrowing range of warrior hills
Whose brooks have bled with battle when thy son
Smote Acarnania, there all they made halt,
And with keen eye took note of spear and hound,
Royally ranked; Laertes island-born,
The young Gerenian Nestor, Panopeus,
And Cepheus and Ancæus, mightiest thewed,
Arcadians; next, and evil-eyed of these,
Arcadian Atalanta, with twain hounds
Lengthening the leash, and under nose and brow
Glittering with lipless tooth and fire-swift eye;
But from her white braced shoulder the plumed shafts
Rang, and the bow shone from her side; next her
Meleager, like a sun in spring that strikes
Branch into leaf and bloom into the world,
A glory among men meaner; Iphicles,
And following him that slew the biform bull
Pirithous, and divine Eurytion,
And, bride-bound to the gods, Æacides.
Then Telamon his brother, and Argive-born

The seer and sayer of visions and of truth,
Amphiaraus; and a four-fold strength,
Thine, even thy mother's and thy sister's sons.
And recent from the roar of foreign foam
Jason, and Dryas twin-begot with war,
A blossom of bright battle, sword and man
Shining; and Idas, and the keenest eye
Of Lynceus, and Admetus twice-espoused,
And Hippasus and Hyleus, great in heart.
These having halted bade blow horns, and rode
Through woods and waste lands cleft by stormy
 streams,
Past yew-trees and the heavy hair of pines,
And where the dew is thickest under oaks,
This way and that; but questing up and down
They saw no trail nor scented; and one said,
Plexippus, Help, or help not, Artemis,
And we will flay thy boarskin with male hands;
But saying, he ceased and said not that he would,
Seeing where the green ooze of a sun-struck marsh
Shook with a thousand reeds untunable,
And in their moist and multitudinous flower
Slept no soft sleep, with violent visions fed,
The blind bulk of the immeasurable beast.
And seeing, he shuddered with sharp lust of praise
Through all his limbs, and launched a double dart.
And missed; for much desire divided him,
Too hot of spirit and feebler than his will,
That his hand failed, though fervent; and the shaft,
Sundering the rushes, in a tamarisk stem
Shook, and stuck fast; then all abode save one,
The Arcadian Atalanta; from her side
Sprang her hounds, labouring at the leash, and
 slipped,

And plashed ear-deep with plunging feet; but she
Saying, Speed it as I send it for thy sake,
Goddess, drew bow and loosed; the sudden string
Rang, and sprang inward, and the waterish air
Hissed, and the moist plumes of the songless reeds
Moved as a wave which the wind moves no more.
But the boar heaved half out of ooze and slime
His tense flank trembling round the barbèd wound,
Hateful; and fiery with invasive eyes
And bristling with intolerable hair
Plunged, and the hounds clung, and green flowers and
    white
Reddened and broke all round them where they came.
And charging with sheer tusk he drove, and smote
Hyleus; and sharp death caught his sudden soul,
And violent sleep shed night upon his eyes.
Then Peleus, with strong strain of hand and heart,
Shot; but the sidelong arrow slid, and slew
His comrade born and loving countryman,
Under the left arm smitten, as he no less
Poised a like arrow; and bright blood brake afoam,
And falling, and weighed back by clamorous arms,
Sharp rang the dead limbs of Eurytion.
Then one shot happier, the Cadmean seer,
Amphiaraus; for his sacred shaft
Pierced the red circlet of one ravening eye
Beneath the brute brows of the sanguine boar,
Now bloodier from one slain; but he so galled
Sprang straight, and rearing cried no lesser cry
Than thunder and the roar of wintering streams
That mix their own foam with the yellower sea;
And as a tower that falls by fire in fight
With ruin of walls and all its archery,
And breaks the iron flower of war beneath,

Crushing charred limbs and molten arms of men;
So through crushed branches and the reddening brake
Clamoured and crashed the fervour of his feet,
And trampled, springing sideways from the tusk,
Too tardy a moving mould of heavy strength,
Ancæus; and as flakes of weak-winged snow
Break, all the hard thews of his heaving limbs
Broke, and rent flesh fell every way, and blood
Flew, and fierce fragments of no more a man.
Then all the heroes drew sharp breath, and gazed,
And smote not; but Meleager, but thy son,
Right in the wild way of the coming curse
Rock-rooted, fair with fierce and fastened lips,
Clear eyes, and springing muscle and shortening
     limb—
With chin aslant indrawn to a tightening throat,
Grave, and with gathered sinews, like a god,—
Aimed on the left side his well-handled spear
Grasped where the ash was knottiest hewn, and smote,
And with no missile wound, the monstrous boar
Right in the hairiest hollow of his hide
Under the last rib, sheer through bulk and bone,
Deep in; and deeply smitten, and to death,
The heavy horror with his hanging shafts
Leapt, and fell furiously, and from raging lips
Foamed out the latest wrath of all his life.
And all they praised the gods with mightier heart,
Zeus and all gods, but chiefliest Artemis,
Seeing; but Meleager bade whet knives and flay,
Strip and stretch out the splendour of the spoil;
And hot and horrid from the work all these
Sat, and drew breath and drank and made great cheer
And washed the hard sweat off their calmer brows.
For much sweet grass grew higher than grew the reed,

And good for slumber, and every holier herb,
Narcissus, and the low-lying melilote,
And all of goodliest blade and bloom that springs
Where, hid by heavier hyacinth, violet buds
Blossom and burn; and fire of yellower flowers
And light of crescent lilies, and such leaves
As fear the Faun's and know the Dryad's foot;
Olive and ivy and poplar dedicate,
And many a well-spring overwatched of these.
There now they rest; but me the king bade bear
Good tidings to rejoice this town and thee.
Wherefore be glad, and all ye give much thanks,
For fallen is all the trouble of Calydon.

ALTHÆA

Laud ye the gods; for this they have given is good,
And what shall be they hide until their time.
Much good and somewhat grievous hast thou said,
And either well; but let all sad things be,
Till all have made before the prosperous gods
Burnt-offering, and poured out the floral wine.
Look fair, O gods, and favourable; for we
Praise you with no false heart or flattering mouth,
Being merciful, but with pure souls and prayer.

HERALD

Thou hast prayed well; for whoso fears not these,
But once being prosperous waxes huge of heart,
Him shall some new thing unaware destroy.

CHORUS

O that I now, I too were
By deep wells and water-floods,
Streams of ancient hills, and where

All the wan green places bear
Blossoms cleaving to the sod,
Fruitless fruit, and grasses fair,
Or such darkest ivy-buds
As divide thy yellow hair,
Bacchus, and their leaves that nod
Round thy fawnskin brush the bare
Snow-soft shoulders of a god;
There the year is sweet, and there
Earth is full of secret springs,
And the fervent rose-cheeked hours,
Those that marry dawn and noon,
There are sunless, there look pale
In dim leaves and hidden air,
Pale as grass or latter flowers
Or the wild vine's wan wet rings
Full of dew beneath the moon,
And all day the nightingale
Sleeps, and all night sings;
There in cold remote recesses
That nor alien eyes assail,
Feet, nor imminence of wings,
Nor a wind nor any tune,
Thou, O queen and holiest,
Flower the whitest of all things,
With reluctant lengthening tresses
And with sudden splendid breast
Save of maidens unbeholden,
There art wont to enter, there
Thy divine swift limbs and golden
Maiden growth of unbound hair,
Bathed in waters white,
Shine, and many a maid's by thee
In moist woodland or the hilly

Flowerless brakes where wells abound
Out of all men's sight;
Or in lower pools that see
All their marges clothed all round
With the innumerable lily,
Whence the golden-girdled bee
Flits through flowering rush to fret
White or duskier violet,
Fair as those that in far years
With their buds left luminous
And their little leaves made wet,
From the warmer dew of tears,
Mother's tears in extreme need,
Hid the limbs of Iamus,
Of thy brother's seed;
For his heart was piteous
Toward him, even as thine heart now
Pitiful toward us;
Thine, O goddess, turning hither
A benignant blameless brow;
Seeing enough of evil done
And lives withered as leaves wither
In the blasting of the sun;
Seeing enough of hunters dead,
Ruin enough of all our year,
Herds and harvests slain and shed,
Herdsmen stricken many an one,
Fruits and flocks consumed together,
And great length of deadly days.
Yet with reverent lips and fear
Turn we toward thee, turn and praise
For this lightening of clear weather
And prosperities begun.
For not seldom, when all air

As bright water without breath
Shines, and when men fear not, fate
Without thunder unaware
Breaks, and brings down death.
Joy with grief ye great gods give,
Good with bad, and overbear
All the pride of us that live,
All the high estate,
As ye long since overbore,
As in old time long before,
Many a strong man and a great,
All that were.
But do thou, sweet, otherwise,
Having heed of all our prayer,
Taking note of all our sighs;
We beseech thee by thy light,
By thy bow, and thy sweet eyes,
And the kingdom of the night,
Be thou favourable and fair;
By thine arrows and thy might
And Orion overthrown;
By the maiden thy delight,
By the indissoluble zone
And the sacred hair.

MESSENGER

Maidens, if ye will sing now, shift your song,
Bow down, cry, wail for pity; is this a time
For singing? nay, for strewing of dust and ash,
Rent raiment, and for bruising of the breast.

CHORUS

What new thing wolf-like lurks behind thy words?
What snake's tongue in thy lips? what fire in the eyes?

MESSENGER

Bring me before the queen and I will speak.

CHORUS

Lo, she comes forth as from thank-offering made.

MESSENGER

A barren offering for a bitter gift.

ALTHÆA

What are these borne on branches, and the face
Covered? no mean men living, but now slain
Such honour have they, if any dwell with death.

MESSENGER

Queen, thy twain brethren and thy mother's sons.

ALTHÆA

Lay down your dead till I behold their blood
If it be mine indeed, and I will weep.

MESSENGER

Weep if thou wilt, for these men shall no more.

ALTHÆA

O brethren, O my father's sons, of me
Well loved and well reputed, I should weep
Tears dearer than the dear blood drawn from you
But that I know you not uncomforted,
Sleeping no shameful sleep, however slain,
For my son surely hath avenged you dead.

MESSENGER

Nay, should thine own seed slay himself, O queen?

ALTHÆA

Thy double word brings forth a double death.

MESSENGER

Know this then singly, by one hand they fell.

ALTHÆA

What mutterest thou with thine ambiguous mouth?

MESSENGER

Slain by thy son's hand; is that saying so hard?

ALTHÆA

Our time is come upon us: it is here.

CHORUS

O miserable, and spoiled at thine own hand.

ALTHÆA

Wert thou not called Meleager from this womb?

CHORUS

A grievous huntsman hath it bred to thee.

ALTHÆA

Wert thou born fire, and shalt thou not devour?

CHORUS

The fire thou madest, will it consume even thee?

ALTHÆA

My dreams are fallen upon me; burn thou too.

CHORUS

Not without God are visions born and die.

ALTHÆA

The gods are many about me; I am one.

CHORUS

She groans as men wrestling with heavier gods.

ALTHÆA

They rend me, they divide me, they destroy.

CHORUS

Or one labouring in travail of strange births.

ALTHÆA

They are strong, they are strong; I am broken, and
    these prevail.

CHORUS

The god is great against her; she will die.

ALTHÆA

Yea, but not now; for my heart too is great.
I would I were not here in sight of the sun.
But thou, speak all thou sawest, and I will die.

MESSENGER

O queen, for queenlike hast thou borne thyself,
A little word may hold so great mischance.
For in division of the sanguine spoil
These men thy brethren wrangling bade yield up
The boar's head and the horror of the hide
That this might stand a wonder in Calydon,
Hallowed; and some drew toward them; but thy son
With great hands grasping all that weight of hair
Cast down the dead heap clanging and collapsed
At female feet, saying This thy spoil not mine,

Maiden, thine own hand for thyself hath reaped,
And all this praise God gives thee: she thereat
Laughed, as when dawn touches the sacred night
The sky sees laugh and redden and divide
Dim lips and eyelids virgin of the sun,
Hers, and the warm slow breasts of morning heave,
Fruitful, and flushed with flame from lamp-lit hours,
And maiden undulation of clear hair
Colour the clouds; so laughed she from pure heart,
Lit with a low blush to the braided hair,
And rose-coloured and cold like very dawn,
Golden and godlike, chastely with chaste lips,
A faint grave laugh; and all they held their peace,
And she passed by them. Then one cried, Lo now,
Shall not the Arcadian shoot out lips at us,
Saying all we were despoiled by this one girl?
And all they rode against her violently
And cast the fresh crown from her hair, and now
They had rent her spoil away, dishonouring her,
Save that Meleager, as a tame lion chafed,
Bore on them, broke them, and as fire cleaves wood
So clove and drove them, smitten in twain; but she
Smote not nor heaved up hand; and this man first,
Plexippus, crying out, This for love's sake, sweet,
Drove at Meleager, who with spear straightening
Pierced his cheek through; then Toxeus made for him,
Dumb, but his spear spake; vain and violent words,
Fruitless; for him too stricken through both sides
The earth felt falling, and his horse's foam
Blanched thy son's face, his slayer; and these being
    slain,
None moved nor spake; but Œneus bade bear hence
These made of heaven infatuate in their deaths,
Foolish; for these would baffle fate, and fell.

And they passed on, and all men honoured her,
Being honourable, as one revered of heaven.

ALTHÆA

What say you, women? is all this not well done?

CHORUS

No man doth well but God hath part in him.

ALTHÆA

But no part here; for these my brethren born
Ye have no part in, these ye know not of
As I that was their sister, a sacrifice
Slain in their slaying. I would I had died for these;
For this man dead walked with me, child by child,
And made a weak staff for my feebler feet
With his own tender wrist and hand, and held
And led me softly and shewed me gold and steel
And shining shapes of mirror and bright crown
And all things fair; and threw light spears, and
    brought
Young hounds to huddle at my feet and thrust
Tame heads against my little maiden breasts
And please me with great eyes; and those days went
And these are bitter and I a barren queen
And sister miserable, a grievous thing
And mother of many curses; and she too,
My sister Leda, sitting overseas
With fair fruits round her, and her faultless lord,
Shall curse me, saying A sorrow and not a son,
Sister, thou barest, even a burning fire,
A brand consuming thine own soul and me.
But ye now, sons of Thestius, make good cheer,
For ye shall have such wood to funeral fire

As no king hath; and flame that once burnt down
Oil shall not quicken or breath relume or wine
Refresh again; much costlier than fine gold,
And more than many lives of wandering men.

CHORUS

O queen, thou hast yet with thee love-worthy things,
Thine husband, and the great strength of thy son.

ALTHÆA

Who shall get brothers for me while I live?
Who bear them? who bring forth in lieu of these?
Are not our fathers and our brethren one,
And no man like them? are not mine here slain?
Have we not hung together, he and I,
Flowerwise feeding as the feeding bees,
With mother-milk for honey? and this man too,
Dead, with my son's spear thrust between his sides,
Hath he not seen us, later born than he,
Laugh with lips filled, and laughed again for love?
There were no sons then in the world, nor spears,
Nor deadly births of women; but the gods
Allowed us, and our days were clear of these.
I would I had died unwedded, and brought forth
No swords to vex the world; for these that spake
Sweet words long since and loved me will not speak
Nor love nor look upon me; and all my life
I shall not hear nor see them living men.
But I too living, how shall I now live?
What life shall this be with my son, to know
What hath been and desire what will not be,
Look for dead eyes and listen for dead lips,
And kill mine own heart with remembering them,
And with those eyes that see their slayer alive

Weep, and wring hands that clasp him by the hand?
How shall I bear my dreams of them, to hear
False voices, feel the kisses of false mouths
And footless sound of perished feet, and then
Wake and hear only it may be their own hounds
Whine masterless in miserable sleep,
And see their boar-spears and their beds and seats
And all the gear and housings of their lives
And not the men? shall hounds and horses mourn,
Pine with strange eyes, and prick up hungry ears,
Famish and fail at heart for their dear lords,
And I not heed at all? and those blind things
Fall off from life for love's sake, and I live?
Surely some death is better than some life,
Better one death for him and these and me.
For if the gods had slain them it may be
I had endured it; if they had fallen by war
Or by the nets and knives of privy death
And by hired hands while sleeping, this thing too
I had set my soul to suffer; or this hunt,
Had this despatched them, under tusk or tooth
Torn, sanguine, trodden, broken; for all deaths
Or honourable or with facile feet avenged
And hands of swift gods following, all save this,
Are bearable; but not for their sweet land
Fighting, but not a sacrifice, lo these
Dead; for I had not then shed all mine heart
Out at mine eyes: then either with good speed,
Being just, I had slain their slayer atoningly,
Or strewn with flowers their fire and on their tombs
Hung crowns, and over them a song, and seen
Their praise outflame their ashes: for all men,
All maidens, had come thither, and from pure lips
Shed songs upon them, from heroic eyes

Tears; and their death had been a deathless life;
But now, by no man hired nor alien sword,
By their own kindred are they fallen, in peace,
After much peril, friendless among friends,
By hateful hands they loved; and how shall mine
Touch these returning red and not from war,
These fatal from the vintage of men's veins,
Dead men my brethren? how shall these wash off
No festal stains of undelightful wine,
How mix the blood, my blood on them, with me,
Holding mine hand? or how shall I say, son,
That am no sister? but by night and day
Shall we not sit and hate each other, and think
Things hate-worthy? not live with shamefast eyes,
Brow-beaten, treading soft with fearful feet,
Each unupbraided, each without rebuke
Convicted, and without a word reviled
Each of another? and I shall let thee live
And see thee strong and hear men for thy sake
Praise me, but these thou wouldest not let live
No man shall praise for ever? these shall lie
Dead, unbeloved, unholpen, all through thee?
Sweet were they toward me living, and mine heart
Desired them, but was then well satisfied,
That now is as men hungered; and these dead
I shall want always to the day I die.
For all things else and all men may renew;
Yea, son for son the gods may give and take,
But never a brother or sister any more.

CHORUS

Nay, for the son lies close about thine heart,
Full of thy milk, warm from thy womb, and drains
Life and the blood of life and all thy fruit,

Eats thee and drinks thee as who breaks bread and
    eats,
Treads wine and drinks, thyself, a sect of thee;
And if he feed not, shall not thy flesh faint?
Or drink not, are not thy lips dead for thirst?
This thing moves more than all things, even thy son,
That thou cleave to him; and he shall honour thee,
Thy womb that bare him and the breasts he knew,
Reverencing most for thy sake all his gods.

ALTHÆA

But these the gods too gave me, and these my son,
Not reverencing his gods nor mine own heart
Nor the old sweet years nor all venerable things,
But cruel, and in his ravin like a beast,
Hath taken away to slay them: yea, and she,
She the strange woman, she the flower, the sword,
Red from spilt blood, a mortal flower to men,
Adorable, detestable—even she
Saw with strange eyes and with strange lips rejoiced,
Seeing these mine own slain of mine own, and me
Made miserable above all miseries made,
A grief among all women in the world,
A name to be washed out with all men's tears.

CHORUS

Strengthen thy spirit; is this not also a god,
Chance, and the wheel of all necessities?
Hard things have fallen upon us from harsh gods,
Whom lest worse hap rebuke we not for these.

ALTHÆA

My spirit is strong against itself, and I
For these things' sake cry out on mine own soul

That it endures outrage, and dolorous days,
And life, and this inexpiable impotence.
Weak am I, weak and shameful; my breath drawn
Shames me, and monstrous things and violent gods.
What shall atone? what heal me? what bring back
Strength to the foot, light to the face? what herb
Assuage me? what restore me? what release?
What strange thing eaten or drunken, O great gods,
Make me as you or as the beasts that feed,
Slay and divide and cherish their own hearts?
For these ye show us; and we less than these
Have not wherewith to live as all these things
Which all their lives fare after their own kind
As who doth well rejoicing; but we ill,
Weeping or laughing, we whom eyesight fails,
Knowledge and light of face and perfect heart,
And hands we lack, and wit; and all our days
Sin, and have hunger, and die infatuated.
For madness have ye given us and not health,
And sins whereof we know not; and for these
Death, and sudden destruction unaware.
What shall we say now? what thing comes of us?

CHORUS

Alas, for all this all men undergo.

ALTHÆA

Wherefore I will not that these twain, O gods,
Die as a dog dies, eaten of creeping things,
Abominable, a loathing; but though dead
Shall they have honour and such funereal flame
As strews men's ashes in their enemies' face
And blinds their eyes who hate them: lest men say,

'Lo how they lie, and living had great kin,
And none of these hath pity of them, and none
Regards them lying, and none is wrung at heart,
None moved in spirit for them, naked and slain,
Abhorred, abased, and no tears comfort them:'
And in the dark this grieve Eurythemis,
Hearing how these her sons come down to her
Unburied, unavenged, as kinless men,
And had a queen their sister. That were shame
Worse than this grief. Yet how to atone at all
I know not; seeing the love of my born son,
A new-made mother's new-born love, that grows
From the soft child to the strong man, now soft
Now strong as either, and still one sole same love,
Strives with me, no light thing to strive withal;
This love is deep, and natural to man's blood,
And ineffaceable with many tears.
Yet shall not these rebuke me though I die,
Nor she in that waste world with all her dead,
My mother, among the pale flocks fallen as leaves,
Folds of dead people, and alien from the sun;
Nor lack some bitter comfort, some poor praise,
Being queen, to have borne her daughter like a queen,
Righteous; and though mine own fire burn me too,
She shall have honour and these her sons, though dead.
But all the gods will, all they do, and we
Not all we would, yet somewhat; and one choice
We have, to live and do just deeds and die.

CHORUS

Terrible words she communes with, and turns
Swift fiery eyes in doubt against herself,
And murmurs as who talks in dreams with death.

ALTHÆA

For the unjust also dieth, and him all men
Hate, and himself abhors the unrighteousness,
And seeth his own dishonour intolerable.
But I being just, doing right upon myself,
Slay mine own soul, and no man born shames me.
For none constrains nor shall rebuke, being done,
What none compelled me doing; thus these things
    fare.
Ah, ah, that such things should so fare; ah me,
That I am found to do them and endure,
Chosen and constrained to choose, and bear myself
Mine own wound through mine own flesh to the heart
Violently stricken, a spoiler and a spoil,
A ruin ruinous, fallen on mine own son.
Ah, ah, for me too as for these; alas,
For that is done that shall be, and mine hand
Full of the deed, and full of blood mine eyes,
That shall see never nor touch anything
Save blood unstanched and fire unquenchable.

CHORUS

What wilt thou do? what ails thee? for the house
Shakes ruinously; wilt thou bring fire for it?

ALTHÆA

Fire in the roofs, and on the lintels fire.
Lo ye, who stand and weave, between the doors,
There; and blood drips from hand and thread, and
    stains
Threshold and raiment and me passing in
Flecked with the sudden sanguine drops of death.

CHORUS

Alas that time is stronger than strong men,
Fate than all gods: and these are fallen on us.

ALTHÆA

A little since and I was glad; and now
I never shall be glad or sad again.

CHORUS

Between two joys a grief grows unaware.

ALTHÆA

A little while and I shall laugh; and then
I shall weep never and laugh not any more.

CHORUS

What shall be said? for words are thorns to grief.
Withhold thyself a little and fear the gods.

ALTHÆA

Fear died when these were slain; and I am as dead,
And fear is of the living; these fear none.

CHORUS

Have pity upon all people for their sake.

ALTHÆA

It is done now; shall I put back my day?

CHORUS

An end is come, an end; this is of God.

ALTHÆA

I am fire, and burn myself; keep clear of fire.

CHORUS

The house is broken, is broken; it shall not stand.

ALTHÆA

Woe, woe for him that breaketh; and a rod
Smote it of old, and now the axe is here.

CHORUS

Not as with sundering of the earth
   Nor as with cleaving of the sea
Nor fierce foreshadowings of a birth
   Nor flying dreams of death to be
Nor loosening of the large world's girth
And quickening of the body of night,
   And sound of thunder in men's ears
And fire of lightning in men's sight,
   Fate, mother of desires and fears,
   Bore unto men the law of tears;
But sudden, an unfathered flame,
   And broken out of night, she shone,
She, without body, without name,
   In days forgotten and foregone;
And heaven rang round her as she came
Like smitten cymbals, and lay bare;
   Clouds and great stars, thunders and snows,
The blue sad fields and folds of air,
   The life that breathes, the life that grows,
   All wind, all fire, that burns or blows,
Even all these knew her: for she is great;
   The daughter of doom, the mother of death,
The sister of sorrow; a lifelong weight
   That no man's finger lighteneth,
Nor any god can lighten fate;

A landmark seen across the way
   Where one race treads as the other trod;
An evil sceptre, an evil stay,
   Wrought for a staff, wrought for a rod,
   The bitter jealousy of God.

For death is deep as the sea,
   And fate as the waves thereof.
Shall the waves take pity on thee
   Or the southwind offer thee love?
Wilt thou take the night for thy day
Or the darkness for light on thy way,
   Till thou say in thine heart Enough?
Behold, thou art over fair, thou art over wise;
The sweetness of spring in thine hair, and the light in
    thine eyes.
The light of the spring in thine eyes, and the sound in
    thine ears;
Yet thine heart shall wax heavy with sighs and thine
    eyelids with tears.
Wilt thou cover thine hair with gold, and with silver
    thy feet?
Hast thou taken the purple to fold thee, and made
    thy mouth sweet?
Behold, when thy face is made bare, he that loved
    thee shall hate;
Thy face shall be no more fair at the fall of thy fate.
For thy life shall fall as a leaf and be shed as the rain;
And the veil of thine head shall be grief; and the
    crown shall be pain.

ALTHÆA

Ho, ye that wail, and ye that sing, make way
Till I be come among you. Hide your tears,

Ye little weepers, and your laughing lips,
Ye laughers for a little; lo mine eyes
That outweep heaven at rainiest, and my mouth
That laughs as gods laugh at us. Fate's are we,
Yet fate is ours a breathing-space; yea, mine,
Fate is made mine for ever; he is my son,
My bedfellow, my brother. You strong gods,
Give place unto me; I am as any of you,
To give life and to take life. Thou, old earth,
That hast made man and unmade; thou whose mouth
Looks red from the eaten fruits of thine own womb;
Behold me with what lips upon what food
I feed and fill my body; even with flesh
Made of my body. Lo, the fire I lit
I burn with fire to quench it; yea, with flame
I burn up even the dust and ash thereof.

CHORUS

Woman, what fire is this thou burnest with?

ALTHÆA

Yea to the bone, yea to the blood and all.

CHORUS

For this thy face and hair are as one fire.

ALTHÆA

A tongue that licks and beats upon the dust.

CHORUS

And in thine eyes are hollow light and heat.

ALTHÆA

Of flame not fed with hand or frankincense.

CHORUS

I fear thee for the trembling of thine eyes.

ALTHÆA

Neither with love they tremble nor for fear.

CHORUS

And thy mouth shuddering like a shot bird.

ALTHÆA

Not as the bride's mouth when man kisses it.

CHORUS

Nay, but what thing is this thing thou hast done?

ALTHÆA

Look, I am silent, speak your eyes for me.

CHORUS

I see a faint fire lightening from the hall.

ALTHÆA

Gaze, stretch your eyes, strain till the lids drop off.

CHORUS

Flushed pillars down the flickering vestibule.

ALTHÆA

Stretch with your necks like birds: cry, chirp as they.

CHORUS

And a long brand that blackens: and white dust.

ALTHÆA

O children, what is this ye see? your eyes
Are blinder than night's face at fall of moon.
That is my son, my flesh, my fruit of life,
My travail, and the year's weight of my womb.
Meleager, a fire enkindled of mine hands
And of mine hands extinguished; this is he.

CHORUS

O gods, what word has flown out at thy mouth?

ALTHÆA

I did this and I say this and I die.

CHORUS

Death stands upon the doorway of thy lips,
And in thy mouth has death set up his house.

ALTHÆA

O death, a little, a little while, sweet death,
Until I see the brand burnt down and die.

CHORUS

She reels as any reed under the wind,
And cleaves unto the ground with staggering feet.

ALTHÆA

Girls, one thing will I say and hold my peace.
I that did this will weep not nor cry out,
Cry ye and weep: I will not call on gods,
Call ye on them; I will not pity man,
Shew ye your pity. I know not if I live;
Save that I feel the fire upon my face
And on my cheek the burning of a brand.

Yea the smoke bites me, yea I drink the steam
With nostril and with eyelid and with lip
Insatiate and intolerant; and mine hands
Burn, and fire feeds upon mine eyes; I reel
As one made drunk with living, whence he draws
Drunken delight; yet I, though mad for joy,
Loathe my long living and am waxen red
As with the shadow of shed blood; behold,
I am kindled with the flames that fade in him,
I am swollen with subsiding of his veins,
I am flooded with his ebbing; my lit eyes
Flame with the falling fire that leaves his lids
Bloodless; my cheek is luminous with blood
Because his face is ashen. Yet, O child,
Son, first-born, fairest—O sweet mouth, sweet eyes,
That drew my life out through my suckling breast,
That shone and clove mine heart through—O soft
        knees
Clinging, O tender treadings of soft feet,
Cheeks warm with little kissings—O child, child,
What have we made each other? Lo, I felt
Thy weight cleave to me, a burden of beauty, O son,
Thy cradled brows and loveliest loving lips,
The floral hair, the little lightening eyes,
And all thy goodly glory; with mine hands
Delicately I fed thee, with my tongue
Tenderly spake, saying, Verily in God's time,
For all the little likeness of thy limbs,
Son, I shall make thee a kingly man to fight,
A lordly leader; and hear before I die,
'She bore the goodliest sword of all the world.'
Oh! oh! For all my life turns round on me;
I am severed from myself, my name is gone,
My name that was a healing, it is changed,

My name is a consuming. From this time,
Though mine eyes reach to the end of all these things,
My lips shall not unfasten till I die.

SEMICHORUS

She has filled with sighing the city,
    And the ways thereof with tears;
She arose, she girdled her sides,
She set her face as a bride's;
She wept, and she had no pity;
    Trembled, and felt no fears.

SEMICHORUS

Her eyes were clear as the sun,
    Her brows were fresh as the day;
She girdled herself with gold,
Her robes were manifold;
But the days of her worship are done,
    Her praise is taken away.

SEMICHORUS

For she set her hand to the fire,
    With her mouth she kindled the same;
As the mouth of a flute-player,
So was the mouth of her;
With the might of her strong desire
    She blew the breath of the flame.

SEMICHORUS

She set her hand to the wood,
    She took the fire in her hand;
As one who is nigh to death,
She panted with strange breath;
She opened her lips unto blood,
    She breathed and kindled the brand.

SEMICHORUS

As a wood-dove newly shot,
    She sobbed and lifted her breast;
She sighed and covered her eyes,
Filling her lips with sighs;
She sighed, she withdrew herself not,
    She refrained not, taking not rest;

SEMICHORUS

But as the wind which is drouth,
    And as the air which is death,
As storm that severeth ships,
Her breath severing her lips,
The breath came forth of her mouth
    And the fire came forth of her breath.

SECOND MESSENGER

Queen, and you maidens, there is come on us
A thing more deadly than the face of death;
Meleager the good lord is as one slain.

SEMICHORUS

Without sword, without sword is he stricken;
    Slain, and slain without hand.

SECOND MESSENGER

For as keen ice divided of the sun
His limbs divide, and as thawed snow the flesh
Thaws from off all his body to the hair.

SEMICHORUS

He wastes as the embers quicken;
    With the brand he fades as a brand.

SECOND MESSENGER

Even while they sang and all drew hither and he
Lifted both hands to crown the Arcadian's hair
And fix the looser leaves, both hands fell down.

SEMICHORUS

With rending of cheek and of hair
Lament ye, mourn for him, weep.

SECOND MESSENGER

Straightway the crown slid off and smote on earth,
First fallen; and he, grasping his own hair, groaned
And cast his raiment round his face and fell.

SEMICHORUS

Alas for visions that were,
And soothsayings spoken in sleep.

SECOND MESSENGER

But the king twitched his reins in and leapt down
And caught him, crying out twice 'O child' and
    thrice,
So that men's eyelids thickened with their tears.

SEMICHORUS

Lament with a long lamentation,
Cry, for an end is at hand.

SECOND MESSENGER

O son, he said, son, lift thine eyes, draw breath,
Pity me; but Meleager with sharp lips
Gasped, and his face waxed like as sunburnt grass.

SEMICHORUS

Cry aloud, O thou kingdom, O nation.
O stricken, a ruinous land.

SECOND MESSENGER

Whereat king Œneus, straightening feeble knees,
With feeble hands heaved up a lessening weight,
And laid him sadly in strange hands, and wept.

SEMICHORUS

Thou art smitten, her lord, her desire,
Thy dear blood wasted as rain.

SECOND MESSENGER

And they with tears and rendings of the beard
Bear hither a breathing body, wept upon
And lightening at each footfall, sick to death.

SEMICHORUS

Thou madest thy sword as a fire,
With fire for a sword thou art slain.

SECOND MESSENGER

And lo, the feast turned funeral, and the crowns
Fallen; and the huntress and the hunter trapped;
And weeping and changed faces and veiled hair.

MELEAGER

Let your hands meet
Round the weight of my head;
Lift ye my feet
As the feet of the dead;
For the flesh of my body is molten, the limbs of it
molten as lead.

CHORUS

O thy luminous face.
Thine imperious eyes!
O the grief, O the grace,

As of day when it dies!
Who is this bending over thee, lord, with tears and
    suppression of sighs?

MELEAGER

Is a bride so fair?
Is a maid so meek?
With unchapleted hair,
With unfilleted cheek,
Atalanta, the pure among women, whose name is as
    blessing to speak.

ATALANTA

I would that with feet
Unsandalled, unshod,
Overbold, overfleet,
I had swum not nor trod
From Arcadia to Calydon northward, a blast of the
    envy of God.

MELEAGER

Unto each man his fate;
Unto each as he saith
In whose fingers the weight
Of the world is as breath;
Yet I would that in clamour of battle mine hands had
    laid hold upon death.

CHORUS

Not with cleaving of shields
And their clash in thine ear,
When the lord of fought fields
Breaketh spearshaft from spear,
Thou art broken, our lord, thou art broken, with
    travail and labour and fear.

MELEAGER

Would God he had found me
　　Beneath fresh boughs!
Would God he had bound me
　　Unawares in mine house,
With light in mine eyes, and songs in my lips, and a
　　crown on my brows!

CHORUS

Whence art thou sent from us?
　　Whither thy goal?
How art thou rent from us,
　　Thou that wert whole,
As with severing of eyelids and eyes, as with sundering
　　of body and soul!

MELEAGER

My heart is within me
　　As an ash in the fire;
Whosoever hath seen me,
　　Without lute, without lyre,
Shall sing of me grievous things, even things that were
　　ill to desire.

CHORUS

Who shall raise thee
　　From the house of the dead?
Or what man praise thee
　　That thy praise may be said?
Alas thy beauty! alas thy body! alas thine head!

MELEAGER

But thou, O mother,
　　The dreamer of dreams,

Wilt thou bring forth another
      To feel the sun's beams
When I move among shadows a shadow, and wail by
      impassable streams?

CENEUS

What thing wilt thou leave me
      Now this thing is done?
A man wilt thou give me,
      A son for my son,
For the light of mine eyes, the desire of my life, the
      desirable one?

CHORUS

Thou wert glad above others,
      Yea, fair beyond word;
Thou wert glad among mothers;
      For each man that heard
Of thee, praise there was added unto thee, as wings to
      the feet of a bird.

CENEUS

Who shall give back
      Thy face of old years,
With travail made black,
      Grown grey among fears,
Mother of sorrow, mother of cursing, mother of tears?

MELEAGER

Though thou art as fire
      Fed with fuel in vain,
My delight, my desire,
      Is more chaste than the rain,
More pure than the dewfall, more holy than stars are
      that live without stain.

ATALANTA

I would that as water
        My life's blood had thawn,
Or as winter's wan daughter
        Leaves lowland and lawn
Spring-stricken, or ever mine eyes had beheld thee
        made dark in thy dawn.

CHORUS

When thou dravest the men
        Of the chosen of Thrace,
None turned him again
        Nor endured he thy face
Clothed round with the blush of the battle, with light
        from a terrible place.

ŒNEUS

Thou shouldst die as he dies
        For whom none sheddeth **tears;**
Filling thine eyes
        And fulfilling thine ears
With the brilliance of battle, the bloom and the
        beauty, the splendour of spears.

CHORUS

In the ears of the world
        It is sung, it is told,
And the light thereof hurled
        And the noise thereof rolled
From the Acroceraunian snow to the ford of the fleece
        of gold.

MELEAGER

Would God ye could carry me
        Forth of all these;

Heap sand and bury me
By the Chersonese
Where the thundering Bosphorus answers the thunder
of Pontic seas.

ŒNEUS

Dost thou mock at our praise
And the singing begun
And the men of strange days
Praising my son
In the folds of the hills of home, high places of Caly-
don?

MELEAGER

For the dead man no home is;
Ah, better to be
What the flower of the foam is
In fields of the sea,
That the sea-waves might be as my raiment, the gulf-
stream a garment for me.

CHORUS

Who shall seek thee and bring
And restore thee thy day,
When the dove dipt her wing
And the oars won their way
Where the narrowing Symplegades whitened the
straits of Propontis with spray?

MELEAGER

Will ye crown me my tomb
Or exalt me my name,
Now my spirits consume,

Now my flesh is a flame?
Let the sea slake it once, and men speak of me sleeping
    to praise me or shame.

CHORUS

Turn back now, turn thee,
    As who turns him to wake;
Though the life in thee burn thee,
    Couldst thou bathe it and slake
Where the sea-ridge of Helle hangs heavier, and east
    upon west waters break?

MELEAGER

Would the winds blow me back
    Or the waves hurl me home?
Ah, to touch in the track
    Where the pine learnt to roam
Cold girdles and crowns of the sea-gods, cool blossoms
    of water and foam!

CHORUS

The gods may release
    That they made fast;
Thy soul shall have ease
    In thy limbs at the last;
But what shall they give thee for life, sweet life that is
    overpast?

MELEAGER

Not the life of men's veins,
    Not of flesh that conceives;
But the grace that remains,
    The fair beauty that cleaves
To the life of the rains in the grasses, the life of the
    dews on the leaves.

CHORUS

Thou wert helmsman and chief;
    Wilt thou turn in an hour,
Thy limbs to the leaf,
    Thy face to the flower,
Thy blood to the water, thy soul to the gods who
    divide and devour?

MELEAGER

The years are hungry,
    They wail all their days;
The gods wax angry
    And weary of praise;
And who shall bridle their lips? and who shall straiten
    their ways?

CHORUS

The gods guard over us
    With sword and with rod;
Weaving shadow to cover us,
    Heaping the sod,
That law may fulfil herself wholly, to darken man's
    face before God.

MELEAGER

O holy head of Œneus, lo thy son
Guiltless, yet red from alien guilt, yet foul
With kinship of contaminated lives,
Lo, for their blood I die; and mine own blood
For bloodshedding of mine is mixed therewith,
That death may not discern me from my kin.
Yet with clean heart I die and faultless hand,
Not shamefully; thou therefore of thy love
Salute me, and bid fare among the dead

Well, as the dead fare; for the best man dead
Fares sadly; nathless I now faring well
Pass without fear where nothing is to fear
Having thy love about me and thy goodwill,
O father, among dark places and men dead.

CENEUS

Child, I salute thee with sad heart and tears,
And bid thee comfort, being a perfect man
In fight, and honourable in the house of peace.
The gods give thee fair wage and dues of death,
And me brief days and ways to come at thee.

MELEAGER

Pray thou thy days be long before thy death,
And full of ease and kingdom; seeing in death
There is no comfort and none aftergrowth,
Nor shall one thence look up and see day's dawn
Nor light upon the land whither I go.
Live thou and take thy fill of days and die
When thy day comes; and make not much of death
Lest ere thy day thou reap an evil thing.
Thou too, the bitter mother and mother-plague
Of this my weary body—thou too, queen,
The source and end, the sower and the scythe,
The rain that ripens and the drought that slays,
The sand that swallows and the spring that feeds,
To make me and unmake me—thou, I say,
Althæa, since my father's ploughshare, drawn
Through fatal seedland of a female field,
Furrowed thy body, whence a wheaten ear
Strong from the sun and fragrant from the rains
I sprang and cleft the closure of thy womb,
Mother, I dying with unforgetful tongue

Hail thee as holy and worship thee as just
Who art unjust and unholy; and with my knees
Would worship, but thy fire and subtlety,
Dissundering them, devour me; for these limbs
Are as light dust and crumblings from mine urn
Before the fire has touched them; and my face
As a dead leaf or dead foot's mark on snow,
And all this body a broken barren tree
That was so strong, and all this flower of life
Disbranched and desecrated miserably,
And minished all that god-like muscle and might
And lesser than a man's: for all my veins
Fail me, and all mine ashen life burns down.
I would thou hadst let me live; but gods averse,
But fortune, and the fiery feet of change,
And time, these would not, these tread out my life,
These and not thou; me too thou hast loved, and I
Thee; but this death was mixed with all my life,
Mine end with my beginning; and this law,
This only, slays me, and not my mother at all.
And let no brother or sister grieve too sore,
Nor melt their hearts out on me with their tears,
Since extreme love and sorrowing overmuch
Vex the great gods, and overloving men
Slay and are slain for love's sake; and this house
Shall bear much better children; why should these
Weep? but in patience let them live their lives
And mine pass by forgotten: thou alone,
Mother, thou sole and only, thou not these,
Keep me in mind a little when I die
Because I was thy first-born; let thy soul
Pity me, pity even me gone hence and dead,
Though thou wert wroth, and though thou bear again
Much happier sons, and all men later born

Exceedingly excel me; yet do thou
Forget not, nor think shame; I was thy son.
Time was I did not shame thee; and time was
I thought to live and make thee honourable
With deeds as great as these men's; but they live,
These, and I die; and what thing should have been
Surely I know not; yet I charge thee, seeing
I am dead already, love me not the less,
Me, O my mother; I charge thee by these gods,
My father's, and that holier breast of thine,
By these that see me dying, and that which nursed,
Love me not less, thy first-born: though grief come,
Grief only, of me, and of all these great joy,
And shall come always to thee; for thou knowest,
O mother, O breasts that bare me, for ye know,
O sweet head of my mother, sacred eyes,
Ye know my soul albeit I sinned, ye know
Albeit I kneel not neither touch thy knees,
But with my lips I kneel, and with my heart
I fall about thy feet and worship thee.
And ye farewell now, all my friends; and ye,
Kinsmen, much younger and glorious more than I,
Sons of my mother's sister; and all farewell
That were in Colchis with me, and bare down
The waves and wars that met us: and though times
Change, and though now I be not anything,
Forget not me among you, what I did
In my good time; for even by all those days,
Those days and this, and your own living souls,
And by the light and luck of you that live,
And by this miserable spoil, and me
Dying, I beseech you, let my name not die.
But thou, dear, touch me with thy rose-like hands.
And fasten up mine eyelids with thy mouth,

A bitter kiss; and grasp me with thine arms,
Printing with heavy lips my light waste flesh,
Made light and thin by heavy-handed fate,
And with thine holy maiden eyes drop dew,
Drop tears for dew upon me who am dead,
Me who have loved thee; seeing without sin done
I am gone down to the empty weary house
Where no flesh is nor beauty nor swift eyes
Nor sound of mouth nor might of hands and feet.
But thou, dear, hide my body with thy veil,
And with thy raiment cover foot and head,
And stretch thyself upon me and touch hands
With hands and lips with lips: be pitiful
As thou art maiden perfect; let no man
Defile me to despise me, saying, This man
Died woman-wise, a woman's offering, slain
Through female fingers in his woof of life,
Dishonourable; for thou hast honoured me.
And now for God's sake kiss me once and twice
And let me go; for the night gathers me,
And in the night shall no man gather fruit.

ATALANTA

Hail thou: but I with heavy face and feet
Turn homeward and am gone out of thine eyes.

CHORUS

Who shall contend with his lords
    Or cross them or do them wrong?
Who shall bind them as with cords?
    Who shall tame them as with song?
Who shall smite them as with swords?
    For the hands of their kingdom are strong.

FROM 'ERECHTHEUS': ATHENS

SUN, that hast lightened and loosed by thy might
Ocean and Earth from the lordship of night,
Quickening with vision his eye that was veiled,
Freshening the force in her heart that had failed,
That sister fettered and blinded brother
Should have sight by thy grace and delight of each
      other,
  Behold now and see
 What profit is given them of thee;
What wrath has enkindled with madness of mind
Her limbs that were bounden, his face that was blind,
To be locked as in wrestle together, and lighten
With fire that shall darken thy fire in the sky,
Body to body and eye against eye
    In a war against kind,
Till the bloom of her fields and her high hills whiten
 With the foam of his waves more high.
For the sea-marks set to divide of old
The kingdoms to Ocean and Earth assigned,
The hoar sea-fields from the cornfields' gold,
His wine-bright waves from her vineyards' fold,
    Frail forces we find
To bridle the spirit of Gods or bind
 Till the heat of their hearts wax cold.
But the peace that was stablished between them to
    stand
Is rent now in twain by the strength of his hand
Who stirs up the storm of his sons overbold
To pluck from fight what he lost of right,
By council and judgment of Gods that spake
And gave great Pallas the strife's fair stake,
The lordship and love of the lovely land,

The grace of the town that hath on it for crown
    But a headband to wear
  Of violets one-hued with her hair:
For the vales and the green high places of earth
    Hold nothing so fair,
And the depths of the sea bear no such birth
  Of the manifold births they bear.
Too well, too well was the great stake worth
A strife divine for the Gods to judge,
A crowned God's triumph, a foiled God's grudge,
Though the loser be strong and the victress wise
Who played long since for so large a prize,
The fruitful immortal anointed adored
Dear city of men without master or lord,
Fair fortress and fostress of sons born free,
Who stand in her sight and in thine, O sun,
Slaves of no man, subjects of none;
A wonder enthroned on the hills and sea,
A maiden crowned with a fourfold glory
That none from the pride of her head may rend,
Violet and olive-leaf purple and hoary,
Song-wreath and story the fairest of fame,
Flowers that the winter can blast not or bend;
A light upon earth as the sun's own flame,
    A name as his name,
  Athens, a praise without end.

HOPE AND FEAR

BENEATH the shadow of dawn's aerial cope,
  With eyes enkindled as the sun's own sphere,
  Hope from the front of youth in godlike cheer
Looks Godward, past the shades where blind men
    grope

Round the dark door that prayers nor dreams can
    ope,
  And makes for joy the very darkness dear
  That gives her wide wings play; nor dreams that
    fear
At noon may rise and pierce the heart of hope.
Then, when the soul leaves off to dream and yearn,
May truth first purge her eyesight to discern
  What once being known leaves time no power to
    appal;
Till youth at last, ere yet youth be not, learn
  The kind wise word that falls from years that fall—
  'Hope thou not much, and fear thou not at all.'

A DEATH ON EASTER DAY[1]

THE strong spring sun rejoicingly may rise,
  Rise and make revel, as of old men said,
  Like dancing hearts of lovers newly wed:
A light more bright than ever bathed the skies
Departs for all time out of all men's eyes.
  The crowns that girt last night a living head
  Shine only now, though deathless, on the dead:
Art that mocks death, and Song that never dies.
Albeit the bright sweet mothlike wings be furled,
  Hope sees, past all division and defection,
    And higher than swims the mist of human breath,
The soul most radiant once in all the world
  Requickened to regenerate resurrection
    Out of the likeness of the shadow of death.

April 1882.

    [1] Dante Gabriel Rossetti died 9 April 1882.

ON THE DEATHS OF THOMAS CARLYLE
AND GEORGE ELIOT

Two souls diverse out of our human sight
  Pass, followed one with love and each with wonder:
  The stormy sophist with his mouth of thunder,
Clothed with loud words and mantled in the might
Of darkness and magnificence of night;
  And one whose eye could smite the night in sunder,
  Searching if light or no light were thereunder,
And found in love of loving-kindness light.
Duty divine and Thought with eyes of fire
Still following Righteousness with deep desire
  Shone sole and stern before her and above,
Sure stars and sole to steer by; but more sweet
Shone lower the loveliest lamp for earthly feet,
  The light of little children, and their love.

ON THE RUSSIAN PERSECUTION OF
THE JEWS

O son of man, by lying tongues adored,
  By slaughterous hands of slaves with feet red-shod
  In carnage deep as ever Christian trod
Profaned with prayer and sacrifice abhorred
And incense from the trembling tyrant's horde,
  Brute worshippers or wielders of the rod,
  Most murderous even of all that call thee God,
Most treacherous even that ever called thee Lord;
Face loved of little children long ago,
  Head hated of the priests and rulers then,
    If thou see this, or hear these hounds of thine
    Run ravening as the Gadarean swine,
Say, was not this thy Passion, to foreknow
  In death's worst hour the works of Christian men?
January 23, 1882.

ADIEUX À MARIE STUART

I

Queen, for whose house my fathers fought,
    With hopes that rose and fell,
Red star of boyhood's fiery thought,
    Farewell.

They gave their lives, and I, my queen,
    Have given you of my life,
Seeing your brave star burn high between
    Men's strife.

The strife that lightened round their spears
    Long since fell still: so long
Hardly may hope to last in years
    My song.

But still through strife of time and thought
    Your light on me too fell:
Queen, in whose name we sang or fought,
    Farewell.

II

There beats no heart on either border
    Wherethrough the north blasts blow
But keeps your memory as a warder
    His beacon-fire aglow.

Long since it fired with love and wonder
    Mine, for whose April age
Blithe midsummer made banquet under
    The shade of Hermitage.

Soft sang the burn's blithe notes, that gather
    Strength to ring true:
And air and trees and sun and heather
    Remembered you.

Old border ghosts of fight or fairy
    Or love or teen,
These they forgot, remembering Mary
    The Queen.

III

Queen once of Scots and ever of ours
    Whose sires brought forth for you
Their lives to strew your way like flowers,
    Adieu.

Dead is full many a dead man's name
    Who died for you this long
Time past: shall this too fare the same,
    My song?

But surely, though it die or live,
    Your face was worth
All that a man may think to give
    On earth.

No darkness cast of years between
    Can darken you:
Man's love will never bid my queen
    Adieu.

IV

Love hangs like light about your name
    As music round the shell:
No heart can take of you a tame
    Farewell.

Yet, when your very face was seen,
 Ill gifts were yours for giving:
Love gat strange guerdons of my queen
 When living.

O diamond heart unflawed and clear,
 The whole world's crowning jewel!
Was ever heart so deadly dear
 So cruel?

Yet none for you of all that bled
 Grudged once one drop that fell:
Not one to life reluctant said
 Farewell.

V

Strange love they have given you, love disloyal,
 Who mock with praise your name,
To leave a head so rare and royal
 Too low for praise or blame.

You could not love nor hate, they tell us,
 You had nor sense nor sting:
In God's name, then, what plague befell us
 To fight for such a thing?

'Some faults the gods will give,' to fetter
 Man's highest intent:
But surely you were something better
 Than innocent!

No maid that strays with steps unwary
 Through snares unseen,
But one to live and die for; Mary,
 The Queen.

VI

Forgive them all their praise, who blot
    Your fame with praise of you:
Then love may say, and falter not,
    Adieu.

Yet some you hardly would forgive
    Who did you much less wrong
Once: but resentment should not live
    Too long.

They never saw your lip's bright bow,
    Your swordbright eyes,
The bluest of heavenly things below
    The skies.

Clear eyes that love's self finds most like
    A swordblade's blue,
A swordblade's ever keen to strike,
    Adieu.

VII

Though all things breathe or sound of fight
    That yet make up your spell,
To bid you were to bid the light
    Farewell.

Farewell the song says only, being
    A star whose race is run:
Farewell the soul says never, seeing
    The sun.

Yet, wellnigh as with flash of tears,
    The song must say but so
That took your praise up twenty years
    Ago.

More bright than stars or moons that vary,
   Sun kindling heaven and hell,
Here, after all these years, Queen Mary,
   Farewell.

A CHILD'S LAUGHTER

ALL the bells of heaven may ring,
All the birds of heaven may sing,
All the wells on earth may spring,
All the winds on earth may bring
   All sweet sounds together;
Sweeter far than all things heard,
Hand of harper, tone of bird,
Sound of woods at sundawn stirred,
Welling water's winsome word,
   Wind in warm wan weather,

One thing yet there is, that none
Hearing ere its chime be done
Knows not well the sweetest one
Heard of man beneath the sun,
   Hoped in heaven hereafter;
Soft and strong and loud and light,
Very sound of very light
Heard from morning's rosiest height,
When the soul of all delight
   Fills a child's clear laughter.

Golden bells of welcome rolled
Never forth such notes, nor told
Hours so blithe in tones so bold,
As the radiant mouth of gold

Here that rings forth heaven.
If the golden-crested wren
Were a nightingale—why, then,
Something seen and heard of men
Might be half as sweet as when
Laughs a child of seven.

DRAMATIC POETS

I

CHRISTOPHER MARLOWE

CROWNED, girdled, garbed and shod with light and fire,
Son first-born of the morning, sovereign star!
Soul nearest ours of all, that wert most far,
Most far off in the abysm of time, thy lyre
Hung highest above the dawn-enkindled quire
Where all ye sang together, all that are,
And all the starry songs behind thy car
Rang sequence, all our souls acclaim thee sire.

'If all the pens that ever poets held
Had fed the feeling of their masters' thoughts,'
And as with rush of hurtling chariots
The flight of all their spirits were impelled
Toward one great end, thy glory—nay, not then,
Not yet might'st thou be praised enough of men.

II

WILLIAM SHAKESPEARE

NOT if men's tongues and angels' all in one
Spake, might the word be said that might speak
Thee.

Streams, winds, woods, flowers, fields, mountains,
    yea, the sea,
What power is in them all to praise the sun?
His praise is this,—he can be praised of none.
    Man, woman, child, praise God for him; but he
    Exults not to be worshipped, but to be.
He is; and, being, beholds his work well done.
All joy, all glory, all sorrow, all strength, all mirth,
Are his: without him, day were night on earth.
    Time knows not his from time's own period.
All lutes, all harps, all viols, all flutes, all lyres,
Fall dumb before him ere one string suspires.
    All stars are angels; but the sun is God.

III

BEN JONSON

BROAD-BASED, broad-fronted, bounteous, multiform,
    With many a valley impleached with ivy and vine,
    Wherein the springs of all the streams run wine,
And many a crag full-faced against the storm,
The mountain where thy Muse's feet made warm
    Those lawns that revelled with her dance divine
    Shines yet with fire as it was wont to shine
From tossing torches round the dance aswarm.

Nor less, high-stationed on the grey grave heights,
High-thoughted seers with heaven's heart-kindling
        lights
    Hold converse: and the herd of meaner things
Knows or by fiery scourge or fiery shaft
When wrath on thy broad brows has risen, and
        laughed
    Darkening thy soul with shadow of thunderous
        wings.

IV

BEAUMONT AND FLETCHER

An hour ere sudden sunset fired the west,
  Arose two stars upon the pale deep east.
  The hall of heaven was clear for night's high feast,
Yet was not yet day's fiery heart at rest.
Love leapt up from his mother's burning breast
  To see those warm twin lights, as day decreased,
  Wax wider, till when all the sun had ceased
As suns they shone from evening's kindled crest.
Across them and between, a quickening fire,
Flamed Venus, laughing with appeased desire.
  Their dawn, scarce lovelier for the gleam of tears,
Filled half the hollow shell 'twixt heaven and earth
With sound like moonlight, mingling moan and mirth,
  Which rings and glitters down the darkling years.

V

PHILIP MASSINGER

Clouds here and there arisen an hour past noon
  Chequered our English heaven with lengthening
    bars
  And shadow and sound of wheel-winged thunder-
    cars
Assembling strength to put forth tempest soon,
When the clear still warm concord of thy tune
  Rose under skies unscared by reddening Mars
  Yet, like a sound of silver speech of stars,
With full mild flame as of the mellowing moon.
Grave and great-hearted Massinger, thy face
High melancholy lights with loftier grace
  Than gilds the brows of revel: sad and wise,

The spirit of thought that moved thy deeper song,
Sorrow serene in soft calm scorn of wrong,
  Speaks patience yet from thy majestic eyes.

VI

JOHN FORD

HEW hard the marble from the mountain's heart
  Where hardest night holds fast in iron gloom
  Gems brighter than an April dawn in bloom,
That his Memnonian likeness thence may start
Revealed, whose hand with high funereal art
  Carved night, and chiselled shadow: be the tomb
  That speaks him famous graven with signs of doom
Intrenched inevitably in lines athwart,
As on some thunder-blasted Titan's brow
  His record of rebellion. Not the day
    Shall strike forth music from so stern a chord,
Touching this marble: darkness, none knows how,
  And stars impenetrable of midnight, may.
    So looms the likeness of thy soul, John Ford.

VII

JOHN WEBSTER

THUNDER: the flesh quails, and the soul bows down.
  Night: east, west, south, and northward, very night.
  Star upon struggling star strives into sight,
Star after shuddering star the deep storms drown.
The very throne of night, her very crown,
  A man lays hands on, and usurps her right.
    Song from the highest of heaven's imperious height
Shoots, as a fire to smite some towering town.

Rage, anguish, harrowing fear, heart-crazing crime,
Make monstrous all the murderous face of Time
  Shown in the spheral orbit of a glass
Revolving. Earth cries out from all her graves.
Frail, on frail rafts, across wide-wallowing waves,
  Shapes here and there of child and mother pass.

VIII

THOMAS DEKKER

OUT of the depths of darkling life where sin
  Laughs piteously that sorrow should not know
  Her own ill name, nor woe be counted woe;
Where hate and craft and lust make drearier din
Than sounds through dreams that grief holds revel in;
  What charm of joy-bells ringing, streams that flow,
  Winds that blow healing in each note they blow,
Is this that the outer darkness hears begin?

O sweetest heart of all thy time save one,
Star seen for love's sake nearest to the sun,
  Hung lamplike o'er a dense and doleful city,
Not Shakespeare's very spirit, howe'er more great,
Than thine toward man was more compassionate,
  Nor gave Christ praise from lips more sweet with
    pity.

IX

THOMAS MIDDLETON

A WILD moon riding high from cloud to cloud,
  That sees and sees not, glimmering far beneath,
  Hell's children revel along the shuddering heath
With dirge-like mirth and raiment like a shroud:

A worse fair face than witchcraft's, passion-proud,
　　With brows blood-flecked behind their bridal
　　　wreath
　　And lips that bade the assassin's sword find sheath
Deep in the heart whereto love's heart was vowed:
A game of close contentious crafts and creeds
　　Played till white England bring black Spain to
　　　shame:
A son's bright sword and brighter soul, whose deeds
　　High conscience lights for mother's love and fame:
Pure gipsy flowers, and poisonous courtly weeds:
　　Such tokens and such trophies crown thy name.

X

THOMAS HEYWOOD

Tom, if they loved thee best who called thee Tom,
　　What else may all men call thee, seeing thus bright
　　Even yet the laughing and the weeping light
That still thy kind old eyes are kindled from?
Small care was thine to assail and overcome
　　Time and his child Oblivion: yet of right
　　Thy name has part with names of lordlier might
For English love and homely sense of home,
Whose fragrance keeps thy small sweet bayleaf young
　　And gives it place aloft among thy peers
　　　Whence many a wreath once higher strong Time
　　　　has hurled:
And this thy praise is sweet on Shakespeare's tongue—
　　'O good old man, how well in thee appears
　　　The constant service of the antique world!'

XI

GEORGE CHAPMAN

HIGH priest of Homer, not elect in vain,
  Deep trumpets blow before thee, shawms behind
  Mix music with the rolling wheels that wind
Slow through the labouring triumph of thy train:
Fierce history, molten in thy forging brain,
  Takes form and fire and fashion from thy mind,
  Tormented and transmuted out of kind:
But howsoe'er thou shift thy strenuous strain,
Like Tailor[1] smooth, like Fisher[2] swollen, and now
Grim Yarrington[3] scarce bloodier marked than
      thou,
  Then bluff as Mayne's[4] or broad-mouthed Barry's[5]
      glee;
Proud still with hoar predominance of brow
  And beard like foam swept off the broad blown sea,
  Where'er thou go, men's reverence goes with thee.

XII

JOHN MARSTON

THE bitterness of death and bitterer scorn
  Breathes from the broad-leafed aloe-plant whence
      thou
  Wast fain to gather for thy bended brow
A chaplet by no gentler forehead worn.
Grief deep as hell, wrath hardly to be borne,

---

[1] Author of *The Hog hath lost his Pearl.*
[2] Author of *Fuimus Troes, or the True Trojans.*
[3] Author of *Two Tragedies in One.*
[4] Author of *The City Match.*
[5] Author of *Ram-Alley, or Merry Tricks.*

Ploughed up thy soul till round the furrowing
 plough
The strange black soil foamed, as a black beaked
 prow
Bids night-black waves foam where its track has torn.
Too faint the phrase for thee that only saith
Scorn bitterer than the bitterness of death
 Pervades the sullen splendour of thy soul,
Where hate and pain make war on force and fraud
And all the strengths of tyrants; whence unflawed
 It keeps this noble heart of hatred whole.

XIII

JOHN DAY

DAY was a full-blown flower in heaven, alive
 With murmuring joy of bees and birds aswarm,
 When in the skies of song yet flushed and warm
With music where all passion seems to strive
For utterance, all things bright and fierce to drive
 Struggling along the splendour of the storm,
 Day for an hour put off his fiery form,
And golden murmurs from a golden hive
Across the strong bright summer wind were heard,
 And laughter soft as smiles from girls at play
 And loud from lips of boys brow-bound with May
Our mightiest age let fall its gentlest word,
When song, in semblance of a sweet small bird,
 Lit fluttering on the light swift hand of Day.

XIV

JAMES SHIRLEY

THE dusk of day's decline was hard on dark
 When evening trembled round thy glowworm lamp

That shone across her shades and dewy damp
A small clear beacon whose benignant spark
Was gracious yet for loiterers' eyes to mark,
    Though changed the watchword of our English
      camp
    Since the outposts rang round Marlowe's lion ramp,
When thy steed's pace went ambling round Hyde
    Park.

And in the thickening twilight under thee
Walks Davenant, pensive in the paths where he,
    The blithest throat that ever carolled love
      In music made of morning's merriest heart,
    Glad Suckling, stumbled from his seat above
      And reeled on slippery roads of alien art.

XV

THE TRIBE OF BENJAMIN

Sons born of many a loyal Muse to Ben,
    All true-begotten, warm with wine or ale,
    Bright from the broad light of his presence, hail!
Prince Randolph, nighest his throne of all his men,
Being highest in spirit and heart who hailed him then
    King, nor might other spread so blithe a sail:
    Cartwright, a soul pent in with narrower pale,
Praised of thy sire for manful might of pen:
Marmion, whose verse keeps alway keen and fine
The perfume of their Apollonian wine
    Who shared with that stout sire of all and thee
The exuberant chalice of his echoing shrine:
    Is not your praise writ broad in gold which he
    Inscribed, that all who praise his name should see?

XVI

ANONYMOUS PLAYS:

'ARDEN OF FEVERSHAM'

MOTHER whose womb brought forth our man of men,
  Mother of Shakespeare, whom all time acclaims
  Queen therefore, sovereign queen of English dames,
Throned higher than sat thy sonless empress then,
Was it thy son's young passion-guided pen
  Which drew, reflected from encircling flames,
  A figure marked by the earlier of thy names
Wife, and from all her wedded kinswomen
Marked by the sign of murderess? Pale and great,
  Great in her grief and sin, but in her death
  And anguish of her penitential breath
Greater than all her sin or sin-born fate,
  She stands, the holocaust of dark desire,
  Clothed round with song for ever as with fire.

XVII

ANONYMOUS PLAYS

YE too, dim watchfires of some darkling hour,
  Whose fame forlorn time saves not nor proclaims
  For ever, but forgetfulness defames
And darkness and the shadow of death devour,
Lift up ye too your light, put forth your power,
  Let the far twilight feel your soft small flames
  And smile, albeit night name not even their names,
Ghost by ghost passing, flower blown down on flower:
That sweet-tongued shadow, like a star's that passed
Singing, and light was from its darkness cast

To paint the face of Painting fair with praise:[1]
And that wherein forefigured smiles the pure
Fraternal face of Wordsworth's Elidure
   Between two child-faced masks of merrier days.[2]

XVIII

ANONYMOUS PLAYS

MORE yet and more, and yet we mark not all
   The Warning fain to bid fair women heed
   Its hard brief note of deadly doom and deed;[3]
The verse that strewed too thick with flowers the hall
Whence Nero watched his fiery festival;[4]
   That iron page wherein men's eyes who read
   See, bruised and marred between two babes that
      bleed,
A mad red-handed husband's martyr fall;[5]
The scene which crossed and streaked with mirth the
      strife
Of Henry with his sons and witchlike wife;[6]
And that sweet pageant of the kindly fiend,
   Who, seeing three friends in spirit and heart made
      one,
Crowned with good hap the true-love wiles he screened
   In the pleached lanes of pleasant Edmonton.[7]

[1] *Doctor Dodypol.*
[2] *Nobody and Somebody.*
[3] *A Warning for Fair Women.*
[4] *The Tragedy of Nero.*
[5] *A Yorkshire Tragedy.*
[6] *Look about you.*
[7] *The Merry Devil of Edmonton.*

XIX

THE MANY

I

GREENE, garlanded with February's few flowers,
  Ere March came in with Marlowe's rapturous rage:
  Peele, from whose hand the sweet white locks of age
Took the mild chaplet woven of honoured hours:
Nash, laughing hard: Lodge, flushed from lyric
    bowers:
  And Lilly, a goldfinch in a twisted cage
  Fed by some gay great lady's pettish page
Till short sweet songs gush clear like short spring
    showers:
Kid, whose grim sport still gambolled over graves:
  And Chettle, in whose fresh funereal verse
  Weeps Marian yet on Robin's wildwood hearse:
Cooke, whose light boat of song one soft breath saves,
  Sighed from a maiden's amorous mouth averse:
Live likewise ye: Time takes not you for slaves.

XX

THE MANY

II

HAUGHTON, whose mirth gave woman all her will:
  Field, bright and loud with laughing flower and
    bird
  And keen alternate notes of laud and gird:
Barnes, darkening once with Borgia's deeds the quill
Which tuned the passion of Parthenophil:
  Blithe burly Porter, broad and bold of word:
  Wilkins, a voice with strenuous pity stirred:
Turk Mason: Brewer, whose tongue drops honey still:
Rough Rowley, handling song with Esau's hand:

Light Nabbes: lean Sharpham, rank and raw by
   turns,
But fragrant with a forethought once of Burns:
Soft Davenport, sad-robed, but blithe and bland:
   Brome, gipsy-led across the woodland ferns:
Praise be with all, and place among our band.

XXI

EPILOGUE

Our mother, which wast twice, as history saith,
   Found first among the nations: once, when she
   Who bore thine ensign saw the God in thee
Smite Spain, and bring forth Shakespeare: once,
   when death
Shrank, and Rome's bloodhounds cowered, at
   Milton's breath:
   More than thy place, then first among the free
   More than that sovereign lordship of the sea
Bequeathed to Cromwell from Elizabeth,
More than thy fiery guiding-star, which Drake
Hailed, and the deep saw lit again for Blake,
   More than all deeds wrought of thy strong right hand,
This praise keeps most thy fame's memorial strong
That thou wast head of all these streams of song,
   And time bows down to thee as Shakespeare's land.

THE PALACE OF PAN

Inscribed to my Mother

September, all glorious with gold, as a king
   In the radiance of triumph attired,
Outlightening the summer, outsweetening the spring,
Broods wide on the woodlands with limitless wing,
   A presence of all men desired.

Far eastward and westward the sun-coloured lands
    Smile warm as the light on them smiles;
And statelier than temples upbuilded with hands,
Tall column by column, the sanctuary stands
    Of the pine-forest's infinite aisles.

Mute worship, too fervent for praise or for prayer,
    Possesses the spirit with peace,
Fulfilled with the breath of the luminous air,
The fragrance, the silence, the shadows as fair
    As the rays that recede or increase.

Ridged pillars that redden aloft and aloof,
    With never a branch for a nest,
Sustain the sublime indivisible roof,
To the storm and the sun in his majesty proof,
    And awful as waters at rest.

Man's hand hath not measured the height of them;
        thought
    May measure not, awe may not know;
In its shadow the woofs of the woodland are wrought;
As a bird is the sun in the toils of them caught,
    And the flakes of it scattered as snow.

As the shreds of a plumage of gold on the ground
    The sun-flakes by multitudes lie,
Shed loose as the petals of roses discrowned
On the floors of the forest engilt and embrowned
    And reddened afar and anigh.

Dim centuries with darkling inscrutable hands
    Have reared and secluded the shrine
For gods that we know not, and kindled as brands
On the altar the years that are dust, and their sands
    Time's glass has forgotten for sign.

A temple whose transepts are measured by miles,
  Whose chancel has morning for priest,
Whose floor-work the foot of no spoiler defiles,
Whose musical silence no music beguiles,
  No festivals limit its feast.

The noon's ministration, the night's and the dawn's,
  Conceals not, reveals not for man,
On the slopes of the herbless and blossomless lawns,
Some track of a nymph's or some trail of a faun's
  To the place of the slumber of Pan.

Thought, kindled and quickened by worship and
      wonder
  To rapture too sacred for fear
On the ways that unite or divide them in sunder,
Alone may discern if about them or under
  Be token or trace of him here.

With passionate awe that is deeper than panic
  The spirit subdued and unshaken
Takes heed of the godhead terrene and Titanic
Whose footfall is felt on the breach of volcanic
  Sharp steeps that their fire has forsaken.

By a spell more serene than the dim necromantic
  Dead charms of the past and the night,
Or the terror that lurked in the noon to make frantic
Where Etna takes shape from the limbs of gigantic
  Dead gods disanointed of might,

The spirit made one with the spirit whose breath
  Makes noon in the woodland sublime
Abides as entranced in a presence that saith
Things loftier than life and serener than death,
  Triumphant and silent as time.

PINE RIDGE: *September* 1893.

A YEAR'S CAROLS

JANUARY

HAIL, January, that bearest here
On snowbright breasts the babe-faced year
   That weeps and trembles to be born.
Hail, maid and mother, strong and bright,
Hooded and cloaked and shod with white,
   Whose eyes are stars that match the morn.
Thy forehead braves the storm's bent bow,
Thy feet enkindle stars of snow.

FEBRUARY

Wan February with weeping cheer,
Whose cold hand guides the youngling year
   Down misty roads of mire and rime,
Before thy pale and fitful face
The shrill wind shifts the clouds apace
   Through skies the morning scarce may climb.
Thine eyes are thick with heavy tears,
But lit with hopes that light the year's.

MARCH

Hail, happy March, whose foot on earth
Rings as the blast of martial mirth
   When trumpets fire men's hearts for fray.
No race of wild things winged or finned
May match the might that wings thy wind
   Through air and sea, through scud and spray
Strong joy and thou were powers twin-born
Of tempest and the towering morn.

APRIL

Crowned April, king whose kiss bade earth
Bring forth to time her lordliest birth
  When Shakespeare from thy lips drew breath
And laughed to hold in one soft hand
A spell that bade the world's wheel stand,
  And power on life, and power on death,
With quiring suns and sunbright showers
Praise him, the flower of all thy flowers.

MAY

Hail, May, whose bark puts forth full-sailed
For summer: May, whom Chaucer hailed
  With all his happy might of heart,
And gave thy rosebright daisy-tips
Strange fragrance from his amorous lips
  That still thine own breath seems to part
And sweeten till each word they say
Is even a flower of flowering May.

JUNE

Strong June, superb, serene, elate
With conscience of thy sovereign state
  Untouched of thunder, though the storm
Scathe here and there thy shuddering skies
And bid its lightning cross thine eyes
  With fire, thy golden hours inform
Earth and the souls of men with life
That brings forth peace from shining strife.

JULY

Hail, proud July, whose fervent mouth
Bids even be morn and north be south
  By grace and gospel of thy word,

Whence all the splendour of the sea
Lies breathless with delight in thee
    And marvel at the music heard
From the ardent silent lips of noon
And midnight's rapturous plenilune.

AUGUST

Great August, lord of golden lands,
Whose lordly joy through seas and strands
    And all the red-ripe heart of earth
Strikes passion deep as life, and stills
The folded vales and folding hills
    With gladness too divine for mirth,
The gracious glories of thine eyes
Make night a noon where darkness dies.

SEPTEMBER

Hail, kind September, friend whose grace
Renews the bland year's bounteous face
    With largess given of corn and wine
Through many a land that laughs with love
Of thee and all the heaven above,
    More fruitful found than all save thine
Whose skies fulfil with strenuous cheer
The fervent fields that knew thee near.

OCTOBER

October of the tawny crown,
Whose heavy-laden hands drop down
    Blessing, the bounties of thy breath
And mildness of thy mellowing might
Fill earth and heaven with love and light
    Too sweet for fear to dream of death
Or memory, while thy joy lives yet,
To know what joy would fain forget.

NOVEMBER

Hail, soft November, though thy pale
Sad smile rebuke the words that hail
   Thy sorrow with no sorrowing words
Or gratulate thy grief with song
Less bitter than the winds that wrong
   Thy withering woodlands, where the birds
Keep hardly heart to sing or see
How fair thy faint wan face may be.

DECEMBER

December, thou whose hallowing hands
On shuddering seas and hardening lands
   Set as a sacramental sign
The seal of Christmas felt on earth
As witness toward a new year's birth
   Whose promise makes thy death divine,
The crowning joy that comes of thee
Makes glad all grief on land or sea.

ON THE DEATH OF MRS. LYNN LINTON

   KIND, wise, and true as truth's own heart,
      A soul that here
Chose and held fast the better part
      And cast out fear,

Has left us ere we dreamed of death
      For life so strong,
Clear as the sundawn's light and breath,
      And sweet as song.

We see no more what here awhile
      Shed light on men:
Has Landor seen that brave bright smile
      Alive again?

If death and life and love be one
 And hope no lie
And night no stronger than the sun,
 These cannot die.

The father-spirit whence her soul
 Took strength, and gave
Back love, is perfect yet and whole,
 As hope might crave.

His word is living light and fire:
 And hers shall live
By grace of all good gifts the sire
 Gave power to give.

The sire and daughter, twain and one
 In quest and goal,
Stand face to face beyond the sun,
 And soul to soul.

Not we, who loved them well, may dream
 What joy sublime
Is theirs, if dawn through darkness gleam,
 And life through time.

Time seems but here the mask of death,
 That falls and shows
A void where hope may draw not breath:
 Night only knows.

Love knows not: all that love may keep
 Glad memory gives:
The spirit of the days that sleep
 Still wakes and lives.

But not the spirit's self, though song
    Would lend it speech,
May touch the goal that hope might long
    In vain to reach.

How dear that high true heart, how sweet
    Those keen kind eyes,
Love knows, who knows how fiery fleet
    Is life that flies.

If life there be that flies not, fair
    The life must be
That thrills her sovereign spirit there
    And sets it free.

LUCIFER

Écrasez l'infâme.—Voltaire

Les prêtres ont raison de l'appeler Lucifer.—Victor Hugo

Voltaire, our England's lover, man divine
  Beyond all Gods that ever fear adored
  By right and might, by sceptre and by sword,
By godlike love of sunlike truth, made thine
Through godlike hate of falsehood's marshlight shine
  And all the fume of creeds and deeds abhorred
  Whose light was darkness, till the dawn-star soared,
Truth, reason, mercy, justice, keep thy shrine
Sacred in memory's temple, seeing that none
Of all souls born to strive before the sun
  Loved ever good or hated evil more.
The snake that felt thy heel upon her head,
Night's first-born, writhes as though she were not
    dead,
  But strikes not, stings not, slays not as before.

THE AFTERGLOW OF SHAKESPEARE

LET there be light, said Time: and England heard:
And manhood grew to godhead at the word.
No light had shone, since earth arose from sleep,
So far; no fire of thought had cloven so deep.
A day beyond all days bade life acclaim
Shakespeare: and man put on his crowning name.
All secrets once through darkling ages kept
Shone, sang, and smiled to think how long they slept.
Man rose past fear of lies whereon he trod:
And Dante's ghost saw hell devour his God.
Bright Marlowe, brave as winds that brave the sea
When sundawn bids their bliss in battle be,
Lit England first along the ways whereon
Song brighter far than sunlight soared and shone.
He died ere half his life had earned his right
To lighten time with song's triumphant light.
Hope shrank, and felt the stroke at heart: but one
She knew not rose, a man to match the sun.
And England's hope and time's and man's became
Joy, deep as music's heart and keen as flame.
Not long, for heaven on earth may live not long,
Light sang, and darkness died before the song.
He passed, the man above all men, whose breath
Transfigured life with speech that lightens death.
He passed: but yet for many a lustrous year
His light of song bade England shine and hear.
As plague and fire and faith in falsehood spread,
So from the man of men, divine and dead,
Contagious godhead, seen, unknown, and heard,
Fulfilled and quickened England; thought and word,
When men would fain set life to music, grew

More sweet than years which knew not Shakespeare
    knew.
The simplest soul that set itself to song
Sang, and may fear not time's or change's wrong.
The lightest eye that glanced on life could see
Through grief and joy the God that man might be.
All passion whence the living soul takes fire
Till death fulfil despair and quench desire,
All love that lightens through the cloud of chance,
All hate that lurks in hope and smites askance,
All holiness of sorrow, all divine
Pity, whose tears are stars that save and shine,
All sunbright strength of laughter like the sea's
When spring and autumn loose their lustrous breeze,
All sweet, all strange, all sad, all glorious things,
Lived on his lips, and hailed him king of kings.
All thought, all strife, all anguish, all delight,
Spake all he bade, and speak till day be night.
No soul that heard, no spirit that beheld,
Knew not the God that lured them and compelled.
On Beaumont's brow the sun arisen afar
Shed fire which lit through heaven the younger star
That sank before the sunset: one dark spring
Slew first the kinglike subject, then the king.
The glory left above their graves made strong
The heart of Fletcher, till the flower-sweet song
That Shakespeare culled from Chaucer's field, and
    died,
Found ending on his lips that smiled and sighed.
From Dekker's eyes the light of tear-touched mirth
Shone as from Shakespeare's, mingling heaven and
    earth.
Wild witchcraft's lure and England's love made one
With Shakespeare's heart the heart of Middleton.

Harsh, homely, true, and tragic, Rowley told
His heart's debt down in rough and radiant gold.
The skies that Tourneur's lightning clove and rent
Flamed through the clouds where Shakespeare's
      thunder went.
Wise Massinger bade kings be wise in vain
Ere war bade song, storm-stricken, cower and wane.
Kind Heywood, simple-souled and single-eyed,
Found voice for England's home-born praise and
      pride.
Strange grief, strange love, strange terror, bared the
      sword
That smote the soul by grace and will of Ford.
The stern grim strength of Chapman's thought found
      speech
Loud as when storm at ebb-tide rends the beach:
And all the honey brewed from flowers in May
Made sweet the lips and bright the dreams of Day.
But even as Shakespeare caught from Marlowe's word
Fire, so from his the thunder-bearing third,
Webster, took light and might whence none but he
Hath since made song that sounded so the sea
Whose waves are lives of men—whose tidestream rolls
From year to darkening year the freight of souls.
Alone above it, sweet, supreme, sublime,
Shakespeare attunes the jarring chords of time
Alone of all whose doom is death and birth,
Shakespeare is lord of souls alive on earth.

INDEX OF TITLES

INDEX OF FIRST LINES

DISTRIBUTORS
for the Wordsworth Poetry Library

AUSTRALIA, BRUNEI, MALAYSIA & SINGAPORE

Reed Editions
22 Salmon Street
Port Melbourne
Vic 3207
Australia

Tel: (03) 646 6716
Fax: (03) 646 6925

GREAT BRITAIN & IRELAND

Wordsworth Editions Ltd
Cumberland House
Crib Street
Ware
Hertfordshire SG12 9ET

PORTUGAL

International Publishing Services Ltd
Rua da Cruz da Carreira, 4B
1100 Lisboa

Tel: 01-570051
Fax: 01-3522066

ITALY

Magis Books SRL
Via Raffaello 31/C
Zona Ind Mancasale
42100 Reggio Emilia

Tel: 0522-920999
Fax: 0522-920666

SOUTHERN AFRICA

Struik Book Distributors (Pty) Ltd
Graph Avenue
Montague Gardens
7441
P O Box 193
Maitland
7405
South Africa

Tel: (021) 551-5900
Fax: (021) 551-1124

USA, CANADA & MEXICO

Universal Sales & Marketing
230 Fifth Avenue
Suite 1212
New York, NY 10001 USA

Tel: 212-481-3500
Fax: 212-481-3534